KYLE JAMES

NOT AFRAID OF THE FALL

Published by Inkshares, Inc., Oakland, California
www.inkshares.com

Edited by J.C. Gabel | Kaitlin Severini
Cover design by Jack Smyth | Interior Design by Kevin G. Summers

ISBN: 9781942645283
e-ISBN: 9781942645290
Library of Congress Control Number: 2016941217

First edition

Printed in the United States of America

My sweet Ash,

This book is dedicated to you. Without your push, we never would have fallen.

I was afraid to leave the comfort of our lives in Denver, but waking up to your smiling face every morning, eager to explore, assured me that everything was going to be okay. I was then afraid of not finishing this book or not being able to find a publisher, but you urged me to keep writing. Ash, you are the wind to my sails and the ink to my pen.

No matter where I go or what I do, the only thing I am sure of is that I want you by my side. Every cliff I jump off, every moped I crash, every morning after a night of food poisoning, every Mediterranean sunset, I want you by my side.

I never want to stop exploring with you, Ash.

Will you marry me?

PREFACE

Let's start from the beginning, shall we? In 1989, I was born a middle child into a middle-class family in Middle America. Yes, I understand it is impossible to be born a middle child. I must have sensed there was a Valentine's Day with my little brother's name on it. I have been an independent middle child since I began crawling. At eight months old, I became bored with crawling and decided to walk. This allowed me to see more of my environment and get a better view of the world. At eleven months old, I discovered that taking my strides faster would cut down on my travel time and decided to run. I took plenty of falls, and in hindsight, I probably should have learned how to hit the brakes first. After third grade, I had learned enough in Ann Arbor, Michigan, and decided to move to Chapel Hill, North Carolina. (That is what I told my third-grade teacher, at least.)

Chapel Hill is my home. Even writing the words *Chapel Hill* makes me feel good. When I graduated from high school, I *decided* to take my academic talents (or lack thereof) to Boone, North Carolina, to attend Appalachian State University. This allowed me to see the world at an even higher bird's-eye view, from 3,333 feet. The view of the mountains was great, but the view of a Southern girl from Lincolnton, North Carolina, was even better. I *decided* to make this girl named Ashley (Ash) mine. It took longer than I thought, and after many failed pickup lines (such as asking for ChapStick but then proclaiming I didn't use the stick), I managed to convince her to go on a hike with me. We fell in love in the Appalachian Mountains that day, traveling across trails and rivers and exploring an area of the world neither of us had ever seen. *The exploration of new things is quite an aphrodisiac.* We graduated from App State, and we *decided* to move to Denver, Colorado, to begin our careers. It was our dream to travel the world together, but we had to work to make money, so we told ourselves we would work for a year and then leave.

Ash was a kindergarten teacher and I worked in fundraising for a nonprofit called Junior Achievement. We lived our lives similarly to many Millennials. Getting through the five days of the week only by looking forward to the weekend. One year quickly became two, and the window to travel was disappearing. I had taken my place in the rat race to ascend the long, steep corporate ladder. As a result of our working lifestyles, our relationship suffered. Ash would wake up earlier than I did to commute to school, and we would not see each other in the morning. After work we would go to the gym. When we got home, one of us would start cooking while the other showered, and then we would switch places. We ate our meals on the couch and watched Netflix, dreading the next workday. On the weekends we would go out with friends and try to pack as much into those two days as we could. It wasn't that we weren't still in love; it was that we weren't exploring new things anymore. We spent time hiking, snow-boarding, and visiting new places in Colorado, but after two years of the same thing, our lives became monotonous.

Desperate for a change, I landed what I thought was my dream job in an athletic program selling corporate sponsorships. I was leaving an amazing job at Junior Achievement with great people. Ash was absolutely devastated. She didn't tell me, but I could see it in her eyes. She knew that this was it, our plants were rooted, and we would be in Denver for a long time. I told her that we needed to do this for our future and that we would take a two-week vacation somewhere amazing. She supported me because she knew I badly wanted this job, but our dreams of traveling the world would be put on hold once again.

I began my new job and absolutely hated it. I spent my entire first day making cold calls. I came home and shared my disappointment with Ash. I have never felt quite as lost as I did that day in January 2015. I felt like my life had spiraled out of my control. So we made the toughest decision we had ever made: we *decided* to follow our dreams and travel the world. We *decided* to risk our future for a happier now.

6/7/15
Denver, USA -> New York City, USA

Ashley (Ash) woke up an hour earlier than I did. She was running around like a five-year-old on Christmas morning, throwing last-minute items into her fifty-liter REI backpack. I got out of bed quietly and snuck out of the room to avoid the tornado. When safely out of the flying-clothes zone, I let my morning routine commence: sitting on the toilet while the shower water heated up and reading my Twitter feed to catch up on general news, politics, and sports. The day we'd been planning for for six months—and dreaming about for years—had come; we were headed to the airport to leave our routine lives and travel across Europe and Southeast Asia with nothing but backpacks and each other.

Our wheels were up by 11:00 a.m. We were passengers B5 and B7 in Southwest's boarding line. (We never did find that mystery B6 person who somehow managed to check in between us online.) After more snacks than we could eat, multiple coffees, and four hours of prep work for our trip, we touched down at LaGuardia Airport in New York City.

Feeling adventurous and eager to test out our backpacking legs, we decided to trek the two miles from the airport to the nearest subway and ride the train into Manhattan. We exited the LaGuardia terminal to the smell of money and cigarettes. *Welcome to New York.*

Google Maps had no walking directions from the airport, but what the hell does Google Maps know? We walked briskly and confidently in the cardinal direction of the subway. Two endless parking garages and a frightening Frogger experience later, our Uber had arrived.

Our Uber dropped us off in the busy neighborhood of the Upper East Side of Manhattan. The feeling I get in New York City is unlike how I feel in any other city in the world; it's almost like I am the star of a movie, and the bustling streets and honking taxis are just the background in my scene. Everyone has his or her own movie in New York City.

Eager for our afternoon caffeine fix, we ventured to the closest Starbucks, a mere fifty yards away. *Did you know there are more Starbucks in New York City than pigeons? That is a false statement that I just made up; you shouldn't believe everything you read.*

We ordered extra-large coffees and then walked next door to an overpriced pizzeria to grab massive slices of New York–style pizza.

We took our calories and caffeine to Central Park, where we nestled into the grass to people watch and wait for our friends Orrie and Rebekah to get home from a wedding.

Orrie and Rebekah are college friends from our alma mater, Appalachian State. We had not seen them in a few years, so we were excited to spend a couple days in their company. They are the type of people who improve every part of your life when you are around them. Their positive energy is both uplifting and infectious. They were the perfect people to send us away as we fell into the unknown world of unemployed backpackers.

We arrived at their tiny Manhattan apartment around 11:00 p.m. and caught up with them for a few minutes before they headed to bed.

6/8/15
New York City, USA

Orrie and Rebekah's apartment window faces the building next door, so the sunlight had almost no way to enter the apartment naturally. We slept until 10:00 a.m. in the dark quarters of the studio. This was still only 8:00 a.m. Denver time, but we felt like lazy slobs nonetheless.

With little motivation to spend any more money than we needed to, Ash, Rebekah, and I hung out in the apartment, chatted about our trip, and waited for Orrie to get home from work. Rebekah was so easy to talk to. Many people, myself included, simply hear people talk, but instead of truly listening, they're just planning what they will say next and waiting to interject. Rebekah honestly and attentively tuned in to whatever was coming out of our mouths.

When Orrie got home, we ventured back into the playground of New York City, enjoying overpriced beer and underpriced company in the West Village.

Orrie and Rebekah decided to take us to their favorite restaurant in Chinatown to save money. As we walked, it amazed me how abruptly the culture changed during the course of a mere ten blocks. From robust bars and fine dining, to busy streets of shops and hole-in-the-wall restaurants with Mandarin painted across the tops of the businesses.

We stumbled upon the dumpling shack Orrie and Rebekah swore by. We nearly missed the sweltering hallway you had to duck down into to grab some grub. (This place looked like it would give me an upset stomach.) The shack was filled with steam and the stench that accompanied it. Despite the suspect conditions, the line of people out the door steadily grew.

All I knew was it was a dollar for four steamed or fried dumplings. Ash and I ordered twenty. *Why doesn't this guy charge more money?* I thought. The line never subsided, and four dumplings for a total price of one dollar seemed criminal. The dumplings were amazing, and Ash and I filled our faces while laughing as if we had figured out a cheat code to low-priced, essential New York City cuisine.

We decided to head home to prepare for our second travel day. We took the subway to our stop and ascended up the stairs only to find that what was once a nice New York City evening had turned into a chilly, rainy night. At a break in the rain, we raced past speeding garbage trucks and soaked trash lined up along the street; the whole city smelled like a wet dog. As we climbed into bed for our last night in the United States, I thought about how great it felt going to places like the dumpling shack, places that only the locals knew about. Hopefully, we could find people as nice as Orrie and Rebekah overseas to show us the local gems.

6/9/15
New York City, USA → Oslo, Norway

Once again, we slept through Orrie and Rebekah's morning routines and awoke at 10:30 a.m. like two bears emerging from their cave. With only one day left in New York, we obviously had to eat breakfast at a New York bagel shop. I ordered the lox and cream cheese, Ash the veggie spread.

We spent the afternoon people watching on Fifth Avenue as thousands of dollars walked by. I thought about how fresh these people looked but also about how stressful it must be to maintain a reputation of wearing clothes so nice. Everyone who walked by was wearing what would have been my most expensive outfit. Speaking of money, Ash remembered we needed to get some euros for our trip, so we strolled to the bank. It took us two Bank of America trips and two Chase trips to achieve this tedious task.

Orrie and Rebekah arrived home from work just in time for us to soak up as much of their positive energy as possible as we said our good-byes.

Our Uber arrived and we sped off to JFK Airport, narrowly missing collisions at every turn. I guess Uber adopted not only the New York City taxi model, but also the driving style as well: accelerate full throttle to close up as much space between cars as possible, and then slam the brakes at the last minute to avoid demolishing bumpers.

Dropping our packs off at the Norwegian Air check-in was a huge weight lifted off our shoulders. *This was it,* I thought as we showed our passports and went through security. As I got a bit nervous about what awaited us, I noticed a mother trying to mask her own crying as her two children stood beside her, weeping. I recognized the tears of saying good-bye to loved ones for an extended period.

I suddenly felt a wave of guilt pass over me. I already missed my family, and I wasn't sure that Ash's and my choice to quit our jobs and take off for several months made a lot of sense. We were only going to be gone for four months. But it wasn't the time that worried me; it was the distance. If anything happened to our families while we were in Denver, it was a quick three-hour flight to get to them in

North Carolina. Soon we would be at least a day of travel away from making it home. I quickly wiped my eyes before raising my hands to prove my innocence to the metal detector.

Our Boeing 787 was brand new, and there were touch-screen TVs behind each seat. Ash and I each chose a movie to start the trip: Ash chose *Wild*, as she had just finished reading the book, and I chose *Interstellar*, because I love engulfing myself with explosive spaceship movies while flying.

We probably should have slept on the plane, as it was already 10:00 p.m., but we were like giddy schoolchildren, adrenaline pumping through our veins.

I noticed food being brought out on trays to passengers. I prepared to give my order to the flight attendant before realizing they were preordered meals. Preordered meals that we hadn't paid for. (Nothing makes you feel more like a loser than watching meals served to the people around you who paid for them ahead of time.) Meanwhile, my stomach was growling. I immediately regretted not paying the twenty dollars back in March for a hot meal. I then saw the dog-food-like mush that was being handed to the rubes who'd ordered it, and my disappointment boomeranged to the notion of how genius we were for *not* buying the meal.

We both finished our movies and popped some melatonin pills to enjoy a deep sleep and strange dreams for the final three hours of our flight to Norway.

6/10/15
Oslo, Norway → Paris, France

We jumped time zones and arrived in Oslo at 10:00 a.m. After fumbling our way through customs, we entered Norway's pristine airport. I say fumbled because for some reason those officers have a knack for making me feel like I am coming into the country to commit an act of terrorism.

"What do you plan on doing in Europe?" the officer asked with a straight face.

"Just visiting," I replied.

"Where are you going and when are you leaving?" she asked coldly, still with a straight face.

"Uhhh, all over Europe, and then we are heading to Bangkok in September." *Shit, that didn't sound good,* I thought.

I never understood these small-talk questioning protocols at customs checkpoints. Even if I were there to commit a crime, why the hell would I just admit it? *Yeah, you caught me. Had you not asked me what I was doing in Europe, I would have gotten away with it!*

The Oslo airport was exactly as you would imagine it: clean, new looking, expensive, and full of beautiful Nordic people. Everyone seemed to travel in a blazer or a full suit. With a six-hour layover and food and drink prices higher than the people in Denver, we decided to build on the three hours of sleep we'd amassed the night before, and slept in comfortable chairs in a corner of the airport.

We ended our short trip to Norway and boarded an older Norwegian Air plane. (Safe to say the honeymoon phase with Norwegian Air was over as I sat in a chair that felt like an elementary school desk, my legs jammed sideways.)

When the all-too-familiar *ding*—"Flight staff, please prepare for landing"—sounded, our six-month preparation and lifelong dream became very real, especially to Ash. She gets giggly when she is excited, and her eyes got as big as I had ever seen them (and trust me, that's big—she has eyeballs for days).

I will admit: there is nothing I love more than seeing her *this* happy. Traveling and the excitement of visiting foreign cities makes her happier than . . . Well, happier than just about anything makes me. I was still unsure about the decision we'd made to quit our jobs and set sail. Before I quit, my boss told me point-blank, "You are making the biggest mistake of your life." But it was too late to second-guess ourselves now.

We bounced into Paris with a rather rough landing and proceeded to baggage claim. The fact that every sign was in English was half a relief/half a letdown. I had this romantic vision of struggling with the language and almost missing trains as we jumped on the rolling caboose just as the conductor yelled, "Last call!"

We exited the tram that took us from the airport to one of the city's main stations. As we looked for our next move, that bittersweet feeling from before quickly lost the sweet part.

We could not figure out where to go and traversed the terminal in search of our train to Bastille. A jolt of panic shot through our spines; it was day one and we were already failing. After some angry exchanges between Ash and me, a sweet French woman pointed us to the right train. We rode in silence, both embarrassed at our anger toward each other.

We then headed aboveground to the Bastille neighborhood of Paris, our home for the next few days. It's hard to describe what we, after twenty-four hours of nonstop travel, felt and saw as we emerged from the depths of the metro into the City of Light for the first time. It was as if Google Images had dumped photos from an "Amazing Paris Neighborhood" search on top of us.

We had that awkward tourist sensory overload moment, too, where we scrambled for our phones and cameras to try to take pictures of every limb of every tree around us all at once, as if every Gothic cathedral would disappear in seconds. Eventually, we snapped out of it and strolled confidently to our first Airbnb destination. *We did it; we are backpackers . . .* or so we thought.

"Are you sure that code is right?" I asked Ash, entering the number from the Airbnb instructions for a third time.

"Yes, Kyle! I am reading it right from the message," she said.

It took us half an hour to realize we were on the wrong road and at the wrong building. *Dammit,* I thought. *We suck, again.* We eventually found the right building and walked up six flights of steep, spiraling steps.

Waiting for us at the top was our Parisian Airbnb host, Clemence, a gorgeous aspiring actress. Clemence showed us around the small studio while she enthusiastically pointed out to the rooftop porch where she spent most of her time. It was a four-by-four-foot roof covered in Astroturf and with no guardrail—it was a long way down to the Bastille street below. As we said our good-byes, she told us we were welcome to sit on the porch if we were "not afraid of the fall."

That day was definitely a learning experience for us, with a few more downs than ups. Our first metro experience exposed something I was worried about on this trip: my tendency to get frustrated easily in stressful situations. Instead of taking a deep breath and relaxing, I got flustered and took it out on Ash. I knew I'd have to remedy this or we'd be staring down some stupid arguments as our sojourn continued. Regardless of the hurdles we had to overcome, we made it to Europe, we made it to Paris, and we made it to our first Airbnb in a foreign city. We were not experts in traveling yet, but we were certainly not afraid of the fall.

6/11/15
Paris, France

It was before 6:00 a.m. when Ash woke up. She kissed my cheek repeatedly and bounced up with excitement like my late grandpa James on the first day of hunting season. It was surprisingly light out for 5:45 a.m., and with no other option but to succumb to Ash's excitement, I got myself up as well.

We had not yet figured out how to get clothes out of our backpacks effectively, so we dumped everything out like kids with bags full of Halloween candy, picked something to wear, and headed down the deathly spiral staircase. Our goal was to get lost in Paris, eventually making our way to the most clichéd but essential destination, the Eiffel Tower.

As we walked down the cobblestone streets of the Sixth Arrondissement, I noticed the all-too-familiar runny nose and throat tickle of an oncoming allergy attack. *Please be a false alarm,* I thought, gazing at the shops of Paris Saint-Germain. We ventured south, as did my allergy condition. Finally, after six massive snot rockets, Ash made me buy tissues.

Then, mid-nose-blow, we saw it at the same time: the Eiffel Tower. Even just a glimpse of the top gave us chills. It was such an iconic structure, and I had seen it hundreds of times in books, magazines, and on television. It was nice to confirm that it was indeed real.

When we reached the tower, we stood in awe and shamelessly took hundreds of pictures, as if one angle would be better than another. Eventually the wonder wore off, and we headed home on the line 9 subway to Voltaire and took a long nap before dinner. Paris, we were finding out the hard way, was *exhausting*.

Our evening was spent picnicking on the deathly rooftop. We put on some music and spread out our sandwiches on the space of the turf that our bodies hadn't taken up. Our first sunset in Paris was spent laughing on the roof at the ridiculous selfies our GoPro had produced. The bottle of champagne certainly assisted. I watched Ash take a selfie and then laugh, but I couldn't see the picture; I was transfixed by her. We were having a blast on this four-by-four-foot Astroturf roof, and we didn't need anything but each other. However, the view of the Paris skyline from Bastille certainly didn't hurt.

6/12/15
Paris, France

On this particular morning, it was I who couldn't sleep. I sat in bed, hungover from my cocktail of melatonin, allergy medicine, champagne, and jet lag. I woke up at six fifteen to the sound of bustling streets outside our window as Parisians hurried to get their Friday over with. I remember the excitement of Fridays. No matter what happened on Friday, I was going to be home free at 5:00 p.m. for the eternity of two days.

While Ash slept, I did some work on the budget we had set up on Google Drive and looked for Airbnbs in Belgium and the Netherlands.

It was a huge concern of mine that we would run out of money while overseas. I wanted to make sure we came home with at least six thousand dollars to get our lives back on track, so I created a spreadsheet on Excel to record our daily spending.

We calculated that from what we'd saved for two years, we could spend one hundred and fifty dollars a day on Airbnbs, food, drinks, and activities for the entire trip and come back with six thousand dollars. We created this dynamic budget so that we could correct the problem early enough if we were blowing money too fast. As I worked on this, I heard Ash stir.

"Kyle?" she said sweetly from the corner of the studio.

She always does this when she first wakes up and I am not in bed. She never needs anything; she just likes to hear my voice to make sure I am around.

"Yes, baby?" I replied.

She received her comforting confirmation and then rolled back asleep.

Ash woke up a few hours later, furious at me for letting her sleep the day away. It was only 10:00 a.m., but the feeling of not maximizing every second of her day stresses her out. In my opinion: quality > quantity. (There are obvious exceptions to this rule, like light beer and Legos.)

Ash got ready (she didn't want to rest her day away, but she had no problem doing her hair and makeup for half an hour), and we left the apartment to go back to the Eiffel Tower. Sure, there were plenty of other things to do in Paris, but most things were expensive. Spending the day basking in the sun on the lawn out in front of the Eiffel Tower sounded great to us.

We took the line 9 metro all the way from Bastille to the Eiffel Tower and got out at the Palais de Tokyo. Before we got to the tower for the remainder of the afternoon, we stopped at a corner store to grab a bottle of wine, two Carlsberg tallboys, and a pack of cigarettes. (We didn't smoke cigarettes, but that made us the only two people in Paris who didn't. We wanted to embrace the culture and do as the Parisians do.)

We then sprawled out in the grass on the lawn of the Eiffel Tower and waited. Every hour, on the hour, the tower would light up and sparkle for five minutes. As we sat there on the pristine lawn, two thoughts came to mind. *First: I can tell this trip is going to be a life-changing experience because it's only the first week and I am completely out of my comfort zone, with no structure to my life right now. Second: Holy shit, I hate smoking cigarettes.*

As the night went on, we had to jump a fence to escape some obnoxious eighteen-year-old kids who were partying loudly. *I mean, wow; I remember my first trip to the Eiffel Tower.* We stepped over a low-netted area and then lay on what appeared to be forbidden lawn to watch the tower glisten. It was extremely romantic. Ash pulling down her entire romper to pee behind a tree was not. It did succeed in making both of us laugh uncontrollably for an entire hour between the tower's glistening. We ended up lying there until 2:30 a.m. before crawling back to the subway, exhausted from our three days in the City of Light.

Unfortunately, it turns out that the subway closes at 2:00 a.m. in Paris. We had just missed the last train. Although Uber was indeed available, it had surge pricing at this hour, which meant a fifty-dollar ride. Even when there are technological shortcuts, they don't always beat the old-school method of public transit. Take the fifty-dollar Uber the six miles home and obliterate our budget? *Hell no,* I thought, *we are backpackers and we can use the exercise.* (At least that was what we told ourselves as we started the six-mile trek home.)

After a few hours, we made it all six miles, and although we were beyond tired, mentally and physically, we were feeling great. What's more: our budget was somewhat preserved. I say somewhat, because although we didn't take the fifty-dollar Uber, we ate an entire pizza, pomme frites (french fries), and a monstrous croque madame from a restaurant that was still open at 5:00 a.m. We were grossly ashamed of our late-night feast, yet unequivocally satisfied.

6/13/15
Paris, France → Brussels, Belgium

Finally, for the first time since we had arrived in Paris, we were both able to sleep in until 10:00 a.m. Not getting to sleep till 5:15 a.m. that morning probably assisted in this feat, but it felt great, either way. We headed out hastily so Ash could shop at Zara. Apparently, Zara was a trendy Spanish store that had locations in the United

States, but it sold wares in our price range. The majority of the stores in Paris, however, were for people not on a budget.

We strolled around Bastille in search of crepes and dresses. Not my ideal morning, but I knew Ash would hold it against me forever if she didn't get to shop in Paris. We walked into a swanky boutique, and I followed in the rough wake of the speedboat-to-spend in front of me. When girls are in their shopping zones, it is almost robotic how their minds and hands work together to sift through rack after rack, only needing a millisecond to analyze and decide what will and will not make the cut. Whether it's not cute enough, too expensive, made from uncomfortable fabric, or too similar to something she already owns, hundreds of items get passed over before the all-too-familiar pause and stare. This is where the man's heart starts racing. *She has a live one,* we think as we immediately begin our own analysis of the item. *How bad is this going to hurt? Is it too early in the outing that she will want to continue after this, or could this be our last stop?* Then my mind begins to wander off on its own: *What are we eating for lunch? Is game five of the NBA finals tonight? Did I put deodorant on today?*

The black top has passed all the preliminary tests, and therefore, we begin the duel.

"What about this one?" she asks.

My answer is carefully based on the results of my previous analysis. If it is not too expensive and could wrap up the day, I'd say: "Yeah, that looks great." In this case, it was our first shop, and the sixty-five-dollar top was made with the same amount of fabric as my boxers. "Yeah, that looks great. Do you love it?" I responded, carefully complimenting her on her choice but sending the decision back to her court.

Ash is very indecisive when it comes to clothes, and sure enough, she replied, "Ehhh, I don't know," and kept moving. I took some fire for this, but left unscathed and lived to see another rack. I passed a fellow boyfriend between aisles and gave him the *I'm in the same sinking boat as you—stay strong* nod. We were comrades in a losing war—this was essential for morale.

After a few hours of following Ash around to other shops, we grabbed espresso and a few croissants and took them to our rooftop porch for one last meal.

I think this rooftop is what I will remember most about Paris. The Eiffel Tower is amazing, the streets and shops are spectacular, but everyone has those memories. The rooftop porch was *our* memory, and the small space symbolized us conquering our fear of traveling together. We enjoyed our last romantic picnic on the roof, feeding each other baguettes, our legs tangled to avoid the fall below.

Our ride to Brussels was coming at 4:00 p.m. We were riding with a guy named Jerome through an app called BlaBlaCar.

BlaBlaCar is a ride-sharing app that is a mix between Airbnb and Uber, but it's much cheaper than Uber and specifically for longer jaunts, oftentimes between countries. We searched the website for trips between Paris and Brussels on June 13 and scanned the list of drivers making the trip to find a departure time and price we liked. It was sixty dollars for Ash and me to ride with Jerome the three and a half hours to Brussels, as opposed to the 240 dollars it would cost us by train. The only catch being that we were essentially hitchhiking with a stranger who could kill us. On the off chance he didn't kill us, that extra 180 dollars would be put to great beer-drinking use in Belgium.

At four on the dot, we were outside looking for the Audi A4 Jerome was driving.

Thirty minutes later we were worried we had messed up our inaugural BlaBlaCar trip, because we had still not seen him. He approached apologetically around four forty-five, greeting us by doing the traditional two-cheek kiss with Ash and then shaking my hand. Not that I was against the two-cheek kiss, but Jerome had studied abroad in New York City and knew our customs.

We zoomed out of Paris, and one thing crossed my mind as I reflected on the first of many cities we would be exploring over the next four months: How does everyone here not die of lung cancer in their forties? The term *chain-smoking* does not do it justice. These people were breathing two parts oxygen, one part nicotine.

I sat in the small backseat of the Audi and noticed the highway etiquette in Europe was superior to that in the US. Everyone drove in the right lane until they wanted to pass. When they reached a car traveling at a slower speed, they simply passed, quickly moving back into the right lane afterward. There were no slow cars coasting in the left lane, and it made for efficient highway driving. In the US, you often have to pass someone on the right as they drink their Starbucks latte and text their friend while steering with one knee in the fast lane.

Jerome graciously dropped us off at the doorstep of our Airbnb in Brussels. He double-kissed Ash again, shook my hand once, and headed off with a *"Ciao!"* We had survived our first BlaBlaCar experience, and although I was soaked in sweat and some grown man had kissed my girlfriend multiple times, we'd managed to save 180 dollars.

We chose an Airbnb in Ixelles. This neighborhood had a young population with great nightlife and was surrounded by residential buildings, bohemian restaurants, and Gothic churches. Our place was only fifty-seven dollars a night, leaving us with ninety-three dollars a day for food and beer. Alizee, our next host, had left a key with a neighbor, as she could not meet us in person. We grabbed the key, climbed the four flights of stairs (beats six), and headed to our home for the next few days.

Well, this place has character, I thought as we dropped our packs and looked around. Right away we both noticed the mannequin pieces. There were heads, torsos, and legs scattered all over the floor and tables. It looked like the mannequins were having a board meeting to discuss Q4, and a grenade went off and blew the body parts all over the place.

Eager to explore Brussels, we left to grab dinner and escape the staring mannequins. It had been an ongoing joke between Ash and me for years that I have a thing for mannequins. I constantly whistle at them as we pass by stores, so this made it that much worse that we were sharing a room with seven and a half of them—lots of competition for Ash tonight.

We walked down our street in the chilly evening and turned a corner to a mini city center. We saw packed restaurants with outdoor seating and cool sculptures that led to a small museum in the middle of the square. Every restaurant seemed to be full of happy people chatting and laughing. We entered a bar called De Haus that Jerome had recommended.

We each ordered a Belgian-style beer. They were only four euros apiece, but both contained 8.5 percent alcohol—twice that of most beers back home. They arrived at our table, Ash's served in a large goblet and mine in a test-tube-like glass held by a wooden contraption. It needed the wood because the bottom of the test tube glass was rounded and wouldn't stand up on its own.

We enjoyed three more because we were finally in the land of beer. I think it was the best beer I've ever had. "Back to the plastic brothel," we joked when we were ready to go home.

6/14/15
Brussels, Belgium

I awoke to the sound of birds frantically chirping outside the window. I understood about as much of the birds' conversation as I did the Dutch and French tongues that surrounded us. Today was our only full day in the capital city, so we set out to explore downtown.

We reached the famous Grote Markt, and it was exactly how I'd imagined Brussels would look: Bavarian-style bars, chocolate and waffle shops every few feet, and most notably, cobblestone roads without cars. Caught gazing at the fairy-tale street ahead, we quickly moved aside at the last second as a horse-drawn carriage click-clacked past us. It was transporting a group of tourists who were nonstop photo zombies, numbingly snapping pictures for social media, too busy staring at Brussels through the image of their screens to experience the city in real life. *Poor souls,* I thought. Unfortunately, those photos would never match the sights, sounds, and smells surrounding us. The problem was, I was no better. I had already taken thirty-five pictures since we'd arrived in the market. I think it was good for me to witness others doing it to realize how depressing it looked.

We followed the crowd down the hill like a current and came upon the Grand-Place, the center square of Brussels, hosting most of the city's tourists. Despite the swarms of people, it was stunning with its pristine perfectness encrusted in each piece of gobertange calcareous sandstone. Speaking of perfect, we spotted numerous orange waffle food trucks. Jerome had recommended these as the best waffles in Belgium. We planned on getting them the next day.

After taking a few hundred pictures of the town hall, we headed to a bar to drink one-liter beers. I'd often imagined myself holding one of those mugs of beer, like I was drinking from a milk carton with a handle. One mug of beer led to another, and we decided today was just going to be one of those drunken days. We were drinking far more than we should that early, but all the warning signs for a daytime shit show of knuckles-down drinking fell into place. Besides, we had clear skies and sunshine in the land of beer, and nothing else to do except spend the rest of our daily budget.

The combination of copious amounts of ale coupled with the aftereffects of the sun beating down on us all day—and disagreeing on where to go next—led to our first real argument of the trip. This is the problem with alcohol-induced euphoria; it got to the point where after fifteen minutes, we didn't even remember what we were arguing about, but each of us wanted to win the argument. Ash and I have plenty of things in common, and this is why we enjoy each other's company. Unfortunately, one of the things we share is our refusal to give in during arguments. It was the classic struggle of trying to have the last word. I know what you're thinking: that seems stupid and childish. Well . . . you're right.

We sat in silence at an outdoor beer garden, an espresso in one hand, a beer in the other. Eventually, I mumbled across the table, careful not to use an apologetic tone, "Do you want to go home?"

"Yeah," she replied quietly, and she stood up and started walking.

Ash and I were coming down from our initial high of traveling. It was becoming apparent how much time we were spending together. We may have lived together in Denver for two years, but we had never spent twenty-four hours a day, seven days a week together. This much togetherness made us argue like an old married couple. We had not quite figured out how much space the other one needed. Personal space is like ibuprofen: you don't always need it, but when you do, you need it bad.

6/15/15
Brussels, Belgium → Antwerp, Belgium

I awoke to a rumbling earthquake, my stomach serving as the epicenter. Unfortunately, we didn't leave ourselves ample time to eat. We had to be home by 11:00 a.m. to finish packing and catch a ride to Jacques Brel metro station to meet Sofie, our BlaBlaCar driver chauffeuring us to Antwerp.

Ash and I were on much better terms today as we set out on a mission to eat waffles from the famous orange food trucks we had heard so much about. Thinking about our next meal is a common excitement for us both. We can usually get through dark times fairly quickly when there is food at the end of the tunnel.

It took thirty minutes of walking before we spotted an orange truck. Our stomachs were furious at this point. You can imagine my disappointment when we discovered that the Brussels city trash trucks were *also* orange.

As we walked, both of us becoming "hangry," I had my first real *What the hell are we doing here?* moment. We were jobless, homeless, with a finite money supply, in a country far from home. Like in the movies, it is the true paradox of love and hate. I loved where we were at this very moment. I loved the girl I was sharing this journey with, and I loved using my time the way I wanted rather than being told how to spend my forty-hour workweek. On the other hand, I hated the constant concern we both had that we'd made the wrong decision, and I was troubled that we didn't have jobs lined up for when we got home.

The fact that I was concerned about having a job four months from now was the epitome of my problems. It wasn't that I wanted to save the earth in four months or research life-changing medicine. No, I wanted a *j-o-b* so that I could make money and feel better about how everyone saw me. I was more concerned with my Facebook status and the public view of me than doing what truly made me happy. I suppose admitting the problem is the first step to recovery, right?

Our search for the orange trucks proved unsuccessful, so we settled for a waffle shop in the Grand-Place. This was like going to New York City and only finding pizza in Times Square. The waffles were essentially doughnuts.

We finally made it home with almost no time to spare. We could not afford to miss our BlaBlaCar ride, but we couldn't get a Wi-Fi signal, which meant there was no way to order an Uber to meet Sofie.

Ash finally found a signal as she sat on my shoulders and stretched toward the router. We sat in silence, our backpacks weighing us down, and waited impatiently for the Uber to arrive.

Unfortunately, we once again failed the test of keeping our cool in tense situations. With all the chaos and stress of missing our ride, we naturally took it out on each other. We had no way else to vent, and ended up yelling at each another, making the lack of Wi-Fi the other person's fault rather than a simple misfortune.

On-screen, our driver looked like he was playing Pac-Man and we were the colored ghosts. Right when he would get close to us, he would then suddenly turn the wrong way. He eventually made it and stopped the car in the middle of the road, laughing as he proclaimed we were his first ride ever. *Of course we were.*

I read him the directions to the train station from my phone as fast as I could, but he remained parked in the middle of the road, fumbling with his app, a symphony of honks blaring behind us. He missed the first turn he was supposed to make. *We're screwed,* I thought as we passed multiple orange waffle trucks.

We eventually reached the station, and we sprung out of the car as it rolled to a stop. We urgently looked for Sofie's green Nissan Note. We had been told to meet her at the station, but that point became moot once we arrived: the station took up an entire city block. "Slow down!" Ash yelled twenty yards behind me as I darted from street to street. I was a bit more nimble with my backpack, as it was about a quarter of my weight while Ash's was nearly half of hers.

As I turned one last corner and was ready to give up, I saw the Note heading away from us. I ran into the middle of the street one hundred yards behind the car and waved my hands frantically in an attempt to make a scene in her rearview mirror. It worked. I saw the bright-red lights of her brakes and watched the Note pull into a parking spot, hazards on.

"Sophie?" I asked in between breaths when I got to the car.

"Hello!" she replied. "I was just about to leave!"

We'd made it.

Sophie turned out to be a sweet Belgian woman in her midforties who worked as a nutritionist, but not in a traditional sense. Her role revolved around creating the information infrastructure for wellness coaches who worked with large corporations.

I wished instead of *What do you do?* as an icebreaker, people asked, *So what makes you the most happy?* I would imagine the people who'd figured out life would have the same answer for both. Sophie dropped us off in the middle of downtown Antwerp, and we paid her ten euros for the ride.

The city of Antwerp was gorgeous. It had that small-town feel like everyone might know each other personally; at the same time, it boasted big-city perks like great stores and restaurants. Ash excitedly told me about all the shops in the promenade she would be exploring. I, of course, mapped out all the closest bars.

Our next Airbnb was in the center of the city. How could we afford this, you ask? We were sharing the space with the owner, Lieze, and her boyfriend. We chose to stay at their loft apartment because it would give us our own private porch overlooking the city, and it was only forty-five dollars a night.

The Airbnbs we looked for in each location had the following criteria: our own place (we didn't want to share the space with any-one unless we had to), air conditioning (this is self-explanatory: European summers are hot, yet Europeans abhor the thought of AC), and Wi-Fi (we needed this to plan our trip, communicate with hosts/drivers, and shamelessly access social media). Most important, we wanted to be in a walkable area of the city to explore its best parts. If there was nothing available with our criteria in a desired part of town, we budged on our own space.

Lieze had left us a key in a lockbox outside. We took the elevator to the third floor, which opened up into the apartment, encompassing an entire floor. There was plenty of room to spread out. We dropped off our packs and headed out to indulge in more local beers.

It is truly amazing how people can create such a great-tasting beer with an alcohol percentage this high. Sure, American beer companies make beers with 9 percent, but most end their names with *Ice* or *Platinum* and taste like piss-infused rocket fuel.

Ash headed off to shop. She left me at the outdoor bar.

I ordered my fourth beer of the afternoon, and sat people watching, alone, alongside a table in the promenade. I saw a young girl hopscotching on an imaginary hopscotch course. She got mad at herself when she messed up. There were people all around, yet I was completely zoned out due to the language barrier. That is the best part of people watching in a foreign country: you can watch uninterrupted because you aren't drawn into other people's conversations. The unintelligible chatter merely serves as white noise as you scan the crowds, reveling in the day without interruption, almost like watching a foreign movie without subtitles.

When Ash returned, we decided to go meet our Airbnb hosts before my tipsy demeanor morphed into full-fledged drunk.

Lieze and her boyfriend, it turned out, were video game enthusiasts. They also had a love for art. We chatted for about fifteen minutes with the young couple before heading back into the village to barhop at the local pubs.

We sampled Orval, Kriek Boan, Maes, Affligem, Westmalle, and De Koninck, a beer brewed in Antwerp. Suzie, a lovely sixty-year-old bartender, told us they only get the Orval supply every couple of weeks because it's made in small batches. Sometimes it even takes a month or two before it arrives. Orval refuses to increase production to meet the demand and risk losing quality. (To an American, this business practice seemed extremely respectable but highly questionable.)

We ended our evening eating dinner across the street from our Airbnb at a place with a little bulldog on the sign. It turned out that the bulldog, whose name was Billie, belonged to the owner. Billie strolled around the restaurant like he owned the place. We drank complimentary beers and chatted with the owner about our travels thus far. A fellow traveler himself, he shared some off-the-beaten-path anecdotes and recommendations for Thailand, but made us promise him we would visit an island called Ko Tao. We happily obliged.

We stumbled home afterward, our tummies full from what had to have been five strong beers each. We attempted to unlock the door of our place for twenty minutes, but we just couldn't seem to get it to open. Lieze and her boyfriend eventually let us in. We all laughed at ourselves in the hallway. They told us it wasn't the key that wasn't working. We were pushing the door instead of pulling.

6/16/15
Antwerp, Belgium

I awoke once the sun found her way into the penthouse loft. My head clearly didn't share my great views on the Belgian beer, and I could hear my pulse in my temples. *Thump-thump, thump-thump.* I needed to shower to kill my headache, but I could not get the shower to reach a temperature below one thousand degrees. Our hosts must have thought that if the water didn't burn off the top ten layers of your epidermis, it wasn't truly clean. I am more of a smidge-above-lukewarm guy myself.

While Ash took her turn in the cauldron, I headed to grab some breakfast from the Albert Heijn grocery store. I was perusing the fruit aisle when a man who quite literally smelled like a Dumpster passed behind me. I have smelled plenty of foul people in my day but none as *nicely dressed as this guy.* He was wearing an expensive-looking three-piece suit, yet he smelled like a fridge of broccoli and fish after a two-week vacation. I figured it couldn't have been him that produced this smell, but after four grocery-cart drive-bys and ten fewer nostril hairs, my suspicions were confirmed.

I returned to find Ash patiently waiting for breakfast on the roof, plates and cups set up. She was a sucker for picnics. We ate our breakfast and got some traveling logistics out of the way. BlaBlaCars and Airbnbs were certainly more luxurious and usually cheaper than hostels and trains, but booking them required *constant* communication with the drivers and hosts. When all the waffles were consumed and logistics sorted, it was time to indulge in one of our guilty pleasures, going to the zoo.

Our first stop in the Antwerp Zoo loop was the house of butterflies, though it *felt* more like a house of baking bread. We walked through a room with a temperature well over eighty-five degrees as butterflies of all breeds fluttered around us. The humming of colorful wings put me in a trance, and I felt like we were on an acid trip. The music was warmly tranquil, and I imagined this was a scene out of the world's nicest island yoga retreats. Just then I thought: *Maybe I should invent a yoga studio with butterflies floating around and call it Butterfly with Butterflies? When they land on you during a pose, you are a true yogi.*

We then made our way to the ape section. Ape viewing, for us two, is where the guilt really sets in. They have a 1 percent difference in DNA from humans. One percent is the only difference between sitting on your couch, watching football on Sunday, and sitting in a jail cell for life without having committed a crime.

The elephants, on the other hand, were in rather spunky moods—throwing dirt around and playing with each other. My sister, Emily, is obsessed with elephants, so I naturally have an appreciation for them every time I see them. It also made it easy to buy her gifts when we were growing up: anything elephant-themed was a hit.

Next up: hippo feeding. As we watched the tank-like animal ravage food atop watery stones, I realized that after two years of visiting the Denver Zoo, I had never seen a hippo out of the water until now. Their legs are abnormally short. I still think I could outrun one charging me. The idea of hippos running fifty miles per hour or being the most dangerous animal in Africa was hard to imagine as I watched this short bowling ball graze on piles of fruit and greens.

NOT AFRAID OF THE FALL   25

The highlight of the Antwerp Zoo was the nocturnal animal building. It contained exhibits unlike any we had seen before. The entire building was pitch black. The featured exhibit this summer was rats. (Yes, rats.) The reason for this was their use in Africa to find land mines. It was awesome to watch the documentary on how these rats were conditioned to find explosives hidden in fields. New York City has an arsenal of rats that could really boost their current résumés of eating trash and living in sewers.

We continued our tour and came to the raccoon and skunk exhibit. The exhibit maps along the way had shown us where the animals normally lived. It was usually some remote area of Asia, Africa, or South America. The raccoons and skunks, however, had North America as the sole location of these "exotic" animals. I couldn't believe those little garbage pests were being showcased at the Antwerp Zoo.

The last area of the small loop housed the reptiles. I spoke Parseltongue to the snakes, but none of them responded. They must have been sleeping. We came to the end of the zoo loop and started the long trek home.

Tonight we were calling it an early night. The zoo was a decent blow to our daily budget, and we couldn't afford another night out in Antwerp, financially or physically. We had had one day of rowdiness and one day of relaxation. (That's what *R&R* stands for, right?)

6/17/15
Antwerp, Belgium → Rotterdam, Netherlands

We strolled through the empty streets of Antwerp at 6:30 a.m. to catch a ride with our next BlaBlaCar driver, Jochen. Thirty minutes had passed with no sign of him. We began to worry we had the wrong place. As we sat there, I noticed a girl had joined us on the bench, facing the same landmark. After we all three stood up at a false alarm (a blue Volvo passed), Ash asked if she was waiting for Jochen as well. She replied that she was and that and she had ridden with him many times on BlaBlaCar, and this was unusual. We had yet to have a flawless BlaBlaCar experience. Jerome was late in Paris, we were late in Brussels, and now Jochen was—hopefully—late in Antwerp.

The other girl—whose name escapes me so let's go with Barblah for obvious reasons—finally decided to call Jochen. She woke him up. He had overslept but was now on his way. "Here he comes!" she said as he approached with the classic *I have been rehearsing in my head how to explain to my teacher/boss why I am so late but I am still shook to perform it* face.

"Sorry, everyone, I slept through my alarm," he said.

You have to love the honesty.

The ride was peaceful and uneventful, and after only an hour, we cruised into Rotterdam. Jochen dropped us off at an agreed-upon train station.

Later, as I sat on the train, I thought about how excited I was to spend the next couple of days in the largest port city in Europe and the third largest in the world behind Singapore and Shanghai. When we arrived at the terminal, I sent a message to our Airbnb host, Philippe, to let him know we were on our way.

Of all the Airbnb hosts thus far, Philippe and I had corresponded the most prior to our arrival. We had booked this place a month in advance, and he had provided us with advice and tips on every location leading up to Rotterdam. Meeting him on his row house stoop was like meeting a longtime pen pal in person.

He greeted us with a heartfelt hello and ushered us inside. His house tour was thorough, to say the least. He showed us every light switch and demonstrated each one's illuminating power. It was awesome that he took his Airbnb hosting seriously, but we were *exhausted*. We had been up since 6:30 a.m. and had just finished a mile-long walk with our fifty-pound packs. The tour finally made it to our room, and we quickly showered and climbed into bed to rest before an evening with the siblings of my soon-to-be brother-in-law, JJ.

JJ had arranged for us to meet up with his two sisters and their families while we were in his hometown. We also had a date with his oldest brother and his family tomorrow night. It was a full schedule, but we were excited to have people to hang out with from the moment we arrived in Rotterdam.

When we awoke from our nap, my stomach growled at me like a Rottweiler does at an intruder. We had dinner plans in a few hours, but walked two miles to Rotterdam's new food market to grab a snack. The Markthal Rotterdam was a massive indoor market with a grid of amazing vendors. There were fresh local cheeses, meats, small restaurants, and desserts.

The variety and options were overwhelming, so we made the logical choice and ordered a cone of pomme frites like everyone else. The casualness with which fries were served in cones was exciting. The only weird part was that everyone dipped the fries in mayonnaise instead of ketchup. We then spent the next fifteen minutes coming up with cheesy-fry-inspired movie titles like *Frytanic*, *Saving Private Fryan*, and *Fryving Miss Daisy*.

Ash left to do some shopping, and I went to use the bathroom. I approached the woman at the counter in front of it. *What, is she taking attendance?* I thought.

"Can I use the bathroom?"

"Yes," she said. "It is seventy cents."

Hmm . . . I didn't particularly want to pay seventy cents, but I didn't have much of a choice, so I forked over the money and took a seat.

Afterward, we finished our fries and grabbed coffee for the road to walk to Erasmuspark, our dinner location. As we reached an intersection, the crosswalk light turned to the stopping hand. This obviously meant we had about four more seconds before the light turned green. So I did what anyone who hates waiting at crosswalks would do: I quickly crossed the road. That was my natural response. On the other hand, Ash's natural response was to stop. After realizing she was not with me, I glanced back to see her wearing this *I can't believe you just left me* face. Her passive nature is one of the many things I love about her, but her lack of sidewalk urgency drives me crazy.

We arrived unfashionably early to the restaurant so we could drink a beer to calm our nerves: we were having dinner with four and a half strangers (there was an infant in the mix) from another country. Ash and I were going to serve as family ambassadors before my sister's October wedding to ease the awkwardness of everyone meeting for the first time at the wedding.

It turns out we didn't need the beer to soften up the conversation. These were four of the most sincere, down-to-earth people we had come across thus far. They felt like family from the moment they arrived. I should have known that if they were anything like JJ, we would love them, but there is always a little fear of the unknown, right? We said good-bye to our four and a half newest family members, and thanked them extensively for not only meeting us out but also showing us such great hospitality over a hot meal and drinks.

We had begun feeling a little homesick on our trip, but JJ's family filled that void and gave us the comfort of sharing laughs you only have with family members.

6/18/15
Rotterdam, Netherlands

Today we were spending the afternoon with JJ's eldest brother, Harke. We said good-bye to Philippe and were off to the Dordrecht metro stop, where Harke was waiting.

We spotted Harke's blue Mercedes at precisely the time and location we were to meet. It was the first flawless pickup of our trip so far. He looked similar to JJ, although a bit shorter. (JJ is six foot seven inches tall.) Harke was on his way home from Brussels for work, but his wife, Heidi, and his two sons, Maarten and Tim, were meeting us later.

Harke cruised into a farmland festooned with windmills, surrounding the big city. We were visiting the windmills at Kinderdijk, a UNESCO World Heritage Site. Harke led the way down the dykes as he gave us some background information. Heidi's grandfather used to work on the mills, and he lived in a small house on the property. Then he abruptly said, "Ah, there is my son." I turned to see Maarten, a three-year-old blond kid smiling ear to ear and running toward us. He looked as if he were going to jump right into Harke's arms, but instead he ran right past us, smiling mischievously to see who would chase him.

We ate dinner in the small mill restaurant where we met Heidi and Tim. Tim was only one year old but loved watching his brother play. We were the only group in the mill restaurant; this worked out well for Maarten. He turned the restaurant into his own personal playground and ran around yelling things in Dutch.

It was another great evening spent with JJ's family. These were the days we'd hoped for when we set off to travel. Experiencing different cultures in a variety of ways, from the food, to the sites, to the people. It felt like we had just gotten the hang of Rotterdam, and it was already time to leave.

We headed home to get some rest before our weekend in Amsterdam. We had a strange feeling this was where the trip was going to take a turn for the *weird*.

6/19/15
Rotterdam, Netherlands → Amsterdam, Netherlands

It was only a short distance to Amsterdam, but today was still a travel day. We had to walk a mile to our BlaBlaCar pickup location, drive for an hour, and then take a train from our drop-off point to our next apartment location. We were discovering that, despite the actual travel distance, the entire day was exhausting as we moved from apartment to apartment, and city to city.

After we cleaned our room, our backpacks loaded, we trekked to the train station. As we walked down the chilly streets of Rotterdam, I did some reflecting. If nothing else, this trip solidified my theory that people make the places. There wasn't an abundance of exciting things to do and see in Rotterdam compared to, say, Paris, but we had an amazing time because of the people we were with. JJ's family wanted us to have a great time in their home country, and they had succeeded. I was definitely no traveling expert, but I could already tell that if we could find friends along the way, it would make our journey far more enriching.

Our fourth time was the charm. Our BlaBlaCar pickup, door to door, was flawless, thanks to our military-esque driver, Carmen. I sat in the back of the car, which was the size of a go-kart; Ash BlaBla'd in the front. She and Carmen chatted about their jobs and hometowns, and made other small talk.

Carmen dropped us off at a train station outside the city center. We were four for four on successful BlaBlaCar trips so far—*successful* being quantified by *surviving*. We purchased two one-trip metro tickets for six euros total and got on a train heading to central Amsterdam to meet Arjen, one of JJ's friends. He generously offered us a studio his parents owned on the Amstel canal.

The studio was incredible: it had a large bed, a washer, a big porch, and a table full of beer, chips, fruit, and chocolate as a welcoming gift from Arjen. We thanked him extensively and planned to get dinner with him and his girlfriend tomorrow. Tonight we had plans with an old buddy from App State, Matt, who had been traveling all over Asia for the last six months and was having a traveling-crew reunion in Amsterdam.

We set out to explore the city and started along the Amstel canal, passing houseboat after houseboat, some new, some old, some modern and chic, and some with moss growing on the tops.

After eating at an Italian restaurant, we left to find cold rain pelting us in this canal-lined city. We embraced the conditions; there was something beautiful about a chilly, rainy night in northern Europe.

We arrived at the bar at the the same time as Matt. There were embraces all around as we headed inside. After the phrase "First shots are for Cambodia!" rang out of the mouths of Matt and his traveling buddies, we had a feeling tonight was going to be unscripted.

The first bar was small, but it packed a punch. We took three shots in a matter of ten minutes. I don't always take tequila shots, but when the mood is right and they are handed to me in a loud, excited fashion, how does one say no? Each shot was chased with a ten-ounce Heineken. So there we were, three shots and five beers deep at 9:30 p.m. *This is a recipe for poor decision-making*, I thought.

The walk to the next bar was a blur. My memory of this transition is a lot of hugging and loud talking. I had reached the point where the next beer was going to put me into the land of no return. Ash had probably already passed the point of no return.

We entered the line for a nightclub that I quickly realized we were underdressed for. I watched as ladies in dresses and men in suits walked in ahead of us. I was wearing jogger pants, a casual button-down shirt, and Nike Lunars, my beard flowing in the wind. Ash was more presentable than I was, but her high-top Vans were no match for the stilettos every other girl had on. But the best thing to do when underdressed is pretend you are such a big deal that dress codes don't apply to you.

We approached the bouncer, and I walked up like I owned the place. The problem was, after the amount of tequila we had just consumed . . . *I didn't even know who I was.* The bouncer looked us up and down twice and, for whatever reason, let us in the club. The rest of the night is truly a blur.

This is the part of the movie where there is a montage of dancing; shots; deep, screaming conversations with strangers; shots; strobe lights illuminating sweaty faces; shots; smoke-filled rooms; and more shots. Five hours later, we emerged from the twilight zone and stumbled into the street. I looked down at my phone to get us directions home and saw 5:15 a.m. staring back at me. We somehow managed to crawl home like babies, unsure if each step would keep us upright. We reached our apartment just as the sun began to rise, splashing dull oranges and reds onto the canvas of the canals.

6/20/15
Amsterdam, Netherlands

Thump-thump, thump-thump . . . My head pounded as I struggled to open my eyes, confused about where I was, only able to focus on the throbbing in my head. Then the eject button in my stomach overpowered my head, and I ran to the bathroom just in time to vomit violently. I could barely recall what we'd done last night. My brain felt damaged.

When we were able to move, we decided to do what we'd tried to do at least one day in every city: get lost. We roamed the ever-changing streets; one minute we were walking past elegant houses on the canal, and the next minute we were cruising through clouds of marijuana smoke.

We arrived at the jungle of the city center. It was a smorgasbord of people basking in the lawless quarter of Amsterdam. Ash went into a Zara, and I sat outside on a curb and people watched.

It was one of the most intense people-watching sessions I had ever enjoyed. I saw the many faces of humans whose minds were so distinctly altered, their eyes were simply emotionless windshields for the brain to make sure they didn't run into objects. They were zombies, lost in deep thought. My own transfixed vision on these tripping souls was broken by the screams of a woman on a doorstep, waving a sign and yelling, "God can still save you! It is not too late!" *Quiet down,* I thought. *Can't you see these people are dreaming?*

It was time to gear up for dinner, so we walked the two miles home, still feeling the effects from the shit show of the previous evening. We took longer than anticipated to get ready for dinner with Arjen, and had to Uber to get to the restaurant on time. Only an Uber Black was available, so we rolled around Amsterdam in a Mercedes C-Class. I wrote this on my bucket list just so I could cross it off.

At the restaurant, Arjen introduced us to his girlfriend, Irene. Irene was such a sweet, charming woman; she perfectly complemented Arjen's generous nature. They had made reservations for us at a new French Alps–inspired restaurant called Les Bistrot des Alpes.

After dinner, we headed to one of Arjen's favorite bars in the middle of the Red Light District. Apparently, it is common for locals to go to bars in the district as if it were just another area. We passed through crowds of people partying in the streets, which were lined with women for sale via department store windows.

It was unfathomable to me how out in the open prostitution was. There were gorgeous lingerie-wearing women just waiting for someone to come to their doors. Before arriving, I was well aware of how things truly were in Amsterdam, but I could not believe how accessible and beautiful the women were in the flesh. Arjen explained that the women posing in the department store windows were union protected and paid much more than prostitutes working on their own.

After consuming better gin and tonics than I had anticipated, we escaped the loud noise of the bachelor parties and buzz of drunken people in the Red Light District and crossed the canal. The difference between the two sides was like night and day. What I would describe as a mix of Mardi Gras and porn convention was a mere three hundred yards from the peaceful Amstel.

Our budget, I should note, was once again obliterated—by the French cuisine, large gin and tonics, and Mercedes rides though Amsterdam. But these nights with new friends were priceless. We would just have to save money elsewhere. We did calf raises up the stairs to the studio and quickly fell asleep. Being Amsterdam VIPs had worn us out.

6/21/15
Amsterdam, Netherlands

We had tons of work to do to secure Airbnbs for the next month, book transportation to our next few cities, write reviews for previous hosts, and send and respond to e-mails. Just because we were unemployed, didn't mean we weren't working.

Before heading to a swanky hotel bar across the street from our studio to work, we decided to partake in Amsterdam's local offerings. Living in Denver had given us a taste of marijuana, but this joint was something much stronger and different. I figured it must have been laced with something, but by then I couldn't unsmoke it. So we did the only logical thing in this situation; we embraced the weirdness of its effects.

Ash was far less impaired than I was, as she had only taken a hit or two. She was ready to leave the apartment and get to work, but I was trying to get the room to stop spinning. I could not get down the stairs without laughing.

We made it to the street and then began the three-block trek. As we walked, Ash tripped over her own feet and nearly fell. I didn't know if her shoes were too heavy for her feet, but she had been tripping all over Europe. Speaking of tripping, *doesn't that dinosaur need to be on a leash?* I thought.

As I sat writing about our last few days in Amsterdam, I noticed how different each experience had been. We'd been explorers in France, beer tasters in Belgium, family members in Rotterdam, and partygoers in Amsterdam. That was one of our main qualms with working our nine-to-fives: the monotonous nature of our days. Sure, we could have spent more time doing different things, but after a long, stressful day at work, it was hard to do much of anything besides work out and eat dinner. I am a creature of habit and find comfort in routines. The problem with feeding this creature a routine was that I rarely found myself out of my comfort zone enough to grow. This trip had not only thrown me out of my comfort zone, but it had opened my eyes to the joys of living life on a tight budget. This was a small price to pay for freedom.

Since we'd left Denver two weeks ago, we'd been waking up every morning not knowing what the day had in store for us. We wandered and explored cities until we felt like we had it all figured out. But by the time this comfort had settled in, our train, bus, car, or plane was waiting to throw us into the next city, the next country, the next culture. We would miss Amsterdam, but we were excited to explore Germany.

6/22/15
Amsterdam, Netherlands → Berlin, Germany

Waking up at 5:30 a.m. was never going to get easier for me. Amsterdam is one of the few cities you can go to sleep and wake up at the same time on consecutive days. This was the second time I'd seen 5:45 a.m. on my phone this weekend. I'd packed my backpack the night before, but Ash went to sleep with early-morning packing ambitions instead. This shortsighted thinking led to her running around like a madwoman, throwing things into her backpack.

Arjen came to grab the studio key from us and see us off. I was grateful we'd gotten to know Arjen this week. He'd made our trip to Amsterdam special.

Our trip to Berlin was not by BlaBlaCar but by FlixBus. FlixBus is a massive double-decker Mercedes bus with onboard Wi-Fi, outlets at each seat, refreshments sold on board, and reclining seats. The buses travel all over Europe, with trips as cheap as five dollars a person. The large green bus began moving, and Ash fell asleep instantly. Ash is very similar to a baby when it comes to moving vehicles putting her to sleep.

After only forty-five minutes, we pulled over at a rest stop and the driver yelled, "Fifteen minutes!" squeezing the words out from the gap between his already lit cigarette and lips. We purchased coffee and waffles from Albert Heijn. Ash had only *just* finished the last bite of her waffle when she fell back asleep. I decided to start transferring my handwritten journals to a Google doc in case I lost them or spilled beer on them or something.

Our bus made one last stop in a small town in the middle of nowhere an hour outside of Berlin, but neither of us budged. Ash was fast asleep, and I was deep into my writing and listening to some German classical music.

Finally, the bus arrived in Berlin. As we gathered our belongings sprawled around our seat from the five-hour ride, a Dutch girl from across the aisle leaned in and asked, "Are you writing a book?"

I responded, "Uh, yeah, I think so."

Before leaving the bus, she smiled and said, "That's awesome; you have been writing for the last five hours! I write a lot, too—good luck!"

This was the first time I truly felt like an author. I hurried to get my backpack out from under the bus and then rushed off to find her. I said, "Hey! What's your e-mail? I'll send you the book when I finish it!" She excitedly wrote down her e-mail and told me she was looking forward to it. *I am too,* I thought. *I am too.*

The first leg of the journey was over; now we had to get to our neighborhood by metro. At this point, all the metro stations seemed essentially the same: people not speaking, kiosks, ticket machines, signs I couldn't read, and facial expressions I could.

As we sat on the metro I began recapping the previous day in my journal. Ash and I both noticed that everyone was watching me write my chicken scratch in furious motions (I am not a graceful writer). I couldn't tell if they were watching because people don't write in public anymore, or if it was because people just don't write very much anymore at all. Typing seems to be the easier and more efficient option in this day and age. I prefer writing because it truly makes me think about what I'm putting on paper. With the ease with which we hit the delete button, we can erase thoughts too quickly. Would I be editing and transcribing on a computer later? Yes. But the therapeutic feeling of writing my daily thoughts was beginning to help me cope with the massive amounts of stress I still carried. Society still had a stronghold on me, and although I was beginning to see the benefits of travel, I still constantly questioned if we had made the right decision. Ash was my therapist. She reminded me that we were doing this for our own growth, the growth of seeing the world, something that very few jobs could give us. I hoped she was right.

We stepped out of the metro and into a world unlike one we'd ever seen: cars and bikes whizzing by with people wearing stylish rags, black-and-white punk outfits, and trendy-hipster clothing. I felt like I was in a Tim Burton movie.

We were staying in the Kreuzberg neighborhood of Berlin. After a short walk, we found our building nestled between a bike repair shop and a hip café. We buzzed our host Sasha and heard the lock on the massive door open.

We got lucky because when we'd inquired about staying with him, he told us he was actually going to be out of town in Istanbul for work. We had the entire flat to ourselves, starting tomorrow. We would be in Berlin for five days, our longest stretch in any city yet. We didn't want to leave without really taking in the customs and culture.

We unpacked quickly so we could go explore the Berlin bustling outside our window. For dinner, we were meeting our good friends Marius and Julia. They were natives of Germany but had spent the

last six months working in Denver. We put the address of the restaurant into Google Maps and started the 1.6-mile walk. The buildings
in our neighborhood were emblazoned with impressive graffiti. We
crossed corner after corner of graffiti all the way to the bridge that led
into what used to be East Berlin.

As we crossed the massive bridge over the Spree River, we looked
down on the railroad tracks, covered in trash. It seemed every person
who'd crossed this bridge had thrown an empty beer bottle over the
edge. The grime and grunginess of the city perfectly encompassed
the culture of the creative individuals who inhabited it. I felt more
alive walking through these streets than I had felt in a while.

6/23/15
Berlin, Germany

With our first full day in Berlin, we set out into the rain to find the
Berlin Wall. We reached the wall at the end of the bridge and gazed
at the famous East Side Gallery. The wall was illustrated with seg-
ments from amazing artists from all over the world. I started panning
across the second segment and came to a picture of abstract faces
with large lips. It was one of my favorite pieces, and the name at the
bottom read, MARY MACKEY DENVER, CO USA. (Well, how about that?)

After walking the entire length of the Berlin Wall, we wanted to
check out Spreepark, an old abandoned amusement park that had
been turned into a city park. It was a long walk, but we found a
shortcut through trails.

It hit me that we had not seen another human in a long time.
Where the hell is everyone? The weird feeling intensified as we passed
a lone tombstone with no writing on it. *Seems like an odd place for
a tombstone,* I thought. I turned from the gravestone just in time to
see a massive German shepherd staring back at me. My fight-*and-
flight* adrenaline lines must have run into each other while coursing
through my veins, because rather than fighting or flighting, I froze
up and tried to keep urine from running down my legs. Suddenly the
dog's owner came jogging around the corner. She smiled at us as the

two of them ran off. Ash and I exhaled and laughed nervously, as if we'd just dodged a bullet.

We exited the shortcut and crossed the street into our original destination of Spreepark. I had not been able to shake this eerie feeling as we entered another humanless path surrounded by thick woods. This particular deserted park was covered in dark-green brush, and, simply put, felt dead. The cold rain dropped off branches and onto the fallen leaves. The sky, meanwhile, was quickly darkening with the oncoming night.

We continued down the path, looking for a sign for the amusement park. We started seeing the remnants of the old park through a barbed wire fence as the sun began setting, and we passed a sign that read, DO NOT ENTER! GUARDING WITH DOGS! DANGER TO LIFE AND LIMB! *Well, that doesn't seem necessary, does it?* The worst part was the singular "limb" as I imagined a German shepherd tearing one of my forearms to shreds.

The one-hundred-foot-tall Ferris wheel stood alone in the cold sky, rocking back and forth, creaking as each gust swelled. We agreed we had seen enough scary parks for one day and decided to get the hell out of there. We still had a mile and a half to cover to get out of the woods, and our phone batteries were dying quickly. We'd started talking about how easy it would be for someone to murder us out there just as we saw headlights approaching.

This was a walking path, and we were in the middle of nowhere. Why would there be a vehicle? I immediately assessed our situation. We were alone in a deserted German park, a mile and a half from civilization. Both of our phones were almost dead, and it was getting dark, not to mention extremely cold (the temperature didn't really affect anything, but it didn't help). The beat-up car continued approaching us and was only 250 yards away.

Weapons. Do I have any weapons? I looked around and found nothing but small shrubs and sticks. I sure wish I had a Swiss Army knife. Then I got it: Ash's Canon camera. This was our largest object and would be heavy enough to do some damage. *If I give a surprise blow to the head and follow it with a quick uppercut,* I thought, *I should be able to rattle the chin enough to knock them out.* If nothing else, it would stun them momentarily, and I could tackle whoever was coming at us while Ash ran.

As I prepped my mind to make solid connections and gave Ash the game plan, the car inched forward, its lights now on dim. Ash slowly handed me the camera, and we took deep breaths. It was the moment of truth: one hundred yards away, and we were clearly in their headlights now. Fifty yards . . . forty yards. When the car was twenty-five yards away, we could make out the silhouette of a large man. He spotted us and stopped. Showtime.

Just as we were preparing to execute our plan, the guy seemed as spooked by us as we were of him. He began an awful attempt at a three-point turn, and executed the seldom-used six-point turn instead. After thirty seconds of inching forward and back, he sped off in the other direction.

We looked at each other and laughed out loud at how shaken up we were. I told Ash I wasn't really *that scared*, but my drawn-out plan of action had clearly given me away. We left the park and made it to our Airbnb by memory (somehow). We were angry with ourselves for allowing both of our phones to die while we were alone in a park, and even to let a situation like that become . . . *a situation like that*. Tomorrow things would be different.

6/24/15
Berlin, Germany

We could not help but sleep in. It was a cold, rainy morning, and the constant pattering on the window produced too soothing a rhythm for us to wake up.

Eventually, our hunger took over the window music. I left to grab breakfast. Nothing looked very appetizing at the market, so I ventured farther down the street, past the shops we'd popped into yesterday. One of the hipster punk shops had a necklace with a *K* emblem on it that Ash had wanted. She didn't end up getting it because it was pricey, but I wouldn't have minded her wearing my initial on her neck all the time.

With no luck finding a place to grab food on this street either, I asked the shop owner to recommend a good breakfast spot. She gave me some vague directions to a place called something "Schmuck." She couldn't remember the first word in the name, but told me it had the best brunch in the neighborhood. If I knew the name, I could google it, but "Schmuck" wasn't registering as a location.

Ash was far from impressed that instead of food, I returned with a great recommendation to a place I didn't know the name of. It was getting close to noon, and if my lady hasn't eaten by noon, she turns into a Hangry Hulkess. I was running out of time before the transformation.

Today we were going to Tempelhof Airport, and we agreed to find food on the way. We strolled in the direction of the abandoned airport and kept an eye out for places to eat. I had forgotten about the mythical "Schmuck" restaurant when Ash pointed out a place that looked good. We approached the quirky-looking diner to see a cursive sign that read SALON SCHMÜCK. *Well, I'll be damned,* I thought.

We took seats at a comfortable table in the café, which had a living room feel, and we ordered two shots of espresso each while we waited for our food. The food arrived, and it was exquisite. The French toast had bacon sprinkled on top, and the *berg auf tal*, essentially a continental breakfast, was a mountain of cheese, meats, fruits and vegetables, and a basket of rolls, toast, and small baguettes. It looked *way too good* to be true. The only thing we were missing was butter for the bread. This was a small price to pay for a heavenly meal. Our trek continued.

The Tempelhof Airport was one of the world's first commercial airports. It was an instrumental hub in World War II Nazi Germany, but it was closed down in 2008 so it could be turned into a park where cyclists, joggers, kiteboarders, and other active people use the former runways for recreational purposes.

We reached the airport and walked along the massive old runway. I realized this was my first time going less than two hundred miles per hour on a runway. There was a harsh chill coursing through the Berlin air, and although we had jackets on, we still had to find a bench on the wheel-beaten asphalt to sit behind to escape the biting wind. If the bench didn't do the trick, I imagined the large beers we'd bought on the way here would. We attempted to play a card game, but the wind was like a pestering two-year-old throwing our cards all over the place. Luckily for the kiteboarders, and unluckily for us, the wind kicked up a notch.

It was great that we were legally allowed to drink in public in Berlin, but the true game changer was that I could legally urinate in public. I took advantage of this legality and relieved my bladder over the fence to make room for my second beer in public. *I could certainly get used to this lifestyle,* I thought as a kiteboarder flew off the end of the runway as if he were taking off.

6/25/15
Berlin, Germany

After a long day doing nothing but drinking on an old runway, our goal was to explore the museum district of Berlin. As we stepped off the stoop of our place and onto the street, I felt like I was waking up in a new city. It was the first day since we had arrived in Berlin that we had seen the sun. All of a sudden "AAACHH-OOOO" erupted from my mouth.

It felt like the scene in *Forrest Gump* where Forrest is in Vietnam and the sun finally comes out after days of rain, immediately followed by a barrage of bullets. The allergies hit me hard and fast as we walked. I popped an allergy pill I found in the bottom of my toiletry bag, despite the label claiming the meds had expired in 2009.

On our way to the museums, Ash stopped to do a little more shopping.

I ventured across the street to the pharmacy as she went through the robotic motions of sifting through clothing racks. I bought some prescription-grade allergy medicine for seven dollars. The pharmacy system in Europe is amazing.

We made it through the shopping district without spending a dime (I was both impressed and surprised Ash had not purchased anything since we had arrived), and three hours later we had arrived at the Holocaust memorial.

This Holocaust memorial in Berlin is called the Memorial to the Murdered Jews of Europe, a gut-wrenching name for a gut-wrenching time. In my opinion, it is an architectural masterpiece. The memorial is made up of thousands of concrete stelae (slabs often serving as gravestones) in rows representing the six million Jewish people killed during World War II. I believe that the memorial's architect, Peter Eisenman, designed it to represent the paradox of chaotic order. Although the concrete stelae were in perfect rows and in grid form, the memorial rested on a hill, and this effect created wide-ranging heights for the blocks of stones. Some were a few feet tall; others towered over our heads. I feel as if Eisenman was trying to symbolize a world of normality and order that had been completely shaken up and destabilized. I quietly walked through a deep alleyway of the memorial and reached a point where the sunlight was blocked by a fifteen-foot-tall stela. Towers of cold concrete surrounded me, leaving me in the dark, bringing on a general sense of loneliness and despair. *Well done, Peter Eisenman, well done,* I thought.

We ordered some Helles Hefe Weizen at a market and then went to the Reichstag building, the meeting place of the German parliament. We didn't want to pay to go in and watch them work—that wasn't really our thing; instead we stayed outside and drank our beers and people watched as everyone took photos in front of the building. It was an amazing-looking building architecturally, but the people taking pictures were much more amusing. The selfie epidemic has reached an undeniable worldwide fever pitch.

We had to part ways with Berlin the next day—already our fifth day. We had fallen in love with the city. Every city had been beautiful, each country unique, but Berlin—Berlin made me feel like we'd conquered something. If Seattle and Brooklyn had a tatted-up toddler in a leather jacket who'd been expelled from preschool for selling cigarettes on the playground . . . that would be Berlin. She was just clean enough to avoid being dirty, the people and temperature just warm enough to avoid being cold, and the history just recent enough to avoid being forgettable.

6/26/15
Berlin, Germany → Prague, Czech Republic

We were on the road again. We walked through our neighborhood toward the Hallesches Tor metro station. It is remarkable how our familiarity and perception of the neighborhood had changed since our arrival. We had eaten at almost every restaurant on our block, and knew the faces of the bike repair shop and market owners. We smiled and waved at them as we left. We reached our station and flew through the ticket machine process without breaking our stride.

After departing the metro station, we found our bus. We were the first ones on, and we took front seats in the double-decker Mercedes. Once we were settled, I left the bus to grab some breakfast from a bistro near the station. We were nearing the noon mark in a few hours, and Ash was closing in on Hangry Hulkess. I pulled the trigger on some croissants and blueberry muffins. I also got some German chocolate. (This was ammo in case Ash got angry with me later. No matter what I did wrong . . . *chocolate solved everything.*)

As the bus smoothly hummed, I dozed in and out in that purgatory zone—the sleep zone where you're awake enough to hear the conversations around you, but not awake enough to respond and defend yourself if someone talks shit about you because they thought you were asleep. Before falling asleep, I kept thinking about getting kidnapped. Then I finally dozed off for good.

I must have been in a deep enough sleep to feel . . . *at home.* I passed a large amount of gas, loud enough that it actually woke me up. The bus was full of strangers and was completely silent prior to this event—everyone had heard it. I quickly ran my crisis-management analysis and had to decide whether to play it off and continue sleeping (I had not yet opened my eyes), or wake up and act casual, like it wasn't me. I tried to move in my chair and replicate the sound of the fart; unfortunately, no movement in my chair mimicked the noise of a bowel explosion. I tried to kick casually at the footrest— that wasn't going to cut it either.

My curiosity about the passengers' reaction to the trumpet sound was too strong, and I opened my eyes and immediately glanced at

Ash, hoping at least she had slept through it. She was staring at me, holding her shirt up to her nose to create a safety tent, not too pleased that the cannon had been aimed in her direction. I stared at her apologetically and slowly pulled the chocolate out of my backpack. She perked up and excitedly began eating the chocolate. Unfortunately, I did not have enough chocolate for the rest of the bus.

We arrived in Prague and were reminded that our euros would not work in a country that used Czech crowns. *Idiots.* We would be here for four days, so we got eight thousand crowns out, which equated to about three hundred dollars. We had four bills total, each worth two thousand crowns. Unfortunately, the train tickets were forty-five crowns each, and the machine wouldn't take our two-thousand crown bills.

It took us going into four shops before someone understood English and our dilemma, and agreed to give us change for a two-thousand-crown bill. We finally got our tickets, and it took two trains to get to our stop.

Eager to see the city of *Praha*, we unpacked everything we could into the empty drawers of our simple Airbnb setup, then hit the city. We put "Prague City Center" into our maps and started the mile-long walk. This was usually a good way to see things. Start at the nucleus. We came to the top of a hill about halfway to the city center, and there she was in all her beauty . . . Ash. And behind Ash, was Prague.

We stopped in our tracks and looked down hundreds of feet at the elegant city made up of castles, churches, Gothic buildings, and bridges that connected the two sides of the Vltava River. There must have been a second or two of silence before Ash blurted out, "Shut the fuck up." I'd only only heard her blurt this out once before, when we first saw the view of a beautiful Costa Rican bay from the porch of our hotel years ago.

The surprise aerial view of the city had distracted us from all the people to our right enjoying the view of the city over their large beers. It dawned on us that we had stumbled upon the beer garden we had read about: Letná Beer Garden, a beer-drinker-and-hilltop-view-lover's dream.

We entered the city center, and it truly was a fairy-tale landscape, replete with horse-drawn carriages click-clacking through the mazes of cobblestone roads sheltered by neoclassic architecture and Gothic buildings. The Old Town Square was humming with happy people dining and laughing. *It's impossible to be in a bad mood here.* What I truly loved about the vibe in this square was that it seemed like everyone acknowledged how lucky he or she was to be in Prague at that particular moment.

We wanted to try genuine Czech food at some point. Tonight, however, we were in the mood for Mexican.

The margaritas made the meal a blur, and food quickly came and disappeared. We grimaced as our waitress brought us the bill for an order of nachos, two chicken burritos, and four margaritas. I did the conversion math and found our bill was the equivalent to only eighteen dollars. "We are spoiled forever," we joked, dishing out crowns like a dentist in the seventies.

Ash and I raced back to the Old Town Square, reenergized by tequila. I noticed a large crowd of people with their iPhones and selfie sticks handy, surrounding a large clock tower. As the clock struck midnight, ancient-looking skeletons emerged from doors around the clock and began dancing. This was the Prague *orloj*, the oldest working astronomical clock in the world (it was built in 1410).

We wrapped up our first night in Prague by sitting in the middle of the square enjoying coffee and dessert. The lit-up towers and soft music had Ash's romance meter soaring. She continued to talk about how romantic this place was, and we held hands as we ate dessert. We had been on the move so much in the last few weeks and trying to see so much that I felt like I hadn't adequately shown Ash how thankful I was that she pushed us to do this.

Before our walk home, I pulled out the *K* necklace from Berlin. That morning when I'd gone to get breakfast, I had snuck back into the store and bought it for her. It wasn't much, and maybe only cost seventy-five dollars, but the look on her face when I brought it out of my pocket was worth every dime. I had planned to save it for a romantic night in Italy, but I couldn't imagine a night more romantic than this. Ash wore Prague well; I took it as a by-product of our not only falling in love with each other all over again, but also falling in love with our journey. We kissed under the Prague moon as the *orloj* struck one.

6/27/15
Prague, Czech Republic

We consumed our morning double espressos in the beer garden overlooking the city. It turned out that the coffee shop up here already served double espressos as their "espresso." So when we'd ordered a double, we'd actually received four shots of the good stuff.

By the end of breakfast I had the shakes. I felt like I was going through heroin withdrawal. The amount of coffee we had just consumed was unhealthy. Now that I think about it, we had been drinking nothing but coffee, beer, and wine since we'd arrived in Europe. I am usually good about hydrating, but when water cost the same amount as beer, water *rarely* won that fight.

We left the coffee shop and made our way toward the Vltava River to roam the New Town. We were trying to decide if we liked Prague or Berlin better, and whether we liked Berlin better than Amsterdam. Then it dawned on me: by ranking these cities, we were quantifying them. We shouldn't try to quantify our experiences; we had loved every city we'd been to thus far, so there was no point in ranking them. Paris may be the prettiest city, but the beer in Belgium, the people in Netherlands, and the energy in Berlin were just as special in their own ways.

We strolled aimlessly and joyfully down the old, pristine roads and wrapped up our first full day in Prague by drinking a bottle of wine at dinner and watching a pub crawl of college kids stamp drunkenly through the streets. They seemed so childish to us as we elegantly sipped our wine, but we realized we were only four years removed from those college days.

Here we were, four years later in the dreaded so-called real world that every adult in our lives had warned us about. I think Ash's and my generation is trapped in a tough period between the perceived lifestyle of the last two generations (the Boomers and Gen Xers) and the technological advancements and worldwide globalization of the last two decades, which has dramatically altered the landscape of the new normal workforce. This has created the paradox wherein so many people in their thirties, forties, and fifties are now taking the jobs that Millennials need in their late twenties. I was starting to realize that traveling the world and taking a step off the ladder for four months may help me find the elevator—that is, the elevator to happiness, which contrary to what I had believed (and had drilled into my head) growing up, may not necessarily be a high-paying job with a great title.

As we walked back across the bridge and started the steep ascent, it turned out to be a tougher climb up—four hundred steps—to get to the beer garden that we'd thought, but the view was worth the work.

6/28/15
Prague, Czech Republic

Today served as a workday for us, and we found a coffee shop with outdoor seating in the bustling city center. We needed to figure out our transportation for the next city and where to stay in Krakow and Budapest.

We finished up the day of work, mapping out a plan. Then we followed the main promenade that brought us back through the Old Town on the way home. We swam through a swarm of selfie stick savages and street performers. The smell of Vietnamese food filled our nostrils. We approached a pho restaurant that made my mouth water like a dog waiting for its dinner. After a few minutes of debating whether we should eat Czech food, we caved. Spring rolls and three different types of pho were brought to the table less than an hour later. This wasn't the first and surely wouldn't be the last time where our eyes would be bigger than our stomachs.

We took our leftovers up to the beer garden to watch the sunset over the city and drink a nightcap. The cool evening air turned into a chilly breeze, and we walked home hand in hand to rest our heads before our final day in Prague.

6/29/15
Prague, Czech Republic

For our last day in Prague, we decided to go to the zoo. I'll save my speech about how we were torn. Prague Zoo was ranked number seven in the world; this was a no-brainer. It was three miles northwest of our Airbnb, but we needed the exercise. We had failed to hit our goal of twenty thousand steps on Ash's step tracker yesterday.

It was nearing noon. We had to get food soon. We passed a crepe place, but let's be honest: *crepes don't fill you up.* We expected to find something soon after, but the route to the zoo led us to the middle of nowhere. Ash started mentioning how we should have just gotten crepes, and I could see her skin start to turn a hint of green. *I am running out of time.* We walked through a gorgeous park and then crossed over a bridge that looked like it took us into a new country. We went from the busy vehicle-covered roads of Prague, surrounded by parks and trees, to an arid farmland with animals roaming flora-less pastures.

I double-checked the map to make sure this was right, and sure enough, the zoo was still ahead. We approached a hut on the side of the road that had a beer sign lit up. There was a slim chance they had food, but I couldn't afford to miss an opportunity to avoid the Hangry Hulkess. We entered and asked the guy if they had any food. He didn't speak English and just kept repeating "Beer?" *Well, what the hell? It's better than nothing.* We left the hut with two big beers for a total of two dollars, the breakfast of champions.

Finally we spotted the only restaurant north of the river, and we didn't even care if they only served crepes at this point.

The zoo may have been in the middle of nowhere, but it *did* have a bar attached to the outside. I love the Czechs' style; they pre-gamed for the zoo. It was now 1:00 p.m., and my daily consumption consisted of two gargantuan beers and one panini. I needed to start questioning my dieting habits at this point in the trip if I wanted to make it to Thailand in September.

We entered the zoo with a good buzz and grabbed maps. I immediately became overwhelmed with how nonuniform and scattered the layout of the zoo was. The map was a huge rectangle but with routes going every which way. How the hell were we supposed to see every animal in an organized manner? That is what I love about the Denver Zoo: it's set up in a large circle, so we can walk around and see all the animals.

We made the best game plan we could and started up the path. It only took five minutes before both Ash and I were extremely annoyed by all the people surrounding the exhibits. Particularly annoying were the kids, screaming in different languages. Hearing a six-year-old say, "Mommy, look, the gorilla is sniffing his own poop!" is normally cute, but when you can't understand the language, the sounds just become piercing high-pitched screaming.

At last we arrived at the best exhibit in the whole zoo—the beer tent. As we took a break and drank our Czech beers, we both Instagrammed pictures of animals. We were in a heated competition at this point for who could get the most likes. I was absolutely getting my ass handed to me.

Now laughing as we walked past exhibits, we'd admittedly drunk a bit too much to truly enjoy the animals. By drinking the breakfast beer, we had pregamed for the pregame for the zoo.

We left the zoo after attempting to see as many animals as we could before the chaos of the layout got to me. It seemed like a good idea to grab another travel beer at the hut on the way home, and this time the guy didn't need to ask; he knew what we wanted.

The long afternoon had wiped us out, and back at our Airbnb we decided to lie down to rest. Ash was struggling with a mean bout of hiccups, and I tried to scare her by yelling, "Zara is going out of business!" She was far from amused and hiccupped again shortly after. As I climbed into bed, I realized I was suffering from two things . . . a hangover and sunburn. (These are two of the most obnoxious pains on earth because of how avoidable they are. Day drinking is a blast until you stop.)

6/30/15
Prague, Czech Republic –> Kraków, Poland

The last few days I had been having trouble sleeping, and it seemed my best hours were in the very early mornings. Night was becoming a long period where I stared aimlessly at the ceiling in the hot apartment, worrying about nothing. It felt like I had just fallen asleep when Ash shook me awake to catch our bus to Kraków, Poland. I had even slept through her frantic bag-packing episode.

We were visiting Kraków for the sole reason that it was the closest big city to the Auschwitz concentration camp. I'd been obsessed with learning about World War II and the Holocaust as a kid, and I'd read tons of books on the death camp. I remember being intrigued by how horrifying the world could be. The fact that these stories of murder camps and one man convincing a whole country to commit genocide were true was actually unbelievable to me. I was drawn to the stories of survival in particular.

When we decided to visit, we decided there was only one Airbnb in the small town of Oświęcim. Not only did the Airbnb not match any of our requirements, Oświęcim was also directly outside of Auschwitz. Something told me we would want to get as far away as we could after experiencing the evil of the camp. We didn't know much about Kraków, but we did know that there was only *one* bus that went there from Prague.

The bus station where we would catch said bus was two miles from our Prague Airbnb, a cakewalk. This trip had already drastically changed the way we looked at a few miles. Back in Denver, a two-mile distance was surely an Uber ride. Now time would be the only reason we wouldn't walk when we saw two miles on the map. On the way out, it was nice to say good-bye to the city in person. Taking the metro would have been like breaking up with someone over text message.

We always built in about an hour of "mistake time" in case we took a wrong turn somewhere or couldn't find the entrance. Our trek was mistake free, and we sat down at gate number 9 and watched as super charter bus after super charter bus, similar to our FlixBus vehicles, drove by. Unfortunately, FlixBus did not go to Kraków from Prague, and we had to venture elsewhere in the world of European buses.

We laughed at the sight of a raggedy-looking bus that entered the station. The pink-and-purple-striped vehicle had clearly been born in the nineties. (It should have died there.) All of a sudden the pink murder mobile banked a hard left and started approaching us. *Oh God . . . please no,* I thought as the driver parked the wretched vehicle at our gate.

"You go to Kraków?" the driver asked as he stepped off the creaking bus. He was a prototypical middle-aged Polish man. Bald, bold, and blunt. Two other Polish men were on the bus with him.

"Uhhh, yeah, but you know, our bus is probably coming soon," I responded, still in denial that one, this bus was running, and two, that he expected anyone to get on it. I turned slowly and shot a quick glance at my ticket to check the name of our bus. When I looked at the cardboard sign hanging by a single piece of Scotch tape on the windshield of the Polish man's bus, my stomach hit my throat. *The letters match up.*

The Polish driver looked at my ticket that I was trying to hide and said, "Yes. This bus," and ushered us on.

Ash and I looked at each other as if to say, *This is our only option,* shrugged, and boarded the putrid-smelling bus for our journey into the heart of Poland. We knew this wouldn't be a luxury ride, but there was no way to predict the awfulness of our next nine hours.

My first reaction was this must be hell. *Dark, hot, and for people that made a really horrible decision in life.* We sat down in seats 25 and 26, next to a band of misfits. Sprawled across the backseat, snoring, was a man with a blanket on, whimpering like a dog having a bad dream. In front of us was a sweaty man with sunglasses on; he had greasy hair and a very smelly neck brace. I only knew this because his seat was so far back. We were far from comfortable, but I figured I could use the nine-hour drive to get some work done. I searched the seat for the outlet the website had promised. I couldn't find anything but trash and flies and went to ask the only one of the three Polish guys who spoke a lick of English where the outlets were.

"No outlet, sorry," he said harshly, with no explanation, and turned back to the other two Polish men who came with the bus. I think they were a family; they were talking pretty harshly to one another and all looked rather mean. The back two rows, we noticed, were made into beds with sheets and pillows. I though this must be a glorified RV. I was assuming they just made their living driving people around on this piece of shit. *No big deal. I have a few hours until the computer dies,* I thought, and headed back to our row, where Ash was trying to get comfortable enough to sleep. I knew this situation was bad when Ash didn't fall asleep immediately. She could sleep in a Dumpster.

I needed the code for the Wi-Fi to access Google docs and do some work, so I headed back to the Polish circle and asked them what the Wi-Fi code was. When the English-speaking one told the others what I had asked, they started laughing. I am unfamiliar with Polish customs, but I am going to go out on a limb and suspect they weren't laughing *with* me.

I hadn't slept last night, so I figured I would try to work on that instead. Before I went to sleep, I went to relieve my overfull bladder. I had drunk a ton of water, trying to hydrate before the ride. I stumbled up the moving vehicle and opened the semi-broken door to the bathroom and found what looked like a bedroom closet. Clothes on hangers lined the small space, and the toilet had been removed altogether. The last thing I heard before falling asleep while holding my bladder shut was someone with broken English from the front of the bus, yelling, "Next shtop, Brno, tree howers."

Ash sat across from me on an empty row of seats so we could sprawl out. I dozed in and out of awful sleep. At one point, I dreamed of someone tickling my face. I woke up to find that two flies had landed on my forehead. *How do flies get on a moving vehicle like this?* I realized I was also sweating profusely. There was clearly no AC on this rolling hellhole, and the seats were made out of that fuzzy material that trapped heat and was often found in old vans. This was a nightmare.

We sputtered to a halt at a city bus stop. There were people waiting there, but they were clearly waiting for a different type of bus, probably a bus that didn't reek and that had a bathroom. One of the family members got off and started to talk to the people. I watched as the others peered through the curtain at the representative outside. The brother (I'd assumed by this point the men were brothers) outside was negotiating with the people, and after a minute or two, a couple of them boarded the bus and handed him some cash. In anticipation of these additions to our crew, Ash came back to her seat next to me. Sure enough, a woman sat down in the seat across from us and began eating.

Suddenly I smelled smoke. I knew this thing was going to break down; I knew it without a doubt. I hadn't expected it to light on fire, though. To my surprise, we didn't slow down to pull over. I looked around to see if anyone else noticed that our bus was clearly on fire. The woman across from us kept eating, the man in the back kept sleeping, and the neck brace guy . . . kept neck bracing. Finally I stood up to see what the deal was and saw the smoke; it was coming from the driver's cigarette. His window unopened. We continued to Brno.

When we finally pulled into Kraków, we hit a bump at the station, and the door of the bathroom/closet fell completely off the hinges and hit the ground. *This bus is literally falling apart.* We quickly exited to gasp fresh air. *Welcome to Kraków.*

I had not done a ton of research on Kraków. We really didn't know what to expect, but I certainly didn't expect this massive, immaculate Kraków Główny station that dually served as a mall. This was easily the cleanest and richest-looking station we had been in yet, and we walked, dumbfounded, through the massive domed area. We passed a nice grocery store, luxury boutiques, and even an H&M that I made sure Ash missed by pointing at a cute baby in the other direction. We had imagined Kraków to be a cold, desolate Polish farmland.

We went outside and started walking through nice quiet roads with lush green parks and cool boutiques. We entered the Old Town by passing a protective castle barrier. I could feel the history of this city with every structure we passed.

After entering the city center, we found our Airbnb for the next few days. It was located in the very center of Kraków and on a classic European street with an ice cream shop, jewelry store, coffee shop, café, and boutique. Kraków looked like it had all the good qualities from the other cities without the negative ones. There were just enough people to make it busy.

Our apartment on the fourth and top floor of the building was amazing. There was a washer and a massive king-sized bed. The bedroom window had a view down onto our street. I took two showers, because the first one just didn't feel adequate enough after that bus ride. I felt like I had cigarette smoke infused into my hair and beard at this point.

We found the best Italian place in Kraków and ventured in that direction. It was only 0.4 miles away, and the walk led us right into the main square. The large open space was as vibrant as anywhere we had been. It is actually one of the largest open squares in all of Europe. There were street performers, shoppers, diners, locals, and tourists crowding the square in an orderly chaos. We had that feeling we had in Prague, where all of a sudden we felt a jolt of energy from all the people enjoying their evenings.

The two towers of St. Mary's Basilica and the Town Hall Tower overlooked the square like proud parents. We promised to spend more time here, but our stomachs would not permit it at the moment. We arrived at Ti Amo Ti.

An Italian family owned the highly rated restaurant, and we were intent on checking it out. We sat down, a little unsure of what to expect, and ordered two big Polish beers called Żywiec. We started the meal with a platter of meats and cheeses that came with pizza crust bread on a giant slab of wood. When it arrived, I looked to Ash and saw her whisper, "Shut the fuck up," under her breath. I was proud of her discretion.

We happily ravaged the food, but there was simply too much to finish. Our young Polish waiter brought out diavola pizza with homemade tomato sauce. After consuming all we could, I decided if I were ever on death row, this would be my last meal.

Kraków had been the biggest surprise of the trip thus far. We were staying right downtown for fifty dollars a night, and had just witnessed a gorgeous city square and eaten a meal sent from heaven for twenty-five dollars. Speaking of heaven, it may have been the hell we went through to get here that made it all so good.

7/1/15
Kraków, Poland

I woke up to turn off my alarm and noticed the word *July* pop up on my phone. This time a month ago, Ash and I were moving out of our apartment and taking all our belongings to a storage unit. Today, Ash and I were resting in a penthouse apartment in Kraków, Poland. . . . A lot can change in thirty days.

To start off the day, we decided to first get lost in the city square. There wasn't very much Kraków, it turned out, to get lost in. As the St. Mary's Basilica clock struck noon, a trumpet popped out of the tower and started playing the "Hejnał Mariacki," a five-note Polish anthem. As the tune played, hundreds of crows flew around the clock tower, only intensifying the medieval aesthetic that haunted this city.

Halfway through the song, Ash had spotted a Zara across the square and darted off. I knew I'd have some time on my hands, so I set up camp at a bar across the square and ordered a half-liter of Polish beer called Okocim.

When Ash returned, again without purchasing anything (I was so proud of her restraint), we set off to explore more of the Old Town. The other main attraction in Kraków was the Wawel Castle. It was amazing that the Gothic walls still stood on the Wawel Hill overlooking Kraków seven hundred years after being built. We circled the large castle and drank espressos every few hundred feet. We couldn't help but indulge in the casual caffeine kicks at a dollar apiece.

We had already decided that although there may have been a better meal somewhere else, we wanted to head back to Ti Amo Ti. There was a fifteen-minute wait before we could be seated, but our Polish waiter from last night spotted us and rushed over. "Hey, I remember you two!" he said. When we were seated, we saved him any sort of speech about specials and ordered the exact same meal as the night before.

"If it ain't broke, don't fix it," is a model many live by. That model should also be taken into consideration in its reverse form, "If it is broke, fix it." A wise man once told me: "If what you are doing is not actively filling you up and giving you as much energy as you are putting into it, stop doing it immediately." Ash and I loved our time in Denver, but after two years, our lives were no longer filling us up. I was very reluctant to drop it all and leave, but we were now three weeks into our journey, and I was starting to see that what we had been doing back home was simply not worth the time we were investing. "Life is short" is a cliché, but have you ever heard a wise elderly person tell you about how long life is and not to worry about exploring the world because you can always do it later?

7/2/15
Kraków, Poland → Auschwitz, Poland

We left our Airbnb at 7:30 a.m. and paid a total of seven dollars at the Główny station for two tickets on the next bus out of town. Next stop: Auschwitz.

I left Ash in line for the bus to grab lunch, and when I came back with subs and bottles of water, there was a swarm of people surrounding her. Nobody looked inclined to follow the first-come, first-serve rule of thumb. When the bus finally pulled up, a group of obnoxious Spanish girls standing at the back of the line rudely rushed up to the front of the bus as it pulled in. They skipped the whole line and boarded the bus first.

Normally this would drive me crazy, but because of where *we were going* today, it forced me to let go of this obsession to be first in line. When the prisoners were transported to Auschwitz, their captors crammed 150 people into cattle cars that had a capacity of 50 people. Many traveled for four days with no food or water and had one single latrine bucket. Scores died in transit to the camp.

We boarded the bus and took seats near the front for the hour-and-a-half ride to the infamous Nazi death camp. As a kid, I wasn't allowed to watch *South Park*, and I had to cover my eyes when Itchy and Scratchy came on *The Simpsons*. Yet my parents urged me to read about the Holocaust from a very young age. As soon as I could conquer chapter books, I was invested in the atrocities of the 1940s, reading *Night* by Elie Wiesel and *The Diary of a Young Girl* by Anne Frank in middle school. Going to Auschwitz had been a lifelong goal of mine because of how much time I had spent reading about it. Some kids dreamed of going to Disney World; I dreamed of visiting Poland and couldn't have been more eager to experience Auschwitz today.

We exited the bus and got in line to enter the camp; thankfully and luckily for us, entering Auschwitz was a choice. I tried to imagine what it would feel like to finally step off a boxcar that had been rotting with the stench of feces and death for four days. *If only for a millisecond*, I thought, *these poor people would have found relief in stretching their legs and emerging into fresh air.* Unfortunately, this relief quickly disappeared when the selection process began.

While waiting in line, we learned that after 10:30 a.m. we had to be accompanied by a guide through the camp for crowd-control purposes. This was probably a blessing in disguise, as we would learn more about the camp and its history from a guide than by simply reading signs. I was surprised at how well organized this place was, but then again . . . organizing herds of people was what this camp had done.

The prisoners of Auschwitz who were brought in on the boxcars had a much different experience than we did. Upon arrival, they were immediately lined up for the infamous selection process with the SS doctors (Nazi doctors famous for performing heinous experiments on prisoners as if they were animals, not humans). If one was deemed "fit" for labor and was over the age of fourteen, they were branded with prisoner identification and stripped of their hair, clothes, belongings, and the life they once knew. Those under the age of fourteen, the elderly, or women with children, were immediately sentenced to death. They were told they were simply showering, or delousing, but once the chambers were filled with prisoners, the SS locked the doors and executed them by way of asphyxiation with the poison Zyklon B.

We followed the guide under the main gate that the workers had returned through after a long day of slave labor. We listened to our headphones as the guide retold all the stories I had read about as a kid. It was obviously much more powerful to walk through the camp while learning about these atrocities. We were breathing the same air, smelling the same smells, walking on the same ground—and in my case, having an allergy attack from the same dust as those prisoners. I thought Spreepark in Berlin felt creepy and full of spirits; this was downright rotten. My stomach churned as we moved through the barracks where the prisoners slept six people to a wooden bed that I could barely fit in myself. When we arrived in the disciplinary building, I was nauseous.

I am not one who sees ghosts or necessarily believes in them, but the energy that engulfed the disciplinary hall and medical buildings was disturbing, and I felt like I was wearing a heavy blanket of cold, damp hatred. And despite it being eighty degrees outside, exploring the disciplinary hall where prisoners had been punished gave me the chills. This was a building where 1.1 million people were mercilessly murdered.

Our last stop was the gas chamber.

I don't know if there is any room on earth that more people have died in. The gas chamber still emanated evil energy that blanketed the concrete. Imagine being in a building where, in the exact place you were standing, over a million people had been killed. People with families and jobs, pets and mortgages; people who had hobbies and dreams; people who made others laugh; people who made mistakes; people who had accomplished goals and set new ones; people who had plans for their future. People like you and me.

Their lives had been stolen from them, and they were murdered for their religion, skin color, or sexual orientation, among other things. I walked through the camp, and as the guide mentioned words like *homosexuality* and *religion* as the reasons for execution, it made me furious. Furious because people today are still fighting the battle to live their lives the way they choose. It's crazy to imagine that a place like this truly existed, but it's even crazier to think it can't happen again. Philosopher George Santayana once said, famously, "Those who do not remember the past are condemned to repeat it." I think it is a good time to start remembering.

We took a much-needed mental break and shuttled to Birkenau, the camp adjacent to Auschwitz. Birkenau was where the selection process actually took place. We walked along the rails and through the iconic entrance to the camp and listened as our guide gave us details of the train arrivals. It was extremely hot and arid; there was no shade. I was having a massive allergy attack from the dust of the old barracks that had been sitting here for seventy-five years. Not the best conditions, but who was I to complain?

Our tour was finished. We walked, dejected, back to the bus. It felt both amazing and awful to have finally seen the place I had read about and imagined my whole life. I'd needed to see it in person; it gave me a sense of closure and helped allay my childhood obsession with World War II and the Holocaust.

We boarded the bus back to Kraków. Herds of people were trying to leave the camp and catch the bus, which only came once an hour. The last two seats were taken, and the bus doors closed on the remaining people in line. You will never guess who the first people to miss the bus were: none other than the obnoxious Spanish girls who'd skipped in front of everyone in line. Not even I was in the mood to laugh at how big of a bitch Karma could be.

7/3/15
Kraków, Poland → Vienna, Austria

We had heard so many great things about Paris and Amsterdam that we'd had an idea of what to expect before we arrived. Kraków, on the other hand, was a surprise for us. The price of happiness here was cheap. We ate amazing food, spent ample time in a vibrant city square, splurged on espresso and desserts, and witnessed a piece of history that lives in infamy at Auschwitz. We would miss this hidden gem of Eastern Europe, but we considered ourselves equal-opportunity travelers, as it was Vienna's turn to impress us next.

We had planned to meet our next BlaBlaCar driver, Michael, at a McDonald's in the Główny station mall. We arrived at the McDonald's with ample time to kill. We grabbed some cheap sandwiches from a market in the mall and sat in a Starbucks, eating the sandwiches and drinking large Americanos. These were Kobe Bryant–style Americanos. We took three shots in a matter of seconds. Then we met Michael and set off for Vienna.

Four hours later, Michael pulled into the Austrian capital. We took the metro to the Volkstheater station, and felt the familiar rush of excitement that accompanied each emergence into a new city. My first impression of Vienna was that it felt like we were in Washington, DC. This city was encompassed by a picture-perfect architectural grid; there was a museum, palace, theater, or stunning government building in every direction. (My sister Emily would love this place. She is a sucker for big, beautiful government buildings, which is why she lives in Washington, DC.)

Our host, Valentia, buzzed us into our building. We walked through a construction zone to get to our home base for the next few days. It looked like the inside of the building had just been demolished. But despite the hard-hat debacle outside, it was a nice one-bedroom flat, and we were in the heart of the city.

There was another strange thing about this place: the Wi-Fi account was named "We can hear you *not* having sex." I couldn't tell if that was a subtle way of asking guests not to have sex, or telling us that they indeed had the place bugged and were listening to us.

We left the flat, ready to take on the city. As we walked through the promenade streets, sharing the space with horse carriages, Ash and I recapped our drive here. Apparently, our minds were now in sync, because we had had the same epiphany during our transit: we were listening to upbeat, feel-good music and road-tripping through the hilly Polish, Czech, and Austrian countryside on a Friday afternoon with complete strangers in a Mercedes. Life was good. There was no other way to put it. I couldn't think of anything I would rather have been doing than sweating and writing, cramped in the back of that car. It wasn't that there weren't better things; there were always better things. I think part of my problem in Denver was that I was continuously thinking about the grass on the other side when I should have been living in the moment. Besides, we all know Denver's *grass* is the *best*.

In the heart of Stephansplatz, the city center of Vienna, a local café caught our hungry eyes. We wanted to eat authentic Austrian wiener schnitzel. My dad had been using the term *wiener schnitzel* my entire life in every way but the right way. He is the funniest person on (my) earth, and I could barely keep it together when ordering. I chuckled through the entire meal and took every chance I could find to tell Ash how good my wiener schnitzel was, or how well my wiener schnitzel paired with my potatoes. Vienna had briefly taken me home, and it felt damn good.

7/4/15
Vienna, Austria

It felt weird to glance at my phone and see 7/4 on my screen after the demolition crew outside had woken me up. This was the first Fourth of July holiday I had ever spent outside of the United States. Even in countries where great beer cost less than two dollars or where I was able to legally pee in the street, I was still proud to be an American.

I debated with myself on whether we could have as much fun as our friends back home today, and it wasn't looking good. They were going to be on boats, drinking beer in the sunshine. Regardless, we set out to enjoy what Vienna had to offer.

Ash found a large outdoor market in central Vienna that had been around since the sixteenth century called the Naschmarkt. We crossed museum lawns and spotted a grid of tents. Desperate for a break from the sun, we were relieved to duck into the commerce canopy.

Ash spotted the jewelry section, so I took a seat on an abandoned crate around the corner. *We could be here for a while.* While people watching, I noticed three or four New York City shirts and hats in a matter of five minutes. New York City has an unbelievable footprint on the world. This wasn't just Vienna. Between Yankee hats and I LOVE NY shirts, we had seen the Big Apple represented in every city we had been to.

We got home and handled some loose travel ends. We had to wrap up the planning for our trip to Croatia next. We decided we wanted to spend more time in the islands near Dubrovnik than in Italy. We could either take a nine-hour bus from Zagreb to Dubrovnik for a total of 50 dollars, or take a plane for a total of 175 dollars. The nine hours on a hot, sticky Croatian bus didn't seem worth saving 125 dollars. We booked the one-hour flight on the prop plane. I was dreading that day already. I hate those small planes where you feel like a Ping-Pong ball floating in class-five rapids. But it beat basking in cigarette smoke, I suppose.

While I booked the plane tickets, Ash's job was to find us something to do tonight. She found out that the Vienna Film Festival was right around the corner from our place. It was the opening night of the season. The free film showing happened every night for two months during the summer. This was a no-brainer. We set out to be film critics.

We knew we had found the right place when we got within a few hundred yards: the sound of the bustling crowd of festivalgoers was ricocheting off buildings, sending vibrations of excitement throughout the neighborhood. The free admission had attracted a large crowd, and the park space was filled with local food and beer trucks with long lines. At the opposite end from the entrance was a cathedral showcasing an absurdly large screen where the film was to be projected. When the show began, we found seats near the front. Ash and I cuddled up on the asphalt, still warm from the hot day's sun.

I didn't know much about Pink Floyd beyond their hits, but this documentary was making me a fan. It was called *Delicate Sound of Thunder*, and the music put us in a trance of happiness. The mosquitoes were starting to get to us, though, and the heat had not subsided as much as we had wished when the sun went down.

Ash had fallen asleep within seconds of our arrival back at the flat. I always had to wind down a bit more, so I lay on our room's floor, reflecting on the day. I just couldn't believe how lucky I was to be with this woman. She had really pushed us to take this trip, and there was no way I would be here without her. Every time she brought up traveling the world while we were in Denver, I came up with four or five reasons why we *shouldn't*. As I thought back to those excuses, none of them would have been worth missing this. I finally joined Ash in bed, kissed her pink forehead softly, and rigorously scratched one of my many mosquito bites. She rolled over in her sleep and groaned at me for moving too much. If only she knew how sweet I was being to her, in my head.

I tried not to wake her, but these mosquito bites were killing me. They covered my sunburned skin like volcanoes. Talk about maximizing my chances of developing diseases. I had potential malaria deposits covering my pre-melanoma skin. Then it hit me: I was lying in bed, drunk, sunburned, and covered in mosquito bites. We had had a traditional American Fourth of July after all.

7/5/15
Vienna, Austria

Somehow I had convinced Ash to go to Vienna's Natural History Museum today. She isn't a big museum person, and frankly, neither am I. History is one of my favorite subjects, though, and the appearance of the museum sealed the deal for us. We entered a building that very closely resembled the Capitol Building in Washington, DC. The neoclassic architecture of the building itself was worth the ten-dollar admission price.

The rest of the museum was interesting, but it felt like a *worse version* of a zoo. So with all the laundry we had been putting off, we decided to pack it in for the night.

Immediately after stuffing our clothes into the makeshift washer, we had the conversation we had every single day. I asked Ash, "What do you want to eat for dinner?" to which she always replied, "I don't care. Whatever you think."

This conversation only occurred because neither of us wanted to admit what we really wanted. We could say, *Let's just go get Italian*, and not beat around the bush. But there we were, every day, circling the bush, beating away.

After the routine script, we inhaled our diavola pizza with spicy pepperoni and plate of spaghetti Bolognese. We ended our trip in the Austrian capital the same way we started it: eating downtown in awe at the architectural perfection of the buildings. The shopping in Stephansplatz was too unrealistic for us to financially entertain. We couldn't afford anything from the designer stores, but it was still fun to pretend we could and walk through the upscale neighborhoods of Vienna, so rich with history, looking through windows as if we were deciding what to buy. Even if I had the money to buy articles of clothing that cost thousands of dollars, I don't think I would. Neither would Ash. But I am sure that is what everyone thinks until they can afford them.

7/6/15
Vienna, Austria → Budapest, Hungary

Ash and I were traveling by way of the Euroline bus to Budapest. Euroline was no FlixBus, but it felt like a Lamborghini compared to the Polish piece of shit we'd taken to Kraków. It was only a three-hour drive, so I chose to write rather than nap. By the time we left the station, Ash was on dream number four.

With no Wi-Fi and no music on my phone, I had limited options for drowning out the noise around me. Ash had one album on her phone, Taylor Swift's *1989*. I "Shook It Off" and "Bad Blooded" all the way to Budapest.

We arrived in Hungary rather hungry. You can imagine how long I have been waiting to use that stupid joke. We could only afford croissants and coffee this morning in the very pricey Vienna— fifteen euros at that. We were excited to be in the land of forints and out of the euro zone. It was only one dollar for both of us to take the metro to our stop in downtown Budapest.

The first thing I noticed when entering the train car was the change in scenery from Vienna. The metro train looked like it was going to fall apart any second as we careened underground. Our train rattled to our stop, and we left the hunk of metal happy to be in one piece.

When we emerged from the metro and onto the street level, we were welcomed by an oven-like humidity. My first thought was that Budapest was . . . *rustic*. It was also very apparent that Budapest definitely didn't have the money that Vienna did. Perhaps this was the result of the post-Soviet years as the country emerged from half a century of totalitarian rule.

I checked the e-mail our host, Ceci, had sent me with a PDF attached titled *Check-In Instructions*. I had glanced at it briefly on the bus but only skimmed to the point of *lockbox*. We walked half a mile through the grimy streets of Budapest, dodging homeless people and pee-covered walls, and arrived, unbearably hot, at our address. I opened the PDF and got to the step of the lockbox. The only problem was there was no code in the instructions to the lockbox. This was literally the most important piece of information in this scenario: the code to get in.

This is where traveling gets tough. Being hot, sweaty, and grumpy are all manageable conditions with an air-conditioned Airbnb light at the end of the proverbial tunnel. But once that light disappears, the mood hits the fan. We didn't have Wi-Fi to get the code from our host, so we had to walk to the closest restaurant that offered Internet. The café around the corner had the three essential *w*'s of traveling: Wi-Fi, water, and WC [*water closet*, or as we call it in the US, *bathroom*). A ham sandwich, two beers, and a mojito later, Ceci responded nonchalantly with the code, as if it were normal for her to forget *the only piece* of check-in material we needed. Our annoyed mood was lightened when the bill arrived and it was seven dollars, generous tip included.

With the code cracked, we entered one of the quirkiest apartments yet: a small studio with fifteen-foot ceilings. There was a set of stairs leading from the living room to a loft over the living space. The kitchen, living room, bedroom, and bathroom were crammed into about 250 square feet. This is what Europe starts to feel like the more you travel around. Everyone does more with less. I was still pretty salty that we'd had issues getting into the apartment, but the box of chocolates Ceci had left on the table made Ash forgive her instantly. Providing chocolate to get out of the doghouse? *Touché, Ceci. Touché.*

7/7/15
Budapest, Hungary

I woke up from the deepest sleep in weeks. I know this because when I stirred, I had no idea where I was. It wasn't just the unfamiliar ceiling; I had no idea what city or country I was in. It took my brain a few cities to come up with Budapest. We had woken up in thirteen different cities over the last thirty days. I felt like a fugitive. Thankfully, we would be in Budapest for six days. We needed some stability to gear up for month two of this journey.

One thing that had been stable for the last couple of weeks was Ash's obsession with eating toast for breakfast. Toast with jelly and butter to be exact. It wasn't the healthiest thing we could eat for breakfast, but it was one of the cheapest. I am not much of a sweets guy. But if she cooked it, I was eating it. We ate two massive pieces of toast from a loaf we had grabbed from a market the day before. This was an awful decision before our first bathing-suit sightings.

"I look okay, right?" Ash asked while turning and tilting her head to see her backside in the full-length mirror.

"Yeah, of course, baby," I responded honestly.

I could tell she wasn't really concerned with my opinion, as she was twirling like a ballerina to see all angles of herself.

"Those two pieces of toast are just sitting right in my stomach. I don't want to go," Ash said as she left the mirror's crosshairs. I convinced her that nobody in Budapest cared what we looked like, and if it meant anything to her, I thought she was beautiful. Besides, we weren't going to look any different between here and the baths. That's like brushing your teeth before going to the dentist. Those cavities aren't going to disappear.

Budapest is known as the "City of Baths," and it is the only capital city in the world sitting on healing, thermal hot springs. There are fifteen public thermal baths in the city proper. Our first thermal experience was going to be at the Gellért Baths. It was one of the least crowded bathhouses. This was important to us, because we wanted to get our bearings on this whole thermal bathing thing. I didn't know whether to expect naked people casually walking around in robes, or a water park with people frantically moving from body of water to body of water.

The hardest part of entering the bath was avoiding looking like amateurs, but when we entered the tranquil building, we felt lost. The fee was only fifteen dollars for a day pass to all the baths, saunas, and steam rooms. That would probably get you a bowl of strawberries at an American spa.

I followed Ash into the glass-domed room hosting an Olympic-size indoor pool with a smaller hot tub area at the end. It was such a peaceful and tranquil room, with people sporting swimming caps and soaking up the calcium, magnesium, sulphate-chloride, and hydrogen-and-carbonate-rich waters. You know . . . basically all the minerals instrumental in healing our joints.

The smaller hot tub area seemed like a good place to start. I sat down against the wall, and the one-hundred-degree water covered my skin in bubbles. The water made my skin tingle, almost as if it were carbonated. We sat under a small waterfall spilling out of a stone gargoyle's mouth and basked in the mineral water for an hour or so before heading to the outside area.

Immediately upon emerging outside, we found a large bathing area that dually served as a wave pool. Every ten minutes, a wave would emerge and send a wall of water scurrying through the crowd of mostly kids. *I think this is Gellért's day-care system.* Although waves were fun, I preferred them in the ocean. I didn't need to convince Ash to stay out of the wave pool. She wanted to relax and lie out, but there were limited chairs available. Luckily for Ash, I consider myself to be a chair hawk. It's not about finding open chairs; it's about finding people who are beginning the exit process.

Once we found chairs and lay down, I made it about seven minutes before my boredom won the fight and led me to finally walk into the steam room. I went through a cleansing cycle, one I had read about online. The cycle consisted of heat, cold, rest, and repeat. I sat in the 131-degree sauna and roasted like a Christmas ham for ten minutes, jumped into the freezing tub to cool off, and once my nipples were hard enough to carve a pumpkin, I rested on my chair before repeating the cycle.

Our day at the bath was filled with relaxation, meditation, and healing. On the way home, we ate at a traditional Hungarian restaurant: platters of goulash and chicken wrapped in dough. Definitely a gut-buster, but it was important for us to squeeze traditional meals into our Italian agenda. Then we stumbled upon one of Budapest's bucket list destinations, a ruin pub.

The sound of music too funky to be found in a regular bar and the energy of weirdness pulled us into a trippy area that looked straight out of a Pixar movie. Ruin pubs are strange bars created from the ruins of old buildings. The place was called Szimpla Kert. There were flying pigs with angel wings in the air, a trabant with a garden growing in it as a table, various rooms for music, a theater, and numerous bars around the canopied courtyard. I could not imagine a weirder place to be than sitting in the trabant, drinking our two-dollar beers and being cooled off by a mist that blew out of a gnome's mouth. Budapest had both ruined and healed us on our first day. *Oh, glorious Hungary.*

7/8/15
Budapest, Hungary

We geared back up for another day at the baths, but we complained about our carb-filled stomachs once again. It feels good as humans to have excuses. "We look fat only because we just ate a bunch of bread" was an easier pill to swallow than "We look fat because aside from walking, we haven't exercised in a month."

Today we were headed to the Széchenyi Baths, the largest and most famous thermal bath in all of Europe. This was the Madison Square Garden of bathhouses.

We confidently entered the Széchenyi Bathhouse. Frankly, we were underwhelmed. Although much bigger than Gellért's indoor baths, the inside baths were under serious construction and in need of a proper restoration. It wasn't until we made it outside that I realized what all the hype was about: the outside bath grounds looked like the landscape of the ancient Ottoman empire. There were three large pools in a massive courtyard. We didn't even know where to begin bathing. It was the moment of overwhelming awe equivalent to walking into a Chuck E. Cheese's as a kid.

We did what any kid would do: we went directly to the closest pool and submerged ourselves in thermal waters, engulfing our skin in minerals. It was just cool enough not to make us sweat, yet warm enough that we could soak in it comfortably all day without getting a chill. We decided to embark on my new favorite hobby: the roast/freeze therapy.

The sauna was four times as large as the one at Gellért, and it was definitely the hottest thing my body had ever endured. We stepped into a long room of humans sweating in silence. After only two minutes of sitting on the wooden benches, the hair on my head was so hot, I could barely touch it. We stayed as long as we could stand it, but it felt like my skin was melting. It was rather embarrassing to be the last people to enter the room, and the first to leave.

Right around the corner from the sauna was the cold tub. It looked like a large hot tub built into the cave walls, but the water was frigid. The first three seconds felt amazing to cool off our scalding bodies, but after that, it was a new type of uncomfortable. It felt like my body's inner thermostat was on the pirate ship ride at an amusement park, quickly swinging from overheated to freezing in a matter of seconds. We brought our bodies' circulation back to normal in the warm showers next to the tub. Ash called it quits after one cycle, and returned to the outdoor baths to relax. I repeated the cycle three or four times, expelling as many toxins as I could.

I decided to take a break from the water and meet Ash for a little while. We sat on our pool chairs and traded war stories of absurd people we had encountered in the bathhouse. While we chatted, I heard a worried murmuring around us. We turned to see some extremely menacing clouds approaching. The sky looked like a bruise after surgery.

A gust came through that flipped some of our belongings off the chairs. There was a distinct smell of oncoming rain in the air. Everyone got the memo at the same time, and began frantically packing their belongings. We ran to our locker and grabbed our stuff, but it was far too late. The rain began to hammer the streets of Budapest.

We definitely would have toughed out the rain and run home, but we were two miles away and had our iPhones, GoPro, wallets, and, most important, my journal. This trek was going to be a game of dry checkpoints. Our first leg was sprinting to the closest subway, a mere one hundred yards away. We took off running, and although the station wasn't far, the short run soaked us as we sprinted across the steaming ground. It was like Budapest was a hot pan just out of the oven that had been placed under running water.

The closest stop to our Airbnb still left us eight blocks away. There were plenty of people huddled inside the tunnel, waiting for the rain to let up. It looked like Pearl Harbor out there, bullets of rain abusing the now flooding sidewalks and streets. I strapped my backpack onto my chest so the electronics were in front, and put my tank top on top of it to cover it the best I could.

"You ready?" I asked Ash, half hoping she would say, *No, let's just wait it out.*

Silly me—not my Ash. "Let's do it," she said, strapping on her sandals as tightly as she could.

We bravely moved past people waiting in the tunnel as they watched us get ready to depart. The last thing I heard before entering the wall of water was an Eastern European voice shouting, "Good luck, friends!"

We were soaked in the first ten steps as we sprinted down the sidewalk, crossing intersections and passing slower people with umbrellas. Those poor fools were fighting a losing battle. Attempting to stay dry with an umbrella was impossible when the rain was blowing in sideways.

This was no routine storm. The lightning lit up the dark sky, and then almost simultaneously the clap of the thunder echoed in my eardrums. I realized mid-stride that I hadn't sprinted like this in over a month. I felt like Forrest Gump breaking free of his leg braces as we jumped over small ponds forming on the sidewalks. It felt amazing to run through Budapest with the love of my life right behind me. I could hear her shrieking with laughter as she landed in puddles too big to jump over.

We made it home in less than ten minutes, soaked from beard to toe in my case. We scrambled to get inside our place. I checked our backpack to make sure everything had stayed dry enough. My phone was blowing up with severe storm warnings for my current area, a little late.

The remainder of our afternoon was spent snacking on chocolate and beer. These delicacies combined with my runner's high made this one of the best days of my life. Sure, that statement was probably false, but I think the goal in life should be to have as many days like that as possible, days that make you question if you've ever had a better day. There is no way to quantify the quality of a day, but if there were, a day spent with your best friend, beer, chocolate, thermal baths, sunshine, lightning, thunder, and Budapest probably scored highly.

7/9/15
Budapest, Hungary

Other than our flight to Dubrovnik, we had nothing planned for Croatia. While Ash worked on booking our Airbnbs in Zagreb and the islands of Croatia, I caught up on my writing.

When we finished our work, we decided to hit one more ruin pub while in Budapest. We looked online for the weirdest one we could find. There was a ruin pub (and an Italian restaurant, which we stopped at first) near our studio. It was called Instant, and it had great reviews for weirdness. Ruin pubs are like *South Park* episodes. The weirder the better.

We arrived at the renovated two-story building and entered a world of the absurd. There was a maze of rooms surrounding a courtyard area in the middle. Some rooms had bars, other rooms just couches and foosball tables. In one room, there was a stage with DJs playing funky electronic music, while in others, there were just strobe lights illuminating the walls. We walked to the main bar and ordered a large Dreher, the local Budapest beer. Directly above us was a six-foot relic of a woman's naked body with horse hooves for feet and an owl head as the head. Maybe this was the Instant mascot?

At this point in the night my stomach was filled to capacity from dinner; in fact, I could barely get each sip of beer down. I tried to walk it off, and we continued touring around the bar. Then we came upon a room with strobe lights and a DJ going crazy in the corner like there were hundreds of people dancing with him. Ash saw the empty room and decided she wanted to dance.

This was a rare occurrence for Ash. She is not a person who usually feels comfortable dancing in public, but she had really embraced the idea of leaving her comfort zone on this trip. I applauded her for her courage, but my stomach was far too full to dance at that moment.

Maybe it was the minerals from the baths; maybe it was the Dreher. Whatever the case was, she didn't give a single shit about the opinions of others. She looked absolutely ridiculous dancing out of control, and her giant smile was the only way I could tell she wasn't having a seizure. Other girls started watching from the side as she did the crazy legs shake back and forth, her knees coming an inch from banging each time as she laughed at herself. More and more people gathered around, probably looking for somewhere to dance, and I could sense Ash was starting to get a bit nervous. I could see her carefreeness slipping. I had been bobbing my head in the corner, laughing with her, but now there were plenty of people congregating in the once-empty room. Ash started to slow down and walk toward me, but I couldn't let those people put out her fire.

I belched in the corner to clear some room in my stomach, and joined in, dancing harder than I ever had before. I wasn't doing a dance; the dance was doing me. I moved uncontrollably to the beat of the lights, not the music. Ash started laughing and jumped back in with the crazy legs. Eventually people couldn't stand us being the only ones having fun, and everyone apprehensively joined in until the entire bar had found this one small stage to dance as ridiculously as possible.

Ash had started a dance party. She didn't like dancing around people because she felt nervous. Here was the dilemma: dancing made Ash happy, and normally the nerves outweighed her happiness, but not tonight. Tonight Ash decided she cared more about her happiness than the judgment of others. As it turned out, she wasn't alone. Everyone wanted to dance; they just didn't want to be the first ones to do so. Ash was the tinder that started a dance fire, a fire that would burn all night. I also threw up when we got home. So there's that. A small price to pay to watch my girlfriend break free from her self-conscious shell and cut a rug.

7/10/15
Budapest, Hungary

Back to the baths we went. We spent our day participating in our now ritual bath activities. Ash spent the day lying out, and I executed the roast/freeze cycle. I found myself addicted to the high of shocking my circulation system. I almost passed out in the shower at one point, and I realized I needed to get off the good stuff. We left the baths calm and dry, the complete opposite scenario from yesterday. Personally, I preferred the adrenaline rush of battling the storm.

We spent our last night in Budapest eating takeout Vietnamese food and drinking cheap wine. We had some transportation booking to finish before we left Budapest. It didn't quite go as planned. Google

Images and two bottles of wine convinced us to stay in Croatia for three weeks rather than our originally planned one week. We had the drunken munchies, and the buffet of Airbnbs on the Croatian islands was too appetizing for us to pass up.

7/11/15
Budapest, Hungary → Zagreb, Croatia

Before we left for Zagreb, we had to make a pit stop at a flea market to get paprika for our families. Apparently, Hungarian paprika is a highly coveted spice for chefs around the world. This was news to me. In my mind, paprika is just the red horns for deviled eggs.

With the red stuff in hand, we started the trek to find our BlaBlaCar driver, Christine. Ash had been communicating with Christine via e-mail, and it was by far the strangest line of communication we'd had thus far. This was her last e-mail to Ash twenty-four hours ago:

> *Hello, Ash!*
>   *Please meet me around the Népliget metro station at 11:00 a.m. on Saturday. I will be renting a Toyota car to drive us to Zagreb. If I am not there by 11:00 a.m., please wait for an hour, and if I am still not there, I apologize. Something must have gone wrong with the rental.*
>   *Thanks,*
>   *Christine*

This was far from reassuring, but we had no other way to get to Zagreb without spending a few hundred dollars. This BlaBlaCar ride only cost us fifteen dollars.

Within the last twenty-four hours, Ash had e-mailed Christine numerous times, trying to get a better description of the car or a more specific pickup location. With nothing other than that last e-mail from Christine to go off of, we arrived at the station at 10:55 a.m. We had no idea what Christine looked like. Her only description in a previous e-mail was that she was a "blonde looking forty!" This was extremely ambiguous, because she could be a young-looking fifty-year-old or an old-looking thirty-year-old.

We stood at the corner, trying to look as noticeable as possible to someone looking for two travelers. After thirty minutes, we were losing hope. Ash went to try to find Wi-Fi to see if she could somehow reach Christine by e-mail, and I stood on the corner like a drug dealer, making intense eye contact with each female driver who passed by. Ash returned fifteen minutes later—no luck. It was now 11:45 a.m. Christine didn't show up, but what had we expected? She hadn't even responded in the last twenty-four hours.

There was little time to sulk about our situation; we had to find a way to get to the capital of Croatia. We'd already paid for our Airbnb in Croatia that night. I went to do some research on trains. Ash refused to leave the corner until 12:00 p.m., but it was 11:57 a.m. and we didn't even know what we were looking for. Ash hates giving up on things. I walked to the corner where she had found Wi-Fi earlier and began searching for plan B transportation. We'd missed the day train an hour earlier, and our last option was an overnight train that arrived in Zagreb at 6:00 a.m for 175 dollars a person. Missing our BlaBlaCar ride, it turned out, was a costly blunder.

I began the booking process for two train tickets and was moments away from clicking "Confirm Booking" when I heard my name being yelled down the street. I turned to see Ash running at me. "Kyle, I found her! I found her!"

We excitedly hurried back up the block to the metro station where Christine was waiting for us. She eagerly shook my hand and apologized for being late. Apparently, she'd rented the car at a Romanian rental company and had had trouble with the translating.

I assured her we didn't mind and that we were just glad we'd found her. I sat in the back of the Fiat, and Ash took BlaBla-ing duties. Christine explained to us that she did not have a cell phone, which made communication difficult. I was in complete awe that someone could succeed in the twenty-first century without one.

As we left the streets of Budapest, Christine handed Ash a piece of paper. "Here is our map to get to Zagreb," she enthusiastically proclaimed. I looked at the map that was hand drawn with what looked like an erasable pen. You know, that obnoxious light blue that always looked like the pen was on its last drop of ink.

The two of them went over the map together in the front as I sat in the back, shaking my head, knowing failure was imminent. To say Ash is directionally challenged is a huge understatement. If Christine was relying on a handwritten map to travel the three and a half hours to Zagreb, she might be challenged, too. They agreed on the first few steps and high-fived as we pulled out. We were off to Croatia, *I hoped.*

Christine was an eccentric French woman currently living in Berlin. This instantly made me like her more. Berlin had a gold seal of approval in my book. She was going to Rijeka, Croatia, on holiday, traveling by herself and couch surfing to save money.

I began writing to kill some time and couldn't keep my journal pages from flapping in the wind and bombarding me in the backseat. Christine must have heard the flapping paper and told us she didn't use air conditioning because it was bad for the environment. She stated this proudly and smiled at us. I was both appalled and impressed. I was appalled that in the one-hundred-degree heat, and in a car with black leather seats, she was willing to sacrifice the relief of AC. I was even more impressed that she believed in saving the environment enough to put two passengers, who would be reviewing her later on a ride-sharing app, through such harsh conditions. I had to respect her dedication to the third planet.

It became apparent that we were lost when we saw signs for Graz, a city in Austria. The highway was packed with traffic, and we came to a standstill on the road. Christine came up with the bright idea to ask someone for directions. (*Finally,* I thought, *a great idea from the Blond Brigade.*)

"Yeah, that sounds good!" I said, thinking we would pull over to a gas station. Christine, on the other hand, had other plans. She parked the car in the middle of the highway exit and left the vehicle. Meanwhile, Ash and I felt like the two young kids in *Jurassic Park* when the tour guide runs from the green jeep. Christine ran to the car behind us, leaving us perplexed in the roasting Fiat. After fifteen seconds of deliberation, she returned, running into the car, and excitedly told us, "I figured it out!" We exited the next ramp and took the highway back the way we came. A short time later, we arrived at the Croatian border.

Croatia was the first country we had entered with certified border control. There were signs advising drivers to slow down and get their documents ready. As we rolled into what resembled a tollbooth in the US, I imagined Christine just speeding through and blowing through the barrier, confessing that she was actually a drug smuggler. My daydream zapped back to reality as the stern Croatian guard asked for our passports. Christine handed him all three and smiled enthusiastically. I thought about how odd it must look to have a French woman driving two Americans in a Romanian rental car. The Croatian guard must have felt the same way, and after careful analysis, he told us to pull over.

Christine pulled to the side of the border station, where the vans full of drugs probably parked. They told us to stay put until told otherwise. We sat in a small patch of shade and waited, leaning against the trunk of the car. I couldn't help but feel like we were doing something illegal.

The border officer returned and handed us our documents.

"So we are free to go?" I asked.

He nodded and looked disappointed that they had not found anything suspicious.

Although safely in Croatia, we still had an hour and a half of driving to go before we reached the capital city of Zagreb. I finished my writing to the sound of Ash's snores.

I woke Ash up to give her the news of our arrival, but somewhere in the celebration, we missed the exit to the city center and had to turn around. Christine dropped us off at the train station, hugging us both, and then sped off to Rijeka to surf on couches. We wished Christine Godspeed.

As Christine pulled away, Ash and I looked at each other, exhaled, and started laughing. There was never a dull day when taking BlaBlaCars across countries, but this one might have taken the cake for the strangest yet.

Our next Airbnb host, Natalija, drove us the short distance to her place. As she explained her loft, she was distressed that someone had once given her a four-star rating due to the pillows because they were "too hard." We assured her she would be getting five stars from us. We give everyone five stars. She gave us recommendations for food and things to do with our time here, and then left us to enjoy Zagreb.

We drank a bottle of wine to assist in the sleep we were looking forward to getting, and headed home, buzzing through the streets. I had been anticipating this moment all day. We were more than ready for rest at this point.

7/12/15
Zagreb, Croatia

Today was a boring day by design. Our month-long journey through Central Europe had diminished our energy levels. There wasn't too much to do in Zagreb on a Sunday (there wasn't too much to do in Zagreb on any day) because all the stores were closed, so we took the opportunity to relax.

We ate an odd but cost-effective brunch of cereal and baguettes. These two foods brought me back to happy places. The cereal reminded me of nights at home with my brother, watching SportsCenter; the baguettes, on the other hand, reminded me of the sunny mornings on the streets of Paris. Even though one memory was years ago and the other only weeks, both felt like the distant past.

After a day of lounging, writing, cooking, and eating, we spent the evening binge-watching TV. It felt good to immerse ourselves in our back-home comforts while experiencing our new European lifestyle. *Grey's Anatomy* had a marathon running on the only channel in English. We laughed and cried at the plotlines before heading to our brick-pillowed bed at an early hour. Today was exactly what we needed to reset our bodies, minds, and souls.

7/13/15
Zagreb, Croatia

I woke up to Ash excitedly getting ready in the corner of the room. By the look of what step she was on in the getting-ready process (her hair), I could tell she had been up for a while. Ash was elated because today was a designated "shopping day."

Zagreb has a long shopping promenade throughout the downtown city center. Ash was going to get her hands dirty at Zara and Forever 21, while I found a coffee shop to get some work done.

I spent the rest of the afternoon planning our travel to the Dalmatian Islands while Ash bought Dalmatian rompers. Zagreb was a perfect pit stop, and although it didn't have the glam and glitz of Paris or Vienna, it was a great place to relax without the abundance of FOMO prizes around town.

7/14/15
Zagreb, Croatia → Kolocep, Croatia

Another swing and a miss in the sleep department. These brick pillows were not getting the job done; I woke up frequently with a throbbing neck. Before I knew it, the sun was coming up, and I had run out of time to lie awake in bed worrying about not sleeping. Natalija would be waiting outside in half an hour to take us to the airport.

We arrived at the airport and hugged Natalija good-bye, thanking her for the wonderful apartment and hospitality. She had picked us up *and* dropped us off from the train station and airport. Without her, we would have spent substantially more time and money.

When it was time to board our aircraft to the southern coast of Croatia, we headed out to the tarmac. The plane was so small, I felt like a celebrity getting into my own private jet.

As we taxied to the runway, I told Ash that these planes always have the worst turbulence. She listened intently as I expressed my concerns. Normally, she tells me I am overreacting, but this time she—Nope, never mind, she was already fast asleep.

It was a surprisingly smooth flight, and by the time we got to our cruising altitude, we had started our descent into Dubrovnik. I wanted to lean out the window and gaze at the coastline, but I couldn't move with Ash sleeping on my shoulder. We soon landed in Dubrovnik.

When we stepped off the plane, it felt like the tarmac was being cooked by the Adriatic sun. Ash and I both paused at the bottom of the plane steps and stared at the unbelievable mountainous landscape surrounding us. I realized I hadn't seen mountains since we'd left Denver. I missed those lumps of earth.

It wasn't hard to find the bus to Dubrovnik; there was only one bus outside of the terminal, and everyone who wasn't paying to take a taxi was boarding it. We rode along the western coast of Croatia and circled down a mountainside. I instantly recognized the setting of King's Landing from *Game of Thrones*. HBO filmed the show here in the midst of the clay-topped buildings in the seaside village.

Our bus careened down the single road leading into the fortress town. We exited the bus at the port but had no idea how to get to Kolocep from there. I had tried to figure this out in the Zagreb coffee shop, but the ferry websites were about as up-to-date as MySpace.

Eventually, we found the ferry going to Kolocep. We sat on the back as it slowly filled up with other travelers. The ferry pulled out of the port and slowly headed to Kolocep, the first of the three Elaphiti Islands. We looked back on the beautiful town of Dubrovnik in our wake, and it made me truly grateful. Grateful to be in the Adriatic Sea, grateful to be with my woman on a boat, and grateful that we did not book Airbnbs in Dubrovnik because—*holy shit, there were people everywhere.*

After only thirty minutes of smooth sailing, the ferry curled around the wilderness of the island to the small port of Kolocep. We stepped off the ferry onto a single concrete dock. The island only had 120 residents, and there were no roads, cars, or civilization aside from two small villages. This was the precise level of remoteness we were looking for after spending a month in the saturated cities of Central Europe.

Our Airbnb host's niece, Dolores, was waiting for us on the dock. She found us immediately because I'd told her I had a beard. I knew my beard game was strong at this point when people could pick me out of a crowd.

We followed Dolores as she led us to our house for the next week. She gave us a brief tour as we walked along the clear blue water. "This is the only market on the island, and it is owned by my grandmother," she said, pointing to a small mini-mart. We continued walking and came to the two restaurants on the island. Both were dockside cafés with bars attached. Then we moved along the beach outside of the large island resort and reached the stone steps—all 150 of them—that led us to our Airbnb.

After traveling by a small car to Zagreb, a prop plane to Dubrovnik, a crowded bus from the airport, and a Croatian ferry, we had reached our last task before we could finally rest. The mountainside staircase was by far the most exhausting part of the day. We were out of calories and were clearly dehydrated. I was already dreading trying to get my soaked shirt off my skin. It would be like trying to peel a green banana.

Our place was near perfect, and the view from our porch was breathtaking. The 150-step staircase, although strenuous to climb, had nestled us in the heavens of Kolocep. We looked down at the dozens of white sailboats resting in the cove the color of a robin's egg. The gentle rolling hills of the island created a perfect backdrop. After taking pictures of the view that wasn't going anywhere, we decided to go grab some groceries for the week before the market closed.

When we emerged from the glorified pantry with our groceries, the sun was setting over the cove, and the sky looked like a watercolor painting. I quickly lunged for the eggs we'd bought, anticipating Ash dropping them upon seeing the sunset. She is a sucker for sunsets. The pink, purple, and orange colors collided with the water, and the explosion of the reflection hit the sailboats with color flak.

We spent the remainder of the evening sitting on a bench by the water and watching as the sun disappeared, leaving only the black silhouette of the mountains around us. The blazing Mediterranean temperature fell with the sun. Aside from Kraków, Kolocep was our first real "discovery" while traveling. What I mean is that we were not planning on coming here when we left the US. We had never even heard of Kolocep. We read reviews on Croatia and found islands strictly by searching on Airbnb. We put in our criteria of own apartment, AC, Wi-Fi, and places under seventy dollars. We found islands near Dubrovnik, and after careful research, chose three of them, Kolocep being the first. It had not been easy to get here, but the trip to paradise had only cost us a total of 212 dollars. We'd wrapped up our time in Central Europe significantly under our transportation budget. We accomplished this by taking BlaBlaCars and FlixBus, and using public transportation as opposed to taxis and Ubers. We definitely weren't backpackers yet, but I would say we'd graduated from being rookies.

7/15/15
Kolocep, Croatia

I woke up to the smell of good eggs and bad coffee. Nobody wants to smell bad coffee, but I definitely prefer that combination to no coffee. Ash was up at the crack of dawn, sitting on the porch and taking in the view of the sea.

We ate on the porch before walking down the stone steps to the sound of children playing in the water, and cicadas arguing among the trees. The small village on the island of Kolocep already felt like home to us, and we waved to a smiling Dolores as she enjoyed an ice cream cone from her grandmother's market. We strolled into the market, and Dolores's grandmother unleashed an arm-opening welcome to us, knowing we would be regulars for the next week. This was what we were after: feeling like locals in a peaceful place on the water where humans lived simpler lives.

We left the market armed with the essentials: water and Ožujsko, the most popular Croatian beer. Next we went to check out renting a kayak, and I approached the woman sitting next to the kayaks on the beach. She looked up, smiled, and said, "Dolores told me you two were interested in kayaking!" The woman told us her name was Narissa.

She gave us the rundown of the two-seater kayak and told us we had until roughly 5:00 p.m. to return it. I was confused at the casualness of this transaction. There was no paperwork, no deposit, and no lack of trust.

"We won't have our phones, so keeping track of time will be tough. We will try to get back by 5:00 p.m., but what if we are a little late?" I asked honestly.

"No worries," Narissa said, smiling. "I will be around, and besides, I know where you guys live."

I pushed the big green kayak into the shallows, jumped in, and we set off into the cove. Ash sat in the front, and I manned the ship from the stern (yes, I had to look up which end was the stern). As we cruised out of earshot of the kids playing, I looked down and saw each individual spike on the black urchins below us as though the seabed were mere inches, and not twenty feet, away.

We hugged the coastline to observe the flora and fauna along the island, and scanned the shore as if we were going to see dinosaurs.

"Ash, look, a Pancakeasaurus," I whispered, pointing at an older naked woman perched on a rock.

Narissa had told us about the nude beach around the corner of the cove, but we didn't anticipate seeing anyone this close. There were more participants than we had expected. We tried to avoid eye contact and continued paddling. Normally, if we saw someone onshore, we would smile and wave, but when they were nude, we treated them like outcasts. What can I say? I guess we were prejudiced.

We had been paddling for an hour or so when we decided to find rocks to jump off of into the sea to let our muscles cool down. We executed a semi-controlled crash into one of the very few smooth rocks on the coastline. This was our first interaction with the rocks of Croatia. They are as sharp and unforgiving as Judge Judy.

We spent half an hour climbing onto rocks and avoiding sea urchins (the one true nemesis of the Adriatic Sea), and jumped into the crystal-clear water. Ash decided she wanted to join the nudist movement and freed herself of the restriction of her bathing suit. As you can imagine, I had no reservations to this.

Back in the kayak, Ash eventually stopped stopped paddling to fully take in the rocky coast. I didn't want to tell her, but my arms and shoulders were nearly numb as I slowly propelled us through the sea. We had reached the western side of the island that faced across the Adriatic to Italy. The current was a little stronger on the side that faced the deep sea, but we quickly wrapped around the corner and came to what would be known for the rest of the week as our "playground," an oasis of crystal-clear pools with not one boat in sight. We docked the boat in an area of the island where we could stand and overlook the pool. Again, when I say *docked,* I mean we chaotically crashed the boat into rocks, screaming at each other to try to steady the watercraft enough to get out.

We sat on the rocks and drank a beer each, occasionally dipping into the salty water to heal our cut-up feet. The water in the Adriatic was saltier than McDonald's fries; in fact, the locals told us that the water was so salty in Kolocep that there was very little marine life. I think Croatia is such a hidden gem that the fish don't even know about it.

After gaining enough liquid courage from our two-liter Ožujskos, we climbed to the top of the rock, twenty feet above the small pool, and analyzed the depth of the sea below. It was definitely deep enough, but the fact that we had not yet done it was the scary part. Ash and I agreed that if we were going to jump, we would do it together. On the count of three, we would jump and face the unknown pool below. Twice the countdown made it to two . . . and Ash shook her hands and bounced up and down, saying, "No, no, no, not yet!"

Jumping for the first time was scary. I wasn't afraid of landing on anything. The water below was clearly twenty feet deep. I also wasn't afraid of drowning; I am not a great swimmer, but I am a magnificent water-treader. What scared me was the fall itself: I was afraid of jumping, because as soon as I left the familiarity of the rock, I was no longer in control. I couldn't decide that I preferred the comfort of the rock halfway to the sea and turn back. It was all or nothing. Gravity would take over, and whether I was ready or not, I would be seeing the rock from a different perspective.

Finally we agreed this was it. I counted down: three, two, one. Despite the fear of the unknown, I decided I had spent enough time on this rock, and jumped. When gravity introduced me to the Adriatic, she welcomed me with open arms. But I'd left the spiky rocks with just enough time to turn in the air to see Ash standing apologetically on the rocks, ashamed at herself for not jumping, before I hit the water.

"What took you so long?" Ash asked upon my arrival to the surface.

"I should be asking you the same question," I replied, salty about her breach of contract. I scrambled onto the rocks and climbed up to the jumping spot. She was still too scared, and decided she just didn't want to jump yet. It was pretty high, and I didn't blame her. Suddenly I heard voices coming from around the cove. I realized Ash was still topless. It had been hours now, and I had simply grown accustomed to her bare breasts. I spotted a boat full of people, and said, "Hey, Ash! Look there are some people over—"

Splash.

"Ash?" I turned and saw a cloud of bubbles below.

Fear was another reason to jump. I won't beat around the metaphorical bush here. We jumped because of the fear of life ending and us not enjoying it to the fullest. We jumped because of the fear of being stuck in the same situation each and every day. We jumped because the routine was eating away at our happiness. Just because the rock was comfortable, didn't mean it wasn't worth jumping to find out what the water was like. In this case, Ash jumped because there was a group of people on a small boat in the pool adjacent to us, and although she was supportive of the "Free the Nips" campaign . . . she wasn't ready to run for office.

Our next stop was the blue cave. We saw boats in the area we were told to go to, and started the long trek across the bay. We followed as a guide dove into the water and swam into what seemed like a one-foot-by-one-foot gap in the wall. *There is* no way *that is an entrance to a cave,* I thought, watching as the guide disappeared. I was up next, and I got closer to the entrance, but the waves propelled me up against the wall. I ducked under at the last second to avoid hitting my head on the spiky rocks, and after a quick plunge through, emerged into what looked like the exotic club in Amsterdam.

The first thing I noticed was the water temperature; it was significantly colder than the water outside. The small bit of sunlight entering the slit in the wall turned the entire cave a blue that resonated off the moist walls. I could not believe how large the cave was, its ceilings as high as fifteen feet. The bottom was covered in soft, smooth sand, unlike the bottom of the pools outside. I quickly turned around to see Ash's priceless reaction as she surfaced into the oasis. "Shut the fuck up," she spit out through salty water. I apologized for the ugly words that had been ejected out of the beautiful mouth of my girlfriend, but the Croatian guide just laughed. I think he had seen this reaction before. I still couldn't believe that small hole had led us to this paradise . . . but you know what they say: never judge a cave by its entrance.

After floating in the blue cave and taking enough pictures/videos with the GoPro to last a lifetime, we decided it was time to get moving to make our 5:00 p.m. kayak deadline with Narissa. We were not sure how much farther it was to finish the circle of the island, but we could see Dubrovnik from our watercraft, so we knew we were on the east side. We paddled for thirty minutes and soaked in the seawater with each splash from our oars. I spotted a massive table-like rock jutting out over the sea. It resembled an Olympic diving platform. I steered us toward the platform to check it out.

Once we made land, we scaled the rocks to the natural diving platform, and I carefully stepped to the ledge to peer over the edge. *Oh, hell no.* To be as frank as possible, the water was *uncomfortably far away.* After making her way to the top, Ash joined me at the edge, and she, too, had no intention of ever leaving this platform.

The dark-blue water had to have been fifty feet deep, as we could not even see to the bottom through the clear water. There was no concern of hitting anything but water. We were just worried about how hard that water would feel. Ash told me to go first. *No chance, woman.* We were either jumping together or we weren't jumping at all.

At this point, we had stood up there and looked into the abyss below for far too long. That is why roller coasters are great. The time spent terrified on the opening hill is finite, and then the drop comes whether you are ready or not. We decided to chalk it up as a loss and began the difficult descent down the rocks. As we started retreating, the words of Clemence, our Airbnb host in Paris, popped into my head. She'd told us we were welcome to sit on the rooftop balcony as long as we were "not afraid of the fall." We had to do it; we had to jump. We could not be afraid of the fall.

Ash agreed with me: if we didn't jump, we would regret not having had the courage. We stepped up to the edge, secured our footing, held hands, and on the count of three, left the rock. As soon as we were airborne, I realized we had just made a huge mistake.

We immediately released our hands as a reflex of unequivocal fear. We were still rising in the air from our initial jump, and I saw Ash began to drop. Apparently, she does not have the hops I do. Adrenaline shot through my veins like electricity as the fight-or-flight hormone took over. It was really more of a fight-the-flight situation as I flailed my arms in a failed attempt to try to either fly or grab on to something. With no luck from either scenario, I began my descent.

The feeling of my stomach hitting my throat felt like I was missing organs in my chest cavity. After a full second of free fall, I blacked out. I had been trying to analyze the severity of my current situation and was experiencing a sensory overload. With both adrenaline and fear taking over, there was no room on my plate for "analysis." My brain shut down like an old Windows computer with too many programs running, and I hit the water. Unfortunately for me, in my blacked-out state, I had missed the announcement: *Ladies and gentlemen, as we start our final descent into the Adriatic, please make sure your legs are straight and your arms are at your sides, with your body in the upright position. Close your eyes, and be sure your bathing suit is securely fastened. Thank you for flying Kyle Air.*

Ideally, colliding with water from high up is best done in "pencil" form. I hit the water in the unfortunate "open protractor" form, and consequently felt immense pain upon impact. I moved my limbs underwater to make sure they all still worked, and remembered I was not in an environment where breathing was permitted. I kicked my way to the surface of the dark-blue water and emerged after a few seconds. I immediately looked for Ash and saw nothing but the area of bubbles she had entered moments earlier. Right before I planned on diving to look for her, she popped up, her face white with fear.

From the look on her face, I think she had had a similar in-flight experience as I'd had. She was smarter than I was, though; she'd executed a perfect pencil dive. This was why she'd been underwater so long; she must have shot in like a dart and cruised down twenty feet. We looked at each other, and when it registered we had survived this exciting yet traumatic event, we started laughing—that real gut laugh, the one where you and your best friend just cheated death.

7/16/15
Kolocep, Croatia

I woke up this morning with a burning, aching, throbbing sensation that covered my entire body. I rolled over, and all the cuts and bruises politely let me know where they were located. Between the razor-sharp rocks and the concrete water, my body was paying the Kolocep Tax.

Today we headed down to explore Kolocep by foot, following the single path that spanned the perimeter of the cove out of the village. While walking, Ash and I took turns smacking a two-liter beer. Our wandering brought us to a gorgeous cove with nothing around us but clear blue water. The comfort of being able to leap off the surrounding rock and into the sea at a moment's notice made the heat bearable.

Ash was slightly ahead of me, and I noticed her stop in her tracks as she went around a boulder. It was at that moment that we broke the cardinal sin of nudist colonies. We had stumbled upon a couple who looked to be in their midseventies, as far from clothed as could be. We immediately averted our eyes to their genitals. I can't tell you exactly why that is where our eyes traveled, but it was just not something we were accustomed to seeing. We continued walking, ashamed by our actions, and passed them as they rotated their bodies to get sun in different places, like rotisserie chicken at a supermarket. There were a few more people sporting birthday suits around the corner, and we saw one guy drive into the cove on his speedboat, naked.

We eventually found a secluded rock that was surrounded by the shelter of boulders, and set up camp. To my delight, Ash decided to participate and took her top off. I also went topless to free my nips, and jumped into the water to snorkel. While in the water, Ash dared me to get naked with her, and after five minutes of bantering, she quit arguing. I took my bathing suit off and threw the wet fabric ball at her face to mess with her. I wasn't worried about anyone seeing me naked underwater.

Just as I started to feel good about participating in the nudist colony and had climbed onto the rock, I heard a Griswold-esque family approaching. A family of six kayaked right past us. The two parents and four kids all looked perplexed and scrambled to stay in their kayaks as this six-foot-three, two-hundred-pound American stood naked a mere ten yards from them. I almost fell off the rock as I tried to cover up. I probably scarred those kids for life, but I wasn't breaking any rules, just walls of innocence.

We had once again stepped out of our comfort zones. What was fascinating about the nudist colony was the lack of sexuality. Nobody was naked for the reasons that we as Americans think of for being naked. Everyone just seemed to enjoy the fresh sea air and warm sun so much that they wanted their whole bodies to get the experience. Was I comfortable being naked? No, not really. But it was a new experience for us, and that was one of my goals for this trip: to try as many new things as possible. Live like a nudist for a day—check.

7/17/15
Kolocep, Croatia

Ash prepared the Continental Kolocep Breakfast (burned toast, decent eggs, and dirt coffee) before we ventured back down to the nudist colony with the GoPro camera. (No, not to take pictures of the nude people, you pervert.) We had to see what all the hype was about with the underwater pictures. Ash prepped our day bag as I trotted down the 150 steps and across the beach to the market to get more sunscreen.

Living like the locals on a small village island in the Mediterranean was something I had always dreamed of, but never thought I would actually experience. But there we were, KJ and Ash, Kolocep locals on a first-name basis with the people who keep this small community intact.

We spent the day jumping off small rocks and taking shameless underwater selfies. Midafternoon, we took a break and sat in a natural pool attached to the rocks. I spotted a tan and tattooed couple who looked to be in their forties seated close to us. We had decided yesterday that we needed to start meeting more people in order to learn from their cultures and experiences. We had spent most of the first month of our trip alone. It was time to change that.

Based purely off stereotypes, I expected these tattoo-covered people to be the grungy motorcycle-gang types. At one point, all four of us laughed at a nursing home's worth of naked elderly people on a boat, and so we took this opportunity to engage in conversation.

"Hi, guys, where are you from?" I asked, assuming they probably weren't Kolocep natives. You can imagine my surprise when the man responded in a proper English accent resembling Hugh Grant's or James Bond's.

Foz and Millie were from a small town in southern England. Foz owned a scaffolding company, and they were here in Kolocep on a two-week holiday. When we told them we had quit our jobs to travel, they both applauded with proper British golf claps. We spent the afternoon drinking with them, and by the end of an epic day, Foz told me to get his info at the bar later tonight. He told us to be sure to find them, as it was their last night in Kolocep.

It was amazing that by simply talking to the first people we saw, we not only made friends with down-to-earth British folks but also got a soft job offer in England. As soon as they left, we had a frantic *Oh my God, are we going to England?* conversation. Would we actually do it? Probably not, but we loved to dream and plan how we would live our lives as Brits. It wasn't always realistic, but then again, there we were in Croatia on a Friday afternoon. This wouldn't have happened without us dreaming on our couch in Denver.

7/18/15
Kolocep, Croatia

Due to our excitement at dinner, we'd overindulged in Croatian beer and in turn got a late start to the morning. To make things worse, we had run out of both eggs and coffee. Neither of us had the energy to get groceries, let alone cook, so we grudgingly made our way down the steps to eat breakfast at the café for the first time. We both ordered "the Breakfast." There was only one option, and it consisted of eggs with bacon, OJ, and coffee. The eggs weren't that bad, but the bacon was more questionable than the Bush/Gore election.

The thought of propelling a kayak forward just to get pictures underwater was daunting, but we had already gone two days without kayaking, and there wasn't much else to do but sit on the beach. So we grabbed the GoPro and snorkel gear and headed to see Narissa.

We argued over who had to get the gear from the house, and I noticed that we'd both been getting agitated with each other lately. It was surprising that we had argued here and there but not *truly* fought since we'd left Denver. But Kolocep was small, *very small*. We were getting stir-crazy, and every little thing that got on our nerves was projected onto the other person.

We had the kayak routine down after our first adventure, and skipped the nudist cove and proceeded straight across the sea to the playground area. On the way out there, I spotted a high rock that looked like a great jumping platform.

I wanted to get an epic GoPro video jumping off the rock, so we pulled the boat over. It wasn't a traditional jump; it was far more dangerous. First, I had to get to the damn platform by scaling the wall. This was harder than it looked from the kayak. But that wasn't the dangerous part; the rocks below the platform that I couldn't see from sea level were the real concern. I could clear them, but I had to really plant my feet to propel myself fifteen feet out from the rocks.

After deciding that getting down by trying to climb the rocks would probably be *more* dangerous than jumping, my mind was made up. I checked with Ash that she was ready to go; she gave me a thumbs-up. I mapped out my three steps and checked the surface to make sure there would be no slipping. After the runway was clear, I started the engines and took off. By the time I leaped, I felt like an idiot once again as I watched the rocks below come far closer than I had expected. I probably cleared them by about three feet. It was admittedly more dangerous than I'd thought, but the video was going to be *epic.*

I swam through the deep blue water to the kayak and carefully distributed my weight to board it without flipping Ash. I was still shaking a bit from the adrenaline. Ash was looking at me weird when I asked how the video turned out. She said the five worst words I could have heard: "I didn't get the video."

"What do you mean?" I asked as she handed me the GoPro. I checked the playback, and she had recorded everything up until the jump and then stopped the video right before I jumped. Then she started a new video as I swam over to her and said, "Yeah, that was really sketch!" She had hit the record button at all the wrong times.

I erupted.

Not only did I erupt, my eruption caused her to erupt. It was like an earthquake that started a tsunami. Obviously, it was an honest mistake, and she felt bad, but I was extremely nearsighted, and the Adriatic was a salty place. Our arguing turned to yelling, and our yelling turned to paddle-splashing and screaming—crashes that probably echoed to Italy. At one point I screamed so loud, I choked, and my throat was on fire.

"Take me home!" she screamed, her arms folded.

"Oh, I'll take you home!" I said, and began dramatically exhausting all my energy to turn the boat around and paddle as hard as I could. Somewhere in my frantic Chris Farley–esque flailing, I had lost one of my flip-flops. I paddled hard on the right side only and turned the boat around. I think Ash thought I had given in and that that was my way of apologizing.

"No, no way. Turn. This. Boat. Around!" she screamed at me, rejecting the apology I hadn't given.

"I've gotta find my flip-flop!" I yelled back.

As I searched for the lost piece of rubber, we both sat in complete silence, nothing but the sound of water slapping up against the rocks. My flip-flop was black and it floated, so it should have been easy to find. I gave up and chalked it up to the Adriatic. We coasted to the playground area. We knew we had come too far to just kayak home. But the strange thing was, I felt great. It was as if the screaming had released all the built-up frustration I had been holding in for the last month.

When we got to the rocks, we both looked at each other and did the apologizing with our eyes. We tied the kayak up to the rocks, and at the exact same time, we noticed the lost flip-flop had been jammed into a crevice in the middle of the kayak. We both started laughing and held hands as we jumped off the rock, spending the remainder of the afternoon exploring the caves and inlets surrounding the playground.

7/19/15
Kolocep, Croatia

I woke up stiff. I know how that might sound, but I actually couldn't move my limbs very well. This made it easier to designate today a workday. We lounged on our porch all morning, writing and listening to music before taking a Greek salad break around 2:00 p.m. As soon as we began the descent down the 150-step staircase, I felt the sun pressing on the sensitive spots on my skin like pressure points. *I must have gotten burned yesterday,* I thought while popping my collar to cover my neck. The truth was, I had not looked at a mirror in days. What was the point? I wasn't shaving, and my hair was going to be soaked in the sea soon enough.

I realized as I walked down the steps that I was sporting a Hawaiian shirt with its collar popped, free plastic sunglasses that happened to be red, and swim trunks only covering half my thighs. I was officially the biggest asshole on the island, taking the crown from the guy who checked that the people at the cabanas actually belonged to the resort.

We had reservations at a restaurant tonight. That's right, a real restaurant. Last night when we'd returned the kayak, Narissa let us know about a reservation-only restaurant at the end of the cove. It was for people who were staying in the resort, but she told us that we could just walk up there and tell them we were in Villa 2 and they wouldn't ask questions. She was right.

Once we were both dressed up, we strolled down the steps and followed the path along the water, stopping at the restaurant rather than continuing to Bronze Boob Bay. They showed us to one of only eight tables overlooking the sea. We could see the entire cove of Kolocep from our elevated seats.

As the sun disappeared past the horizon, so did our budget. We ordered a nice bottle of Croatian wine and inhaled the complimentary homemade bread the waiter had brought over as soon as he turned away. I realized this was our first real "date" of the trip. Obviously, every night was a date, but we'd made reservations here. That made it feel more *real.* I can't remember being on a date with Ash where she was as carefree as she was right then. Her unkempt hair blowing in the soft breeze and makeup-less face glowing with natural beauty.

Ash was gazing at the sunset, her camera in hand, and an English couple next to us must have noticed because the gentlemen leaned over and asked, "Would you guys like a picture?" He and his wife smiled.

Stephen and Diane were celebrating Diane's fifty-fifth birthday *and* her retirement. She had worked at a university in Newcastle, England, and this was her first holiday on her own time. Stephen had been retired for the last three years and was happy to have her finally join him. They were such a charming couple, and they were extremely intrigued by our traveling story. Our date turned into a four-person dinner, and we couldn't have been happier to share a meal with these folks. Diane and Stephen finished their meal before us, and we thanked them for their company and for letting us share in their dual celebration.

Then a younger couple sat down at the table next to us. We recognized them from the bar the night before. (With one bar on the island, it was easy to spot familiar faces.) When the man ordered the catch of the day, they brought him the fish on a platter to inspect. It was clearly fresh out of the water, and it looked amazing in its raw form. It was hard for us not to look on, and before long, we started talking to them as well. The wine had made us extremely friendly.

Neil and Bryony were from Loch Ness, Scotland. (Yes, the home of the famous monster. No, they have not seen it. Yes, of course we asked.) They were our age and like-minded. They were active travelers who enjoyed beer and adventures. Each couple finished their respective bottles of wine, and we chatted until the restaurant closed. They were staying at the resort (*actually* staying there), and told us we could probably sneak into the bar area and drink with them for free if we wanted to tag along. It was an all-inclusive resort.

We strolled back to their resort, a pep in our step that only comes from the combination of new friends and good wine. Sure enough, we walked right in, and I put on my *Of course, I belong here; don't even think about asking me* face. (The same one I'd given the bouncer in Amsterdam.) They told us they had booked a kayak tour for tomorrow and were not really looking forward to it. We convinced them we could be better tour guides than the resort staff, and they canceled their excursion so they could accompany us. We then swapped phone numbers and somehow ended the night watching hippo attacks on YouTube. *This* was when I knew we would be great friends.

7/20/15
Kolocep, Croatia

Despite not seeing a clock, I could instantly tell we had overslept
when I opened my eyes. I could just feel it. I checked my phone to
see 10:03 looking back at me. We had planned to meet Neil and
Bryony at ten fifteen to kayak. Ash and I jumped out of bed frantically and started handling the essentials. I used one hand to brush
my teeth while the other rubbed pointless circles of sunscreen on my
stomach. Ash was trying to get her bathing suit on while attempting
to open a can of tuna. (Tuna for breakfast was a first and last for me.)

I was finished getting ready before Ash (the sun also rose this
morning), so I ran down and met Neil and Bryony at Narissa's at
10:20. I used the honesty method the BlaBlaCar driver in Antwerp
had used. "Hey, guys! I apologize, but we both overslept."

"No worries," Neil said. "We just got here too, and we're getting
the rundown from Narissa!"

These two were the best.

After Ash arrived, we led the way to Copper Cheeks Cove. The
next stop on the tour was where I'd jumped and Ash had missed my
heroic video. Neil and Bryony seemed perplexed that anyone would
consider jumping from that rock. (I did it for the video, okay?)

When we arrived at our playground, Neil and Bryony couldn't
believe their eyes. They paddled into the main pool area in awe as we
pointed out our favorite places to lounge, jump, snorkel, climb, and
drink beer. As we sat and watched Neil and Bryony jumping from
the cliff, I thought about our surroundings: Two months ago I was in
an office, working on balance sheets for someone else's money, constantly checking the clock with the hopes that somehow 5:00 p.m.
would arrive faster than usual. I was now in a country that we had
not even planned on coming to, in a small cove in the Adriatic Sea,
drinking good beer with great company. This seemed like a scenario
that I couldn't have even begun to think of a few months ago. There
were many reasons not to make this trip happen. But reality now
started to creep in, little by little: What would we do when we got
back? How could we justify spending all the money we had saved for

two years? What if we couldn't get jobs? These were all valid points, and frankly, all these things were *still* weighing on me *heavily*. Despite these concerns, at this precise moment, on this remote island, I was witnessing the fringe benefits of long-term travel firsthand. I didn't know if it was the unbelievable scenery, the new friends with Scottish accents (who we felt like we had known forever), or the now ever accumulating warm beers in my stomach thinking for me, but I felt like we might have made the right choice. I often hear people in their twilight years dole out advice along the lines of, "Live life like it's your last day on earth." If this were my last day on earth, I would die a happy man.

7/21/15
Kolocep, Croatia → Mljet, Croatia

When I realized this was the last time I would wake up in this single bed full of sand and dried blood, a deep depression fell over me. We had been having so much fun on this island that I had forgotten we had to leave soon. Part of me wanted to scratch the rest of the trip and settle down here. Start a family and a small business that only provided enough money to live on. Maybe help Narissa out with the kayaks or assist the island grandmother in moving her fresh produce from the ferry to her market.

I had not yet gone to bed in Kolocep without being bloody, drunk, sunburned, or bruised, yet I had loved every minute of it. Although we were already six weeks into our trip, this was our first real adventure. The metropolitan cities of Central and Eastern Europe were amazing and well worth the visits, but they were similar to the United States in many respects. Kolocep, on the other hand, was as slow and simple as a sloth. This rugged mass of land in the Adriatic had brought out the best and worst in us. Kolocep had set free the organic parts of our souls that had been dying to escape for years.

We took our final walk down the 150 steps and parked our packs at the bar to share one last beer with Neil and Bryony. Our boat was "supposed" to arrive soon, but the ferry rarely arrived right on time—another aspect of island living we could get used to: not caring as much about everything having to be *on time*. We ordered one more big beer and watched as the massive boat curved around the corner of the island and into the cove. Neil and Bryony graciously offered to buy our beers as we pounded them, and then we got in line, waving farewell to our new friends.

We asked the man if this boat was going to Mljet, to which he replied, "No, you need to go to Dubrovnik first." We nodded and boarded the ferry. The rest, it seemed, we would figure out later.

Our next two hours were spent sitting on top of the boat as we cruised past Kolocep and the other two Elaphiti Islands. We watched the sun set over the water and enjoyed the slight chill of the occasional mist that would wash over on the side of the boat and spray us. Normally, water in our faces would be annoying, but the Adriatic was like our baby girl: she could do no wrong.

We heard over the intercom that we were approaching Mljet, and we headed down into the cabin to prepare to depart the catamaran. When the boat pulled into the port, we were slightly confused. There was a gas station, a rental car shack with a few cars, and a single bus sitting on the one-lane road. The only piece of information we had was that we knew we had to get to the village of Sobra. We stood there aimlessly as everyone seemed to disperse to his or her respective methods of travel. Fortunately for us, we could use the elimination process as good as the next couple, and we walked to the bus.

"Sir, are you going to Sobra?" I asked the bus driver, hoping he spoke English.

He looked at me and said, "Sobra, ten kuna."

That'll work, I thought, and handed him the equivalent of a dollar fifty.

The bus then dropped us off and disappeared up a hill. Sobra is a community of houses on a hill, with those closest to the water only yards from the sea. Ash and I stood aimlessly yet again, trying to load the directions from our phones to find Anita, our next Airbnb host. We must have stood out because a woman approached and said, "Hello, I am Anita." I was surprised she didn't even ask if we were Kyle and Ash. Must not be too many random tourists around these parts.

We walked to our studio on the water, and it was then that she told us we had been upgraded to the full apartment rather than the studio at no additional fee because we had arrived so late. (I was unsure how this had worked out, but I was not complaining.) We walked into our room and, well . . . *it had character.* The view from our long bay windows was amazing—there was nothing but the sea, only twenty feet from our apartment. The rest of the place was a bit more rustic. The bed had one sheet for us to use as covers, and the AC was not on. I quickly turned on the unit, and it sputtered like an old car. We left for dinner to try to give the place time to cool down.

After a nice dinner with the cool ocean breeze as an appetizer, we walked home along the water, ready to call it a night, and prayed that our apartment had cooled off. I had closed all the windows in an attempt to let the AC unit do its job. This plan backfired worse than Prohibition. Our apartment was a hotbox. We both started sweating profusely upon arrival. We were not in Kolocep anymore. How I longed for our porch up on the hill, with the blasting AC and matching twin beds.

7/22/15
Mljet, Croatia

We didn't wake up—that would require us to have been sleeping in the first place. Frequently throughout the night, we would take turns walking to stand in front of the air conditioner to escape the heat of our bedroom. Every time I would doze off to sleep, I would quickly be shaken awake by my good friend homeostasis, advising me to get my thermostat down if I wanted to rest.

When the sunrise snuck through the cracks in our windows, we agreed it was an acceptable time to wake up and start cooking the breakfast we'd picked up at the small market the night before. We ate eggs and the off-brand version of the off-brand version of Kellogg's Corn Flakes. After breakfast, I went to take a cold shower to rinse the sweat of the night off my skin when all of a sudden the light turned off.

"Ash, knock it off. I am in no mood for shenanigans."

But she replied with the five worst words since "I didn't get the video."

"The power just went out."

No big deal, I thought. *I don't need the light to shower.* I dried off and went to read the rest of the news on my Twitter feed. *Shit, no Wi-Fi.* Now heating up again, I walked to the AC unit to get some sort of relief, but there was no air coming out. I wanted to alert Anita of our situation, and went to send her a message about our power outage. *Shit. No Wi-Fi.*

Wi-Fi and AC were the two most important of our four prerequisites when looking for an Airbnb; now we were without both. Unable to do much else, we left to rent mopeds so we could get around the island for the week we were here.

The port was only two miles away, so we started the trek up the hill. The heat was blistering, but the view of the water refreshed us as we continued to climb.

Halfway up the hill, my left knee started throbbing. This knee sucked. I know that is pretty vague as far as a diagnosis goes, but I've never figured out what is wrong with it. I am assuming it's some type of tendonitis, but without an MRI, there's no way to be certain. I inherited my uncle Dave's bad knees. I can only hope I inherited some of his writing skills as well. He is a wizard with words, the Dumbledore of poetry.

We arrived at the moped shack, but there was no one inside. I walked to the souvenir shop next door and asked if the woman knew where the moped rental shop owner was.

"I am the owner," she proudly proclaimed. She walked out from behind the souvenir counter and into the shack next door. This was one way to cut labor costs.

We told the woman we wanted to rent two mopeds.

"Okay, do you have experience driving mopeds?" she casually asked.

Ash immediately blurted out, "Nope," honestly and cheerfully. *Dammit, Ash, this is like when the laser tag instructor asks if you have ever played laser tag. You always reply yes to skip the tutorial of "Here is your trigger; aim the gun at everyone you see." Just hand me the laser, boss, so I can light these six-year-olds up.*

To my surprise, the lady didn't even offer a tutorial; she just said she could not rent one to Ash. She told us there had been *far* too many people injured recently on the island, and that there was no hospital; so if anyone was seriously hurt, they had to get a helicopter to Dubrovnik for treatment. This fact actually worked out well, because they had big mopeds equipped for two people, and renting only one for the week would save us 150 dollars.

Before we left the shop, Ash walked over to the Mljet visitors' office to meet a girl named Metka. Ash's dad worked with a man whose daughter happened to be on the island. The man and his family were from Zagreb, but they had a vacation house here, and Metka and her mother were visiting for the summer. Ash returned with plans to hang out with Metka and her mom at the Mljet National Park tomorrow. Then she got situated on the back of the moped, holding on to my sides and leaving me just enough space to get my feet on the pedals. We sped up the hill.

The wind in my face felt so good. I imagined this was what it must feel like to be a dog with a face full of fur. When we reached the intersection to go back to Sobra, we banked left and headed to the villages in the other direction.

When you don't have seat belts and are just sitting on a seat in the open air, going forty-five miles per hour feels like going ninety. We flew down the coast on a road that resembled Highway 1 in California. To our left was the rugged mountainside, and to our right, a deep cliff hanging over what looked like endless light-blue sea. We were in a moving postcard.

We spent the rest of the afternoon village-hopping up and down the south side of the island. There were only a few villages, and some had just a couple of houses and markets, but in each place we found someone selling some sort of food or beverage.

We zoomed down the mountain to the last village of the day: Prozura, a small fishing town nestled on the banks of a cove surrounded by islands. Upon arriving in the village, the road that also served as a sidewalk quickly turned into one lane. I felt like I was in a video game as I weaved past street vendors, fishermen hauling their daily catches, and parked cars that looked like they were from the eighties. There were waitresses walking between cafés and the patio seating on the water. I sped under a fortress-like arch made of stone and skidded to a halt outside the last café in the village. Call me Bond. (Kyle) James Bond.

We stayed in Prozura until dusk, watching the sailboats change colors with the sky. As it got darker, it became much more dangerous for moped travel, so we headed home. When we arrived in Sobra, we careened down into our village.

The power was indeed back on, but the AC unit had to be manually restarted. The place was once again a furnace, and the power flickered off and on again. It was going to be a long night of restarting the AC unit. Sleep was a distant thought at this point.

7/23/15
Mljet, Croatia

We managed to get a bit more sleep than the night before, as the island air had cooled down to the low eighties overnight. This was chilly as far as Mljet was concerned. I couldn't imagine being excited to sleep in eighty-degree temperatures back home. We ventured down to the café to meet up with Metka and her mother to go to the national park.

These two were very serious people. Not in a negative way; they were just serious. At the same time, they were extremely nice. It just wasn't the Southern charm–type of nice that has hidden motives and fluffy, bullshit compliments—no, their kindness was sincere.

The check arrived, and Metka's mother grabbed it. (I keep saying Metka's mother because I can't pronounce her name, let alone spell it. My best guess would be Svetsaladana. Let's go with Svets for short.) So Svets grabbed the check, but Ash asked if she could pay for our pizza. Svets put her finger in Ash's face and said sternly, "No." Then she smiled and walked to the register.

On the twenty-mile ride across the island to the park, Svets led the way in her car as Ash and I followed on our moped. Svets had offered to drive us, but I wanted to cruise the coastline on our bike and feel the fresh sea breeze.

Thirty minutes later, we reached the Mljet National Park and cruised through the village of Polače, located inside. This town reminded me of a mini-Dubrovnik and was vibrant with fishermen and restaurants. (This is where we would have stayed had we known anything about Mljet before this week.)

By the time we'd parked and put our helmets in the compartment of our moped seat and walked to the kiosk, Svets had already paid for our entries to the park. She handed us a few day passes.

The four of us walked slowly down a hill, passing olive tree fields until we reached the centerpiece, Veliko Lake. Svets led us onto a small taxi-boat to cross the lake to St. Mary Island.

After a short ride across the water, we reached an island that hosted an old Roman Catholic church that had been there since the twelfth century. We toured the ancient structure as Svets gave us a history on the ancient ruins and the island as a whole. One particular story stood out to me.

It turns out, Mljet used to be infested with venomous snakes. It became very dangerous for its inhabitants, as they had no antivenom anywhere on the island. If someone was bit, they had to go to Dubrovnik to recover. Not an ideal situation. So they brought in Mongoose Team 6. The mongooses slowly cleared the island of snakes.

It took us an hour to circle the monastery before we headed back to the boat to ride to a small lake. As we were waiting to board, Svets pointed out a tall yellow-flowered plant. It looked more like a tree, as it rose ten feet in the air.

"The agave flower," Svets said, pointing to the large bud. "Agaves only bloom once, and their flower stands beautifully in the air above all other plants, out of reach of animals. But once they die, they die forever and do not rebloom." She boarded the boat as I stood there, contemplating this flower.

These plants, somehow through evolution, decided that it was worth it to live a shorter yet more magnificent life than a monotonous, longer life. Sure, they only got to bloom one time, but would you prefer to bloom once and live a magnificent life, swaying in the sky, or bloom every year and get eaten by obnoxious rodents or stepped on by toddlers? I would choose YOBO: You Only Bloom Once.

We headed back across the glass-like water on our small skiff, and when we reached the cars and began our heartfelt good-bye, Svets waved her finger and invited us to come eat watermelon. It seemed like an odd request, but there was no way we were going to turn it down.

Svets told stories about her life in the region while she sat smoking Croatian cigarettes. I noticed a hole in the middle of the concrete and asked Svets if it was some sort of drainage system. "No," she casually replied. "That is the top of a large anthill." She told us the ants had survived all the construction, so by the time they'd laid the terrace with concrete, she'd left a hole at the top of their colony so they could continue to survive. If they had survived all that construction, they deserved to live.

"Well, what happens if they start infesting the house?" I asked with honest curiosity.

"Well, then we close the hole," she replied, smiling and blowing out the last of her cigarette smoke.

7/24/15
Mljet, Croatia

I woke up covered in sweat as Ash buzzed around, going through her morning routine. It was amazing how this routine was transforming from our days in Denver. To start, it began around 9:00 a.m. rather than 5:45 a.m. (contributing to a major difference in attitude and overall morale). Second, she used to take an hour to pick out an outfit, put on makeup, and "fix her hair" (as it if were broken). Now her routine had been trimmed down to fifteen minutes and consisted of putting on a bathing suit with a tank top and gym shorts, lathering on sunscreen, and putting her hair in pigtails or a topknot.

We jumped onto the moped to get the show on the road. When we reached the end of a long street, we followed the path to a secret beach that Metka had told us about. She'd also told us that a few venomous snakes that had survived the mongoose slaughter had recently fallen out of trees, landed on people, and bitten their faces. With this knowledge, we kept our helmets on as we walked under the thick brush overhead.

I captured Ash's beautiful features with her Canon camera all afternoon as she played along the rocks. I had become overly fascinated with taking pictures with the camera since arriving in Croatia. The landscape obviously assisted in this newfound passion, with its arid cliffs, powder-blue water, and lush forests.

7/25/15
Mljet, Croatia

We decided to head back to the national park today to take advantage of the free passes Svets had given us. We got situated on the moped, and I tried to start the ignition. The damn thing sputtered for five seconds but wouldn't catch. I tried it again—nothing. *I filled her up yesterday, so what's the problem?* On the third try, she turned on just long enough for me to rev the throttle and get going. This was a great feeling, similar to finally getting the lawn mower to start after minutes of out-of-control cord cranking.

As we headed up the hill and banked onto the main road, I noticed it was blistering hot. Most days the air became cooler when we'd sliced through it, but today the heat stood its ground. We made it halfway to the park and were in the middle of nowhere when we spotted an amazing view of the coast between two mountains where the canyon below met the sea. I pulled the moped over to snap a picture. As I was taking the shot, I heard the moped turn off behind me.

"You don't have to turn it off, baby," I said through squinted eyes, trying to capture the perfect shot.

"I didn't touch anything," Ash replied, confused.

I walked back to her and the bike and wiped my brow. From only standing there for one minute, my entire forehead was soaked in sweat. I tried to restart the moped, but she just sputtered once again. I tried numerous times, but the sputtering began to simmer down to a soft hum. By the fourth or fifth try, there was no noise at all. She was completely dead. And I was afraid we were too.

We hadn't seen a car since we'd left Sobra twenty minutes ago, and there were very few vehicles on this island. So we began to panic a bit. Other than taking a snake to the face, this was probably the worst-case scenario: we were at least ten miles from the closest civilization, and it was high noon. There is no such thing as casual traffic on a seventy-five-square-mile island of 1,100 people. *Okay, Kyle, don't panic, don't panic.*

"We're screwed!" came blurting out of my mouth, as I clearly hadn't taken my own advice.

I propped the moped against a tree. At this point, I looked like I had just taken a shower with my clothes on. It was ninety-seven degrees and there was no shade in sight. Our only water bottle was half-empty. The situation became dire, and I tried to think back to any of the survival skills I'd stumbled across while camping growing up. All that came to mind was how to make a fire. Not only was this the last thing we needed, but I was never able to get a flame going anyway. As I turned to give Ash my concession speech, I heard a rumble in the distance. There was not a cloud in the sky, which meant one thing: a vehicle.

We both stared at the long stretch of road until a black dot appeared in the heat waves. There was no way we were going to risk missing the only car we had seen all day and what may be our only shot against heat stroke. Forget the thumbs-up hitchhiking sign; I stood and waved my hands like a football ref asking for the clock to stop.

As the beat-up car got closer, I started to panic again, but not because the car looked like it had been sitting in a front yard in

Kentucky for thirty years; I was panicking because it wasn't going to stop. It got within twenty-five yards and then, *whoosh*. At least the blast of air as the car flew by felt great.

All of a sudden, the car screeched to a stop fifty yards away. A man with long brown hair turned around and put his hand on the passenger seat as he reversed to us at the same speed with which he'd driven by. He was clearly coming to rob or kill us. As an American, I had a natural fear of hitchhiking. If I saw someone with their thumb out, I didn't pick them up because they would probably kill me. If I were walking on the street and someone offered me a ride, I wouldn't get in the car because they, too, would probably kill me. Everyone gets killed in American hitchhiking folklore.

He stopped directly next to us and sat in silence. I peered through the passenger window and said, "Hey, man, our moped broke down. Are you headed to the national park?" This was a rhetorical question, as everyone going this direction was going to the national park. There was nothing else on this side of the island.

"Yes, yes, come on in." He motioned with his hands.

Well, here goes nothing. . . .

We left the moped on the side of the road and got in the car. This man gave me a whole new perspective on speed. I remember how I felt as a four-year-old on Mr. Toad's Wild Ride. This was extremely similar. I had never felt someone accelerate downhill until there was a turn and then slam on the brakes while curving around the corner. We were slowing down *just* enough to not fly off the mountainside. I couldn't complain; he had just removed us from certain death, like picking up two roasting worms on a summer sidewalk and throwing them into the moist grass.

I made small talk in the front and found out that he had lived in Mljet his entire life and owned a restaurant in Polače. This made me feel a little better about traveling at the speed of fright. We flew into Polače, and he slowed down to avoid hitting pedestrians like frogs.

"Do you know where the moped rental shop is?" I asked, as he was probably wondering where to let us out.

"Oh, I am taking you there now," he casually proclaimed as he kept driving.

He pointed out the window and said, "There is my restaurant." By the look of his car, I'd expected a hole-in-the-wall, but it was easily one of the nicest places on the island. The brick oven was twelve feet high, and the place had its own pier area with seating. I looked back at Ash, whose mouth was open in awe. I was proud of her for not blurting out what she usually did in these situations.

He took us all the way to the rental shop and led the way inside. By the time we'd followed him in, he was finishing the conversation in Croatian about our situation. The rental people nodded at him like he was their father, and then handed us keys. He turned to us and said, "They will pick up your moped. The red one outside is now yours." He clearly had some pull around here. We thanked him, but he just shrugged, smiled, and walked back out to the car.

I was in awe of what had just happened. The amount of kindness this stranger had shown us was inspiring. It made me want to search the island for stranded people and pick them up. Although this man was the first person to come by, I had a feeling we would have received the same level of kindness from anyone who had happened to pass us. The people in this country took care of one another. They were a true community. Their kindness was contagious, and Mljet was attacking our depleted traveling immune systems.

7/26/15
Mljet, Croatia

It was our last day in Mljet, and this meant our time on the islands of Croatia was already two-thirds over. Traveling was a constant roller coaster of emotion. We cycled through the pattern of undergoing the stress of getting to a new place, adapting and falling in love with it, and then being depressed that we had to leave. This got me thinking about returning home for good, and what I feared most: getting another job.

It wasn't even a nine-to-five that I didn't want to return to. I just wanted to do something for a living that I actually cared about. I think people who live the longest and happiest lives have figured out how to maximize their happiness-stress ratio. Stress is the single most deadly thing on earth to me, because it can be a subtle demon. When something acute happens to make you unhappy, you can recognize it and fix it. Stress is a gradual killer that eats at your sleep, daily joy, and quality of life in general. Our stress levels were so low at this point in the trip that booking our next accommodation was our biggest worry. That wasn't even stress, just an obligation. Again, this trip was finite; we had to go home in a couple months, but we were learning to live happily and stress free. Hopefully just a taste of this life would change how we lived the rest of ours.

Spending the day in Prozura, drinking beer and espresso, was exactly the kind of lazy day we needed before traveling tomorrow. We didn't want to stay out too late, because we had an apartment to pack up. So we paid our tab with the friendly bar owner who had served us all afternoon, and cruised home for the last time.

The sun was setting over the water, and we were delighted to feel a slight chill in the air as we walked up to our apartment. *Maybe we will sleep tonight.* We were halfway done fixing the explosion that had happened in our backpacks when we heard a knock at the door. *Hmm, we aren't expecting anyone. Hell, we don't know anyone.* I opened the door to see our Airbnb host's daughter, accompanied by a young British couple.

"Hello?" I said as we all looked at one another, confused.

It didn't take long for us to realize that our upgrade from the studio to the apartment had resulted in a double booking. I invited the couple in while the host's daughter attempted to call Anita. The couple seemed very nice but a bit ruffled by the situation. I could definitely understand; if we arrived after a day of travel in the blistering heat and our place wasn't available, I would be much madder than they were. Luckily, I had just the cure. I cracked open a two-liter beer, and they happily obliged as I passed around glasses. Not long after, we were all laughing over the situation like old friends.

Laura and Tom were from London, and they had just finished university. We noticed Laura called Tom by his last name, Withers, so we followed suit. They were traveling together before Laura started a six-month internship back in England. We had only spent fifteen minutes with the young couple, and I could tell we were highly compatible. Anita had found them another place, and we told them if that place sucked, they were more than welcome to stay with us in the other bedroom. Regardless of where they stayed, we planned to meet them for drinks later on.

Ash and I left to fill up the moped before we returned it tomorrow, and when we got back to Sobra, Withers and Laura were already at the bar, with large beers and matching smiles. They welcomed us to the table and told us they had decided to stay with us if it was all right, as the other place was in an awful location up the hill. Of course this was fine with us. We loved their company, and the room at the other end of the apartment had been vacant all week.

With new friends/roommates, we enjoyed a dinner of mussels from the sea a mere ten feet from us. We were in that typical honeymoon stage of any relationship where our new friends could do no wrong in our eyes. We were just happy that they wanted to hang out with us as much as we wanted to hang out with them. The more time we spent with these two, the more I saw ourselves in them. Laura was a very confident, strong woman who loved adventure and seemed to have fun in any situation. She had lived in Cuba shortly, similarly to Ash when she'd taught English in Costa Rica. Withers, on the other hand, was a smart, savvy guy who truly listened to us when we talked, and he asked great questions about our journey. So basically, Laura reminded me of Ash.

The beers continued to go down easily, and Withers rolled us cigarettes from tobacco he took out of a pouch. Eventually we had gotten drunk enough to call it quits, and all four of us walked home, our arms around one another's shoulders like middle school friends taking a last-day-of-school picture. Laura and Withers were added to the list of great friends we had made in Croatia.

7/27/15
Mljet, Croatia → Korcula, Croatia

I woke up with the worst case of the thump-thumps since Amsterdam. The combination of two liters of beer and three rolled cigarettes was too much for my head and stomach. I crept out of bed quietly so as not to wake Ash, tiptoed to the bathroom, and violently threw up— this woke up Ash instantly. *Aww, baby, I knew those cigarettes were a bad idea. Are you okay?* is what I wish she had said, but all I heard from the room was a groan and her roll over on the squeaky mattress.

As we prepped to leave our apartment, we realized there was a component we had failed to plan for: our massive backpacks. There was no way we and our backpacks could both fit on the small moped. These are the things you fail to plan for at 11:00 p.m. when drinking with your new best friends. It took me four trips to get the backpacks, Ash, and Withers to the port. I took Withers so he could rent his own moped for the rest of the week.

As we returned our moped and prepared to board the ferry that had just pulled into the bay to take us to Korčula, we had a heartfelt embrace with Withers and wished him and Laura great luck on the rest of their journey.

I took one last look at the beautiful, rugged coastline of Mljet, waved to Withers as he drove up the hill for the first time on his own rented moped, and walked across the footbridge onto the ferry to set sail for Korčula.

It felt like we had just walked into an oven. This ferry was different from the others in that there was no outside seating. We would have loved to sit outside and let the fresh air wash away our hangovers, but there we were, in the muggy cabin full of other people's exhales. It was like basking in one giant room of bad morning breath.

I was coaching Ashley on breathing like she was in labor as the boat slowly moved around the island and reached the port in Polače. A large group of people left the ferry to visit the fishing village, and we found seats as close as we could to an open window. At this point I was nearly blacking out from heat, nausea, and lack of sleep.

An hour later we stepped off the torture tank, and the fresh air pleasantly filled my lungs. I didn't realize how bad it truly was until we'd exited the ferry. I looked around and realized we were not in Kolocep or Mljet anymore. Korčula was a busy city with cars honking and businesses booming. It reminded me of a Mediterranean version of Key West. It had the aura of a pretty girl who knows she is pretty.

I checked my phone for instructions from our Airbnb host, Darinka, and scanned the pier area until we found her granddaughter. Croatian hosts usually send their younger kids because their English is better. She had a sign with our names on it.

The granddaughter drove us through the Old Town and the two and a half miles along the coast to our apartment, which sat on top of their house. It was perched high up on a hill overlooking a bay. This apartment was stunning, with a huge outdoor terrace that had couches and tables and overlooked the water, a king-sized bed, and freezing-cold AC. The best part: it was only seventy dollars a night, which left us eighty dollars a day to spend on fun. We unpacked excitedly, a nap at the end of the tunnel, and showered to get rid of the morning breath we had soaked in earlier.

I woke up around 4:00 p.m. and sighed with relief when I felt no pain in my head or stomach. I could barely remember the morning. It was as if I were waking up today for the first time. I looked around for Ash, and found her sitting outside on the couches, reading. We agreed to walk to the Old Town for dinner to explore and get some exercise.

The path along the water took us past docked boats in the gentle sea. When we reached a stretch of beach, we transitioned our walk to there, scanning the smooth rocks for sea glass. Sea glass always takes me back to when I was a kid in Lake Huron with my grandparents. My grandma loved collecting sea glass, and her house was always decorated with mason jars chock full of it. She kept water in the jars to let the old glass shine. Every chance we got to add to her collection, we eagerly accumulated pieces. I cherish those summers.

We approached a castle-like structure in the Old Town that resembled the inside of King's Landing. I know the show is filmed in Dubrovnik, but I wouldn't be surprised if scenes had been shot here as well. The city walls encompassed all the shops, restaurants, and vendors as if they were still protecting them from intruders. We strolled on the cobblestone walkway as music seemed to resonate from the rock walls. A sign for affordable seafood stopped us in our tracks.

We were ready to settle in and see what Korčula had to offer, as it was our last home in Croatia, an incredible country all around. We had a week in this land of castle-like structures, and we planned on taking this time to relax and gear up for Italy.

7/28/15
Korcula, Croatia

For the first time in a long time, I slept soundly and through the night. I don't know if it was having the temperature at sixty-seven degrees or if it was the dark room with comfortable pillows, but I was refreshed.

Ash and I had planned on heading into Old Town early, but the couches on our porch, which were strategically placed behind curtains of shade, were too hard to leave. We had spent so much money on mopeds in Mljet that we could not afford to rent them here. This gave us an excuse for pure relaxation.

Hours were spent watching sailboats arrive and depart the small cove, but we still had a mission today: to ride a slide that fed into the sea. Yesterday we'd passed a yellow slide, similar to one you would find at a kid's park that propelled its riders directly into the water. The slide was the only object perched on the edge of a large slab of concrete; it was also home to numerous sunbathers and their rambunctious offspring frolicking in the water.

When we reached the platform, we laid out our towels and sat down to get our bearings. Being propelled from a slide into the warm sea truly takes you back to your childhood.

I filmed Ash slide down, and whatever reservations we had about being the only adults on the slide were long gone. She screamed like a child and laughed the entire way. Before we knew it, we had joined the eight-year-olds in the cycle of slide, swim, climb, slide. This continued until the sun began setting and we returned home, pruned from the water and scorched by the sun.

The sun had both exhausted and roasted us. Some days the sun was great and we loved soaking in her generous rays, but on others she abused us like naughty schoolkids in the twenties. We grabbed pizza from a highly reviewed place on TripAdvisor and sat on our porch, letting the breezy night cool off our skin. Our first day was a success.

7/29/15
Korčula, Croatia

The next day, as we sat on our porch and sluggishly ate breakfast, we came to the realization that we were physically beat. There were no other words for it. After a week of rock climbing and rigorous sea kayaking, our bodies and minds desperately needed rest. Our living conditions in Mljet had not provided this. We'd slept awfully in immense heat on a board they called a bed for six days. The last two weeks had caught up to us, like a Monday-morning cold after a weekend-long bender in college.

After finishing breakfast, I brought in the dishes from the terrace and passed a mirror. I had to look twice because I hardly recognized myself. My head and facial hair had both grown so long, it was hard to tell where one area stopped and one started. The skin on my face resembled the leather of a rodeo-worn saddle, and the valleys under my eyes were Grand Canyon–esque. I was transforming. I couldn't tell if I looked stronger or weaker, but I was glad that this trip was changing me either way. I had come too far to stay the same.

By midafternoon we felt the need to leave our terrace and trek to the Old Town. It was by far the coolest part of Korčula, and we had not been since the first night. We walked the treacherous sidewalk-less road and arrived at a hill that filtered down to the castle walls.

After a seafood dinner, I was ready to go home and get a third good night's sleep in a row, but Ash had other plans: she wanted to find something she could always remember Croatia by. It took numerous trips through the street markets for her to decide on some handmade wooden earrings made from an olive tree. I, too, got into the Croatian spirit and decided to seek out a memento. Ash refused to walk near me the entire way home, trying to suppress her laughter, as I proudly wore my white-and-blue-pinstripe sailor hat (think Greek fisherman's cap) all the way home. This sailor hat with the Croatian flag on it would surely bring me back to my kayak-captaining days.

7/30/15
Korčula, Croatia

Ash had finally reached her relaxation threshold, and she shook me awake at 9:00 a.m. to get to the Old Town. Before we walked outside to start our trek, I noticed something different. My skin wasn't being roasted, and there was some strange sensation on my face that both woke me up and provided relief. Could it be . . . wind? There was a breeze on the island, and it gave me that feeling of finishing my last final in college. A breeze might be an understatement; a gust of wind launched our bug spray across the patio floor, making an obnoxious sound of aluminum ricocheting off stone.

We moseyed around our apartment for much of the day before eventually reaching the Old Town at 5:00 p.m. We took seats at a cool-looking restaurant in one of the alleys that snaked around the castle. A young man strolled up to us like he wanted to chat. We had just looked at the menu and realized we couldn't afford the food here, but we wanted to be nice to the waiter, who seemed like he was ecstatic to see customers. We each ordered a glass of wine from whom we would soon find out was one of the happiest humans we had ever come across.

Tadej was a tall, lean twenty-one-year-old spitfire of a Croatian who spent his summer waiting tables here in Korčula. He had no other customers, so he took a seat against a ledge near us and listened intently as we told him about our travels thus far. He then told us about his time spent working with the American Red Cross in Zagreb. Before long, we were talking like old friends (really like his big brother and sister), offering advice on life and commending him on his work with the Red Cross. Then he stopped, smiled, and said abruptly, "Do you guys want try our local brandy?" We thanked him for offering, but politely told him we were taking a break from drinking. Just kidding, of course we obliged.

He returned, beaming and carrying three large shot glasses full of brandy. He recited a Croatian cheers and we clinked glasses. Then I proceeded to pound my shot in one fell gulp. Ash and Tadej calmly sipped theirs and continued talking. When I realized what I had done, I tried to casually sip my empty glass. Tadej noticed, quickly smiled, and took his like a shot as well. Ash looked confused until she saw mine was gone, and then we all burst into laughter.

Our conversation continued, albeit slightly drunker at this point. Somehow we got on the topic of coffee, and I told him I probably drank four to five cups a day. He slammed the table and said, "I will make you guys the best coffee in Korčula," and proudly strolled into his café.

He returned with large espressos. This was a crucial pick-me-up, as the brandy and two glasses of red wine were trying to take me down. Eventually we came to the realization that we needed to eat, so we told Tadej we were going to head to dinner, because we couldn't afford his restaurant, but that we would be back tomorrow to see him. He ran inside and returned with the check: six dollars with only *one* glass of wine on it. Good man.

We left him a twenty-dollar tip (the equivalent to around one hundred dollars for a Croatian with their cost of living) and felt great about it. We stood up for this first time in hours, and the impact of the drinks was apparent. Instead of taking our usual twenty minutes to decide where to eat, we went to the same seafood shack as the first night.

8/1/15
Korcula, Croatia

Ash woke me up and reminded me with a sad voice that it was our last day in Korčula, which also meant our last day in Croatia. I couldn't believe it had been three weeks since we had laid eyes on the beauty of the Adriatic. The days had felt slow, but the weeks had gone by fast.

Before heading out for the day, I decided to rebudget for Italy. We knew the cost of living there was going to be elevated, and we wanted to expand our budget for those days. I totaled all the "money spent" columns on our Excel model and compared them with our bank statements. I found a two-thousand-dollar discrepancy. *This can't be right.* I did it again and found the exact same total differential. *Shit . . .*

After digging into each withdrawal, I found the issue. Nineteen hundred dollars was taken out in Vienna from Ash's bank account. Not only would we never have taken out nineteen hundred dollars for any reason, we had not taken out *any* money in Vienna. It was the last city that we'd been in that used the euro, and we'd had leftover money from previous cities. Someone must have stolen her credit card information.

We had always heard about the high risk of identity theft in Europe, but we never imagined we would be victims. *Numerous* painful phone conversations left Ash extremely agitated with each clueless transfer. We'd had quite a scare. My fantasy football keeper player, Odell Beckham Jr., was not participating in scrimmages. Oh, and our credit card information had been stolen in Austria. Thankfully, we got our money back right away. Disaster averted.

We left for the Old Town to say good-bye to Tadej, but we could not find the alley where he resided. Just before we were going to give up, we heard a cheerful "Americans!" echoing down the alley. We turned to see Tadej, his arms open for an embrace. We said our good-byes and found each other on Facebook so we could stay in touch. We also made him promise that if he ever came to the US to let us host him. I know we will see Tadej again someday. Our lives wouldn't be nearly as happy if we didn't. He is a special kid.

We wrapped up our Korčula experience the same way we wrapped up most cities—depressed and face deep in a pizza. This had been the best part of our trip thus far, and Croatia was a country that would hold a place in our hearts forever. It was very visceral; it brought out the rawness of our emotions. Every person we'd met—from Neil, Bryony, Foz, Millie, Diane, and Stephen in Kolocep, to Withers, Laura, Metka, and Svets in Mljet, to Tadej in Korčula—would forever be in our hearts for making these three weeks special for us. These weren't just people we'd spent time with; they were true friends. Croatia had given me the peace of mind I needed to cope with this trip and leave the life we'd known behind. Central Europe was still a bustling empire of economies and rat races of their own. Croatia, on the other hand, was simply a land of peace.

8/2/15
Korčula, Croatia -> Dubrovnik, Croatia

It was the first time this week we were woken up by anything other than a splash of 10:00 a.m. sun sneaking through the blinds.

When Darinka's husband dropped us off at the port, I shook his hand and thanked him for the hospitality and sharing the apartment above his home with us, but he didn't speak a lick of English. The language barrier was fierce between us, but I think he got the message; smiles and handshakes are a universal language.

When it was time for boarding, Ash and I walked to the back of the boat where there were a few seats outside. The area was in the middle of the sun with no shade, but the seats were the only two together, and after the hellish trip here, we preferred fresh air. We sat next to one of the guys we had been chatting with in the waiting area.

"Long time no sea," I said, chuckling. Then I realized he couldn't hear how I was spelling *sea* in my head and felt like an idiot.

Mark was a Dutch sailor from Amsterdam. He was down in Korčula working as a skipper for a family on their yacht. When he told us he was trained to be a skipper on freighters that traveled around the horn of Africa, I asked him the obvious questions.

"Yeah," he said, "I've had a run-in with pirates." He said it didn't get as crazy as in the movies, but he was out near the African coast around Somalia when a boat with a small light on suddenly came out of nowhere in the middle of the night. The boat was not on the radar that documented registered vessels, and it came closer and closer toward them. Mark turned on all the ship's floodlights, as well as all the fire hoses. He said the hoses were now completely covering their freighter, and if a small boat got anywhere close to it, it would surely sink the boat in seconds. He told us that when the hoses turned on, the light on the small boat turned off and they didn't see it again. I was almost upset the story didn't end with some sort of gunfight.

Our flight was early tomorrow morning, and rather than stay in Dubrovnik, we figured we would spend thirty-five dollars to sleep a mile from the airport. The bus driver told us two dollars for both of us, and we happily boarded a bus that was probably from 1955. Our quality standards for transportation had plummeted.

When the bus driver announced Konavle, we looked out the window at the desolate land before us and asked him, "Are you sure?" He smiled and nodded as if he found it humorous that we'd ended up here. Konavle was a one-horse town. It had one residential area, one restaurant, and one gas station. It also had one Airbnb. We'd booked it for proximity to the airport, but we were now second-guessing our decision.

We sat down in *the* restaurant, ordered beers, and messaged our host, Sunshine, to let her know we were here. She told us someone would be there shortly to pick us up in "either a black Mazda or a white car." Again, our standards were so low at this point that she could have said, "The next car that shows up is yours," and we probably would have gotten in.

Sure enough, a black Mazda showed up, and a tall smiling kid maybe twenty years old got out and shook our hands. We drove up a hill and arrived at our place. We told him we were leaving at 7:00 a.m. the next morning, and asked about some sort of taxi service.

He smiled and said, "I will be your taxi," and offered to take us for ten dollars.

This was definitely more than we had been paying for public transportation, but the ease of having our ride waiting that early in the morning and not having to find a taxi was worth it. We agreed and planned to meet at seven. He seemed overly thrilled, as if we had just agreed to pay him one million dollars instead of ten.

Our place was awful, two stiff beds in a room with a bathroom. This was why it was thirty-five for the night. It reminded me of the dorm rooms at my basketball camp when I was a kid. The AC worked and the Wi-Fi (sort of) worked, so we had three of our essentials. The amazing part to me was how nice they'd made this place look on the website. I was thoroughly impressed.

8/3/15
Dubrovnik, Croatia → Rome, Italy

When we woke up in Croatia for the last time, our backs were sore from the wood with four-inch mattresses and we were more dehydrated than we preferred to be. It felt right.

We left our Airbnb at precisely 6:40 a.m. and walked down to where the smiling kid lived. I expected that he would not be awake to drive two strangers to the airport, but lo and behold, there he was, perched on his Mazda, smiling from ear to ear and slapping the hood of his car to commence the trip.

As the '96 Mazda stick shift exited the residential area and reached the airport in fifteen minutes, the kid told us about how Konavle had been rebuilt after the war only twenty years earlier. For a once war-torn country from the Soviet Bloc, it seemed awfully peaceful now.

The customs officer stamped our passports with the Dubrovnik seal, and soon after they called the flight to Rome over the intercom. The passengers raced to line up to board the flight. It was assigned seating. *Why the hell are these people so eager to board?* I thought. But when I laid eyes on the overhead space that *might* fit a fifth-grade lunch box, it made sense. Fortunately for us, we'd checked our back-packs and were free-bagging it. Ash was asleep before they finished the seat belt demonstration, and I put on T. Swift and cranked out some writing for the entire pond jump over the Adriatic.

When we landed at Fiumicino Airport, it was a culture shock. Our last three weeks had been spent on island time. The Rome air-port reminded me of an American airport, and it was packed with in-ternational travelers either ready to get their holiday trips underway or to get home and face the depression of returning to work.

It took us two hours to get through customs and get our bags, but we didn't mind. The free Wi-Fi and AC were enough for us to be complacent.

With backpacks securely in tow, we boarded the train headed to central Rome, along with damn near everyone else in the airport. I sat down at a window seat, and when I felt the weight of the cushion shift as someone sat next to me, I turned to talk to Ash and saw it wasn't Ash but an old woman beaming at me. I smiled and turned to see Ash three seats behind me. Ash had the directions on her phone, so I told her to let me know when we got there.

After half an hour or so, our stop was next, so I put on my back-pack and turned to ask Ash where we went from here, only to find her asleep on the window, snoring and probably dreaming about pasta carbonara. *Shit, I forgot this was a moving vehicle!*

"Ash," I said, trying not to make a scene. She didn't stir. I was going to say it louder, but the old Italian man next to her smiled at me and pointed at her as if to say *Want me to wake her up?* I nodded at him and thanked him, and he tapped Ash's shoulder until she awoke, embarrassed. We stepped off the train into the gorgeous oven that was Rome, Italy, and walked up to our apartment.

To use any word but *perfect* to describe our Airbnb would be do-ing it a disservice. We were located in the middle of arguably the best neighborhood in Rome, with a large AC unit *in* the bedroom of our apartment. I always put an emphasis on the AC part because of the nights we were without it. The spacious apartment had a glamorous decor and possessed a large bathroom and a shower with great water pressure. At this point in the trip we needed the pressure to dispel the dirt and sweat. We had forgotten what luxury felt like since being in Croatia for so long. We even had a washer and dryer in our place. Our clothes smelled like sweat and bad hand soap.

With our travel day safely behind us, we ventured into squares that were filled with energetic people wrapped up in romance, and old buildings sporting tan, beige, and red outfits. A place with great seating caught our attention, and we proceeded to study the menu. Ash smiled at an older gentleman near us who was seated with his large family, and he could probably tell we were contemplating whether or not to eat here. He said, with an elegant Swiss accent, "The food is amazing," and smiled.

We thanked him and sat down at the only available table, which happened to be near them. We ordered a bottle of Chianti and took in the view around us. I was gazing at a cathedral across the street when Ash started chatting with the daughter of the gentleman who had convinced us to eat here.

Siofra was a Swiss woman traveling with her three kids and her father in Rome for two nights before heading to Zanzibar for holiday. Siofra seemed to take life as it came, and she exercised the parenting style we hoped to one day have as she truly listened to her kids instead of shoving screens in their faces.

They finished eating well before we did. On the way out, Siofra took Ash's phone number and told us that if we were ever in Switzerland to call her and come stay with her and her family. (That was an offer we were clearly going to her take up on.)

After dinner, we were too drunk and energetic to go to bed so we decided to grab *one* more bottle of Chianti and drink it on the Ponte Sisto Bridge over the Tiber. The bridge hosted amazing street performers and painters who had set up camp for the night. Feeling rather drunk and creative myself, I took pictures of how beautiful the glowing lights made Ash look as she perched on the ledge and pretended to gaze off into the distance. After our second bottle of wine, we contemplated one more.

"When in Rome," I said jokingly, realizing this was the first time in my life that this sentence made sense. We laughed harder than we should have, and drowned the night in the dark-red Chianti.

8/4/15
Rome, Italy

I had a feeling that every time we woke up in Italy, I would experience a slight headache and a full stomach. (That is what you do in Italy: you eat until you are sick, and then you chase that feeling with Tuscan wine.) I was surprisingly not as hungover as I would have imagined. I think this was due to the quality of the wine.

With no room for breakfast in our gastro chambers, we settled on espresso and geared up for a day of sightseeing. We were strapped for Roman time and had only booked two full days here to make room for the rest of the Italian cities we wanted to visit. Our unplanned trip to Croatia had really put a time constraint on our Italian journey.

Our Airbnb was conveniently a mile from Vatican City, so we started off to chat about worldly issues with ol' Pope Francis. Eventually, we had no need for our Google Maps; I had a hunch that the dozens of tour groups all wearing matching shirts were going to the same place we were.

We arrived at the Vatican, and I instantly got goose bumps. Walking through the gate to St. Peter's Square and staring up at the basilica was an awe-inspiring moment for the two of us. I am an unapologetic Dan Brown fanboy, and *Angels & Demons* is my favorite book after the Harry Potter books. I often compare myself to his main character, Robert Langdon, despite the fact that we share no discernible similarities.

Suddenly a Swiss guard approached me standing in the square and told me in a thick Italian accent that we had to leave the square immediately.

"Excuse me?" I replied, confused and looking around to see if I had done anything illegal (always a possibility).

"The Pope is coming to speak to a private group at 6:00 p.m.," he responded sternly. "We need to clear the square by 1:00 p.m. You need to leave immediately."

Long story short, we were kicked out of St. Peter's Square by a Swiss guard for the Pope's safety, almost identical to a scene out of a Dan Brown book. I suppose Robert Langdon and I have more in common than I thought.

Next up, the Pantheon. It was hard to get to the Pantheon from Vatican City. It wasn't the distance that made it tough; it was the tourists. There was no city we had been to yet, or that I had been to in my entire life for that matter, that had more tourists than Rome did in August. You would have thought there was a one-million-dollar prize for the best selfie taken in Rome today, and everyone there was competing.

Once we escaped the area outside of the Vatican that was littered with tourists and vendors selling mini St. Peter's Basilica magnets and fake purses, we reached the area of Rome we fell in love with.

The alley streets east of the Vatican were lined with multicolored buildings with lush overhanging plants on the balconies. Outside of the many cafés, art galleries, and coffee shops sat old men smoking cigars and drinking wine at 1:00 p.m. in the afternoon, talking about what I imagined to be mafia things and their women troubles. But then we reached the Pantheon and the magic had worn off; it was back to tourist hell.

The dome of the Pantheon was covered in biblical paintings and it was stunning. The gray granite pillars holding up the building resembled the trunks of redwoods, and the marble steps still glistened 1,900 years after being built (1,892 to be exact). I wished I had noise-canceling headphones to enjoy the beauty in peace. The constant applause of camera snaps was overwhelming.

As I looked around and noticed every single person taking pictures in the Pantheon (including Ash and me), I wondered what it was like visiting a place like this in the eighties or nineties, before smartphones and high-quality cameras. Why don't they treat these ancient landmarks like classy museums and forbid pictures and loud noises? Social media has ingrained this addictive need to capture every piece of our lives. Almost to the point that if we don't capture it, we feel like it didn't happen. I guess I was just born too late to experience life before technology had taken over the world. At least I won't get polio and I get to eat Chipotle. You win some, you lose some. I looked up into the dome one last time. *Ah, fuck it,* I thought, snapping a GoPro picture.

We decided to head home to get ready for dinner. But before we got a mile closer to home, Ash spoke the five worst words since "The power just went out."

"Hey, look! There's a Zara."

The Spanish clothing store had become my archnemesis. After safely dropping Ash off in the romper and jean shirt mecca, I headed back outside to look at some of the local shops. I passed by a suit shop that looked like the Italian version of JoS. A. Bank. The sign read something along the lines of BUY TWO SUITS AND GET A FREE HOUSE, HEALTH INSURANCE, MAIL-ORDER BRIDE, AND SEGWAY! I could use some health insurance soon. Ash returned with a maxi dress that was surely going to trip her every time she wore it. *We shall see,* I supposed.

We capped off the night with a candlelit dinner at a café in Trastevere and found ourselves quickly venturing down the familiar path of Chianti. Ash was glowing with happiness. I couldn't believe the trance this food was putting her in. Every bite was followed with a noise of extreme satisfaction and then a gulp of acidic wine that left her smiling and ready for the next bite. Gentlemen, if you want to put your woman in the best mood ever, feed her pizza, pasta, chianti, and gelato—the Italian cheat code to a woman's heart.

8/5/15
Rome, Italy

I woke up and immediately braced for impact, but the blow of the hangover never came. I felt like I was dodging bullets every morning, which was good, because today we were heading to the final remaining "must-see attraction" in Rome, the Colosseum. I was pumped to see the largest amphitheater ever built and check it off my monument list. Growing up and learning about the epic battles between warriors and beasts and the gruesome executions that took place had made me infatuated with the Colosseum. I was starting to realize I'd loved all that crazy shit as a kid.

The walk from Trastevere to the Colosseum was far less visually stunning than strolling through Vatican City the day before: it required crossing large, busy roads and took us through a desert-like park (Circus Maximus) that looked like it hadn't seen rain in years.

With every one hundred yards closer to the stadium, the amount of tourists grew exponentially. I saw the Arch of Constantine and knew we were close. We passed under the arch and through a crowd of selfie sticks as everyone captured themselves with the famous landmark. I was cussing out some Asian tourist under my breath who'd just hit me in the head with a phone, when I laid eyes on the old battleground.

When we reached the entrance, one thing quickly became very apparent to us—after visiting such attractions as the Eiffel Tower, the Berlin Wall, and the Grand-Place . . . nowhere was even as *close* to as swarming with tourists as the Colosseum. There were hundreds of people taking the exact same picture (the one you see when you Google "Colosseum"). There were lines in front of the rocks outside. These rocks were probably a foot tall and gave the tourists a somewhat better shot as they stood above the rest of the nimrods taking pictures. Actual lines just to stand on rocks. *I cannot believe how ridiculous this whole social media/photo craze has gotten,* I thought as we patiently stood in line for a rock.

When we reached the inside of the stadium and rushed to the top, I realized it was *much* bigger than I'd imagined it to be. It felt like we were in the sky. I also expected the inside of the stadium to be a field of dirt stained with old blood, but they were renovating the area where the battles took place, so instead of a dirt-covered field we saw the belly of the Colosseum, the hypogeum. This was technically under the battleground and was a series of cages where the animals and gladiators had been kept before contests.

We stood in the upper seats like peasants and continued to casually inch closer to a tour guide nearby. Every time he turned to face the group, we would pretend to take pictures and be uninterested. Classic case of Tour Guide Red-Light, Green-Light.

The guide told the group (and us) that when the gladiators entered the ring and fought, there were two possible exits: the gate of life, where the winners exited and partied all night in the town square, or the gate of death, where the dead bodies were dragged by a man dressed as Charon, the ferryman of the underworld. I tried to wrap my mind around watching the Tar Heels wax NC State and the losers being dragged out of the stadium and to their deaths. I disliked NC State as much as the next sane person, but that seemed a bit extreme.

We had one last meal in Rome before heading to Florence tomorrow. Ash asked a man in his fifties changing the sign for his wine shop where to eat. He told us to walk four blocks to the east. Then he smiled and said, "Eat anywhere on the right side." Seemed like a strange piece of advice, but we trusted the locals.

Four blocks later, we saw the restaurants on the right side; they were all packed with people, but not tourists. When the waiter came around, he said, "Ciao," followed by more Italian. We looked at each other and responded, "Ciao, do you speak English?"

"Ah, Americans," he said, raising his arms. "You came to the right place!" He sounded proud of us for finding him.

We asked him to do us a favor and just get us the best starter and two entrees on the menu (reasonably priced, of course). He returned with some variation of eggplant as an appetizer. We chased our eggplant with a homemade pici dish, and then split the grilled lamb to finish. I am still unsure what the appetizer was, but what I can tell you is, it was *easily* the best meal we had in Italy.

Why we pretend to know what the best thing on the menu is when we go to restaurants, I do not know. I understand having preferences on types of food, but if there is something amazing the staff recommends, we should let them paint our palates with the best colors. The waiters who work and live at these places have a much better understanding of their ingredients and specialties. You also don't always know what you like until you try new things. Would we have ordered eggplant and lamb had we made our own decisions? No, absolutely not. Would we have even found this restaurant had we not asked a local? No, absolutely not. What travel blogs don't tell you is that if you want to find the best restaurants, ask a local, and if you want the best food the restaurant has to offer, ask the waiter.

8/6/15
Rome, Italy —> Florence, Italy

I woke up well rested in our large bed, nestled in a cloud of conditioned air. This Airbnb had been amazing, from its location in Trastevere to its amenities inside. We couldn't have asked for a better place. We'd had back-to-back great Airbnbs. We were hoping for a three-peat in Florence.

Our BlaBlaCar driver was picking us up outside of town, and the only way to get there was taking a train from a station near the Colosseum. Rome resembled a boiler room, and my forehead was perspiring at an alarming rate as we trekked across the Circus Maximus track. The sweat drops occasionally traveled to the corners of my mouth and gave my taste buds a jolt of salt. Half of me was proud of my body's ability to carry this heavy backpack while adequately cooling itself to remain near homeostasis; the other half wanted to stop fucking sweating.

I thought I was relieved when we reached the metro station and hopped on the train heading south; that is, until I realized the AC in the train was weaker than a Red Rover chain of toddlers.

We reached our stop and searched through waves of heat for a white compact car. Forty-five minutes went by, and we were sure we had missed the pickup. Either that or the driver, Dominico, had not come at all. (By this point, our BlaBlaCar experiences were getting more and more unreliable.)

As we looked for a white car, a man and a woman stepped out of a van in my peripheral vision. It looked like the van had just broken down or run out of gas. The man approached us, a black tank top tucked into his ripped jeans. His mustache was one that could only belong to a pedophile or porn star. He resembled an Italian version of Napoleon Dynamite's uncle Rico. The poor guy probably wanted to call someone to pick him up. He approached us, and I was prepared to tell him we had no service when he asked, "Ashley?"

Dear God, no way. No, no, no. Come on, Ash; analyze this situation thoroughly. Think this answer through. We can take a bus, ride a train, walk, crawl, or even crab-walk to Florence.

"Yes, are you Dominico?" she excitedly replied.

Fuck.

Dominico and his female counterpart were from Italy and made their living as laser show performers. I am still unsure what that career entails, but the flyer they passed back to us showed them surrounded by smoke, wearing *Alien vs. Predator* costumes, and holding massive fake laser guns. And by the look, smell, and feel of their touring van, business was far from booming.

Dominico explained that his other vehicle, the white compact car, had broken down. I found it hard to believe this was the reliable vehicle. The entire third row and trunk of the van was covered with equipment for their show. I nicknamed this van the "No Van": It had no AC, no seat belts, and there was absolutely *no* way we were going to survive the four-hour trip to Florence.

Then Dominico turned around and said, "One more."

One more what? We stopped abruptly at a house, and a beautiful young girl in a rather racy outfit walked up to the car. Luckily, we picked her up on Ashley's side. If I were smashed up next to this girl, sweating in the backseat for four hours, Ashley wouldn't be excited. Our backpacks now sat on our laps . . . Add "No room" to the résumé of the van.

Two minutes down the road, Dominico said something to the young girl in the back and passed her a laser show shirt. She replied, *"Grazie,"* and then proceeded to take her shirt off right in front of us, exposing her bra and stomach. My vision traveled from big tan breasts to big blue eyes with a change of focus. Ash looked at me as if to say, *You have one second to turn around before I punch you in the mozzarella balls.* I quickly averted my eyes and looked out the window, shrugging it off and murmuring excuses under my breath.

We *finally* got moving up the road to get out of Rome when Dominico took the next exit. *If we pick up another person, we are out of here,* I thought, still not looking to the right of the seat in front of me. Dominico had pulled into a gas station to fill up. (Add "No gas" to the ever-growing list of the No Van.) Dominico exited the car and walked up to my window and asked if we had the BlaBlaCar money. "Yeah," I replied, confused. He stuck his hand out and said something along the lines of "I need it for gas." Holy shit, add "No money" to the list.

A few hours later, Dominico dropped us off along the Arno River, and after my first four steps out of the car, I almost collapsed. I hadn't realized how crunched my knees had become in the car. I must have looked like a newborn giraffe walking for the first time. My knees were cracking like fresh morning knuckles. As we prepared to leave behind this nightmare, Dominico said, "Heyyyy, I'm sorry," and held his hands out to his sides apologetically. The funniest part was he didn't even apologize for anything specifically; the No Van was just a bad experience all the way around. We told him not to worry about it. Despite the no AC, no seat belts, no room, no gas, and no money, we'd survived. We started the trek to our Airbnb for the next three days.

Florence had the small-town charm of Kraków, the authenticity of Prague, and the Italian culture of Rome. *This* was exactly how I had imagined Italy to be—historical churches and museums around every block. It was no wonder so many artists and painters spent their time here. Ash fell into this category. She had spent six weeks here studying abroad in college. By *studying abroad,* I mean she took a food-and-wine-pairing course and couldn't remember a single recipe.

Our Airbnb was in the heart of Florence, surrounded by cathedrals, cafés, and, unfortunately for me, shopping. We were only a few blocks from the Uffizi, Duomo, and Ponte Vecchio. Our place was rather pricey, but not many Airbnbs in Florence had AC, and that was an absolute necessity at this point in the summer.

Our host's assistant, Giovana, did not speak any English. It was a game of smiles and hand gestures. At this point, we were masters of the Airbnb intro exchanges. Give us the keys, Wi-Fi code, and AC remote, and we're good to go. Giovana gestured to us as if to say, *Got it all?* and smiled. We nodded back and told her, *"Grazie!"* The only issue was the immense heat, and I wished we could have paid an extra ten dollars to have had the AC cranked *before* we got there. We turned it all the way down to sixty-two degrees, showered off the No Van germs in freezing water, and headed to explore Florence for dinner. Today had taken its toll on us, and we were in desperate need of comfort. With our apartment scalding, it wasn't going to come in the form of rest. *We needed food.* But before we could eat, Ash wanted to take me to the Duomo.

I had never seen the Duomo, and frankly I'd barely heard of the thing. She promised me it would be worth seeing before food. I didn't even need the Duomo; I was in awe at the sculptures scattered among random piazzas. I kept stopping and pointing at statues and buildings, and she would reply impatiently, "I know, Kyle, but wait until you see the Duomo." Then we arrived.

"Shut the fuck up," I casually blurted out, and attracted many a disgusted look from mothers with children. "Sorry," I said to everyone who could hear me. *So this is how Ash feels.* This was *easily* the most impressive cathedral I had ever seen. It looked like a massive Gothic soccer stadium. How had I never seen or heard of this before? It felt like I had just found a thousand dollars in my back pocket. The pink, green, beige, and brown colors were perfectly faded to complete the architectural perfection. Ash laughed as I walked up to touch it. I don't even know why I did this—maybe just to make sure it was real. We promised each other to return tomorrow and set off in search of food.

La Cantinetta was the name, and perfection was its game. I rarely go into great detail about meals, because who wants to read about food? Food is like baseball: great if you are there and can experience it, but you don't want to hear someone tell you about it.

But this wasn't food; it was art. We ordered a bottle of Chianti that our quintessential mustache-sporting Italian waiter recommended. We then asked him what we should order to eat. He turned our bottle around and said, "With this Chianti, the linguine with buffalo sauce and our homemade pici with bacon, garlic, hot pepper, and ricotta cheese." *Sold.*

The food and wine were both amazing on their own, but when we took a bite of our respective dishes and chased it with the wine, there was some sort of Italian chemical reaction that occurred in my mouth, and it sent an explosion of flavor to my taste buds. The food was a grenade, and the Chianti pulled the pin. We paired every single bite with wine and laughed in excitement.

We left the restaurant after complimenting every person in the place we could, and walked home to wrap up our first night in Florence.

8/7/15
Florence, Italy

The streets of Florence were steaming hot, but they paled in comparison to the heat basking inside our Airbnb. We arrived home last night and thought the place would be cooled down from turning on the AC, but it was hotter than when we had left. The unit was clearly not conditioning our air to do anything but cook us alive. To try to get any amount of sleep, we had to resort to our emergency sleeping-in-the-heat protocol.

Phase 1 started with pounding three large glasses of water. We were going to sweat profusely; there was no way around it. To not wake up with a pounding headache and cottonmouth, we had to get ahead of the dehydration storm. Next, we took showers as cold as our bodies could stand and then got into bed immediately to try to retain a cool shield to the heat. Unfortunately, I was sweating within a matter of minutes, and the frigid feeling of moments earlier was long gone. It was time for Phase 2.

Phase 2 required teamwork. This was not ideal at 1:00 a.m. We were both exhausted and annoyed by the heat, but we had to find a way to fight the temperature together. We grabbed ice cubes from the freezer and took turns giving each other ice cube wipe-downs, gliding the frozen water across our backs to cool off. This seemed to cool us enough for sleep to be in sight. Time for the knockout punch of Phase 3.

Phase 3 was drugs. *When in doubt, rely on man-made drugs.* Our drug of choice (and only option) was melatonin. We each took two pills and hoped for the best. It worked for Ash; she fell asleep in fifteen minutes. I did not have such luck. It was hours before I tricked my body into not being awake.

Around 9:00 a.m. we exited the boiling room. The fresh air and cloudy sky was as refreshing as a cool shower on sunburned skin. We agreed to play the Google Maps Monument Game. Oh, you've never played? Here's how it works: we opened our map and walked to random monuments that stood out nearby. First was the Piazza Massimo D'Azeglio, followed by Piazza Cesare Beccaria, and lastly the coolest of the three, the Basilica di Santa Croce.

This Basilica di Santa Croce was not as stunningly beautiful as the Duomo, but it held the tombs of Michelangelo, Machiavelli, and Galileo—three of my top five Italians. The other two obviously being Mario and Luigi from Super Mario Bros.

Our next stop was the Uffizi Museum to get tickets to see the statue of *David* the following morning. This was the "must-see" in Florence, and arguably the most famous sculpture in the world. Ash bought the tickets while I grabbed espresso so we could refuel for the evening. She returned and told me we had a date with *David* at 8:30 a.m. There's nothing like massive stone genitals for breakfast.

When Ash was here studying, she'd frequently gone to an amazing overlook of the entire city, and she wanted to take me there. There was no wonder this view was going to be amazing; hiking to the top was grueling. There was a long staircase that looked never-ending from the bottom, and there were vendors selling selfie sticks, stickers, paintings, and sculptures at each platform between flights of stairs. These were smart salesmen; they knew people were going to be making plenty of pit stops.

At the top, we walked along a path that led to a stunning view of Florence. The only problem was everyone seemed to know of this view. Ash commented that almost no one was here when she'd visited four years ago. This was the main difference between Italy and Croatia: Croatia had almost the same amount of beauty with exponentially fewer tourists. Unfortunately, the food didn't even come close in Croatia. If you want advice on your next trip, I would do both. Go to Italy to eat, then cross the Adriatic for peace in Croatia.

We took pictures (along with *literally* everyone else) of the beautiful city and sat on the large amphitheater-style steps until the selfie sticks and fellow view-enjoyers became too much to handle. At one point I went to take a picture of Ash, and she was sandwiched between two selfie sticks. The couples responsible for the sticks didn't even notice her. I snapped the symbolic shot.

8/8/15
Florence, Italy

Holy Duomo, what an awful night. I would have preferred to sleep in a den with howling wolves or a thousand cats in heat than spend one more night like this last one.

Our 8:30 a.m. appointment was the best decision we could have made. We skipped the entire line and stepped inside the 436-year-old museum. First we entered the Botticelli rooms. Botticelli was a famous Florentine widely considered one of the best Renaissance painters. He was most famous for his two pieces: *Primavera* and *The Birth of Venus*, both of which were hanging in the Uffizi. It wasn't hard to spot *The Birth of Venus*. The roughly six-by-nine-foot painting dominated the attention of everyone in the room—all four of us. Botticelli was amazing, but we were here to see *David's cajones*, so we left to find him.

We found a curator sitting silently along a wall, waiting patiently for a random observer to ask him a question about one of the eight paintings in the room. We asked him where we could find *David*, and he replied the five worst words since "Hey, look! There's a Zara."

"*David?* In a different museum."

"I'm sorry," I replied. "You mean a different wing of the museum?"

"Nope, *David* is at the Galleria dell'Accademia," he replied, almost excited that he was about to witness one of us get extremely mad at the other.

I turned slowly to Ash, whose face was red with embarrassment. "Oh yeah, that's right. It *is* in a different museum," she said, half smiling, clearly with her proverbial tail between her legs.

I should have done more research, but she'd lived here once. We marched home, dejected, then grabbed slices of pizza and napped. I was too tired to care.

By evening, La Cantinetta was calling our name. It was our last night in Florence, so we returned to the land of taste bud explosions. We had planned on getting the exact same meal as before, but I sent my brother, Carter, a picture of the appetizers to get his advice. He knew much more about food than we did. He chose a platter of local Tuscan meats and said, "Those meats will knock your socks off." My socks were stuck to my feet from the sweat, so these meats would have to be *pretty amazing*.

After we ordered, I watched as the butcher pulled gargantuan cured meats from hangers and shaved off pieces onto our plates. I noticed a sliver of a piece that was rather small, and the chef threw it away, as it was not to his standard. Cutting corners was not an option for an Italian chef. This was not work; this was his passion, his craft. Against all odds, consider me sockless.

8/9/15
Florence, Italy → Siena, Italy

I slept absolutely great. It felt amazing to get a good night's rest. I'm kidding; it was another night in Airbnb hell, a miserable experience I won't get into. Thankfully, Airbnb issued us a 150-dollar voucher for our catastrophe in Florence.

There were no BlaBlaCars to take us from Florence to Siena. I guess we had to do what travelers did in past decades—we started the mile-long walk to the train station. The route from our Airbnb to the station took us past the Duomo. As we walked by the giant one last time, I realized I was in the backdrop of at least five selfies.

Two tickets to Siena cost thirty euros total. This was painful for us to pay after so many BlaBlaCar trips in the single digits, but I had to admit, the ease of walking up to a kiosk and printing tickets to the next train was extremely relaxing. No waiting in the blazing heat for lost drivers or trying to communicate via stolen restaurant Wi-Fi. We knew exactly where the train would be and when. We couldn't say that about many BlaBlaCar drivers.

We arrived in Siena an hour and a half later, and to be quite honest, neither of us knew a damn thing about this city. We'd never even planned on coming here until we got to New York City and Orrie and Rebekah had told us that Siena was a city we *had* to visit. We fully trusted their opinions, so when we got around to planning Italy, we penciled in a few days.

The station was small, and we immediately noticed Siena was very different from Florence. It was more of a Tuscan village than a city. Rolling countryside and lush vineyards surrounded us. As we scanned the hillside, we spotted a small white car in the visitors' lot. Alessandra, our next Airbnb host, hugged us immediately and welcomed us to Siena.

The roads in Siena were insanely tight and hugged beige and tan buildings with what seemed like only a foot of space between car and building. We continued to climb the mountainside and passed under the large gate in the city walls. "Only resident cars allowed in town," Alessandra told us as a guard checked her windshield.

She took us to our place in the very heart of town and parked on the side of the road. "This way!" she told us excitedly, and skipped onto a side road that was so steep, there was no way a car could get up it. I was basically falling forward and throwing one leg up at a time in front of me to gain enough momentum to keep from tipping backward with my backpack on. I turned around to see Ash on all fours, climbing and laughing with joy. She was already obsessed with Siena.

Alessandra gave us the quick run of our awesome apartment before heading out. We followed her out the door to go downtown, and she pointed up the street and yelled, "That way!" before speeding off down the hill. A few blocks down an empty steep hill and we arrived at the main attraction of Siena, the famous Piazza del Campo.

The Piazza del Campo is a huge flat area made up of hard dirt and surrounded by restaurants and shops. My only question was why there was so much unoccupied room in the middle. I thought it might have been some sort of sports field, but there were no goals or lines. We found a café along the outskirts of the field and started talking to the owner, who was sitting outside. I asked him about the Piazza del Campo, and he looked at me, confused, and then said something about Palio horses and laughed at me. *Holy shit . . . this is where the Palio race is?*

I'd learned about this as a kid, and now when I looked it up (borrowing the same man's Wi-Fi code off his menu), it all looked familiar. The Palio race is held twice a year in this city square and around a windy course lined with people. It is a famous race like no other in the world, closely resembling rally car races . . . but for horses. We'd missed the last race by a couple of weeks, and that explained the lack of people in the village.

After seeing the largest attraction in Siena and walking through the tiny alleys for a few hours, we grabbed two nice bottles of five-euro Chianti from a local market and found a view of the Basilica of San Domenico. We sat on a stone wall and drank the Chianti right out of the bottle. Actually, I was the one drinking it straight from the bottle; Ash had purchased a small one-euro measuring cup from the market because she is a classy gal.

We headed home to get ready for the evening, and as I showered, I heard Ash's stomach growl from the other room. *Uh-oh, she is about to be hangry.* I heard her come running, and I braced for impact in case she had already transformed into the Hangry Hulkess.

"Kyle, did you hear that thunder?"

"Oh, uh, yeah, yeah, I heard it," I said, getting up out of the fetal position.

We hadn't seen a drop of rain since Budapest, let alone a storm. It had been in the midnineties for weeks now. We ran to the window, and I immediately felt a cool, pre-rain gust, releasing mountain ranges of goose bumps on my body. We felt like kids at Camp Green Lake from the movie *Holes*, and ran outside to dance euphorically down the street in the first drops of rain.

Not sure how we didn't pick up on this piece of the puzzle, but the light drizzle and distant rumbles of thunder turned into a torrential downpour. We had our phones, wallets, and Ash's camera all in prime condition to be ruined so we ducked into the closest café and ordered a bottle of wine to watch the rain. The ten-euro bottle of quality wine was a steal, but this was our third bottle of wine today, and Ash was clearly feeling it. She sported the googly eyes you stick on arts and crafts.

Halfway through our pasta, she let out a hiccup that would have woken up Sleeping Beauty. I almost dropped my fork. I looked at her as her face turned red with embarrassment. It was a mix between a hiccup, a burp, and a slight scream. We both knew what was coming next, but there was nothing either of us could do, and moments later another hiccup blurted out. I couldn't help but laugh, and the couple next to us chuckled too. Ash tried holding her breath and drinking upside down, neither of which could prevent the onslaught of hiccups barraging our table.

The hiccups continued until we arrived home, and then Ash began throwing up red wine. I felt bad for not being sick with her, but red wine doesn't affect me like it does most people. I come from a grape-loving family, but Ash comes from a family of light drinkers.

I tried to console her and rub her back, but she gets really mad at me—and everyone else around her—when she is sick. I also tried to make her feel better by reminding her that at least she didn't have the hiccups anymore, but she was far from amused. I sat on the bed and listened to make sure she was okay, and once it seemed like she had finally stopped throwing up, I walked to the bathroom to take care of her. At the precise moment I reached the door, I heard another loud hiccup. I turned right around and went back to the bedroom, an abundance of cuss words at my heels.

8/10/15
Siena, Italy

What a night. The fan blowing cool air on us was great. The rain, meanwhile, continued to pour all day, so we found shelter under a cathedral and caught up on work.

The owner of a pizzeria outside of the cathedral told us we looked hungry and asked if he could feed us. We loved the sincerity in his voice. Ash ordered a glass of wine with her personal pie. Talk about getting back on the horse. She was like a pestering fly on a farm.

After lunch we continued relaxing. It was hard for us to relax like this (harder for Ash than for me), but once we came to terms with the fact that we couldn't afford to shop and had visited most of the famous places yesterday, it was an easy decision. I grabbed another bottle of wine from a market as Ash took refuge from the rain under a church ledge. We are sounding more and more like alcoholics, but I swear, it was casual drinking here.

When I returned to find her reading on the brick wall under the ledge, she looked gorgeous. She was perfectly at peace with her life, and she almost blended in with the wall and pillar of the cathedral. I took a picture of her reading on the wall, and to this day it is my favorite of our entire journey. Ashley wore Italy well.

By the time we got to dinner, we were still forty dollars under budget. This had the possibility of being the first night in Italy we were under budget. But somewhere between sitting on the wall in the rain and walking to dinner, we started arguing about something stupid. Whatever it was, it wasn't what we were actually fighting about. It was just the last piece of tinder that was needed to spark a wildfire, and neither of us felt like being a fireman right then.

The Chianti catalyst wasn't helping. Red wine is like that high school idiot who stands behind an argument and chants, "Fight! Fight! Fight! Fight!" The argument intensified. We only took breaks to politely order food and put on our "fake waiter smiles." Ash ordered pasta, which inevitably came out before my pizza. During her meal, we self-prescribed the silent treatment. At this point, we could finish each other's sentences, so arguing just became a chess match.

She finished her food, stood up dramatically, and said, "I am going home," leaving me to wait on my food. She had my king in her sight: check.

I ate half my pizza and boxed it up, although I wasn't overly worried about her getting kidnapped in Siena. I passed a gelato shop that I couldn't resist, and blew our last five dollars for the day on the frozen treat. At least we were right at our budget. By the time I got home, I found Ash sitting on the stoop outside our place. I could feel the heat from her fuming ears. I'd had the keys all along. I guess it wasn't checkmate; I'd had that random rook in striking distance. She stood up furiously and proclaimed, "I can't do this with you any- more. I think we should travel alone for a while and meet back up in Greece, *and* I used our last five dollars on gelato on the way home, so update the budget accordingly." Hmmm, little did she know I'd also used . . . Never mind.

Her statement was clearly a bluff. I mean, without me she would fall asleep on a train and end up in the middle of Paris all over again, but what else could she say to get under my skin? Neither of us was going anywhere, and we both knew it. I needed her just as much as she needed me. That was the dangerous part about fighting on this journey: no words or actions could take away from the fact that we needed each other and we were in this together.

"Fine," I told her. "I will look for my own Airbnbs tomorrow." I called her bluff and went inside to sleep. She slammed doors and drawers as she got ready for bed, making sure I could hear her anger. The wine put me to sleep instantly, and I dozed off until she got into bed. Once again, she made sure I felt her anger with every movement under the covers.

8/11/15
Siena, Italy → Genoa, Italy

I woke up and had forgotten about our fight. This made things exponentially worse for me.

"Morning, baby, what time are we meeting Alessandra again?" I said, rolling out of bed.

She just stared at me blankly, shook her head, and walked into the bathroom. I had slept so well that my REM sleep had washed away all the previous night's arguments. There is nothing to make you look dumber than trying to reenter argument mode after clearly being over it. I had no other route to take than to apologize.

"Ash, I'm sorry for whatever we were fighting about," I said, "but we have a long day today, so let's just let it go."

"Fine," she said, and then she walked out the door with her backpack. This was going to be a long day, and apparently we were meeting Alessandra now.

With no BlaBlaCars or affordable buses going from Siena to Genoa, we had to resort back to the Italian rail system. We had tried to find the route on the website, but it was extremely confusing and non-user-friendly. We walked inside the station and asked the woman behind the ticket counter if we could get tickets to Genoa. She looked at us like we were trying to buy an iPhone 2 from an Apple Store. "Yes, but you will go to three cities and have two layovers."

We had no other options. "Okay, great, two tickets please," I replied.

We boarded the first train of our journey to Genoa, and noticed we were two of three people on it, the third being a woman who looked to be in her late eighties. With the confidence that she wasn't going to steal our backpacks (if she did, she deserved them), I went to sleep.

I dreamed I was a substitute teacher in a class I couldn't control. I tried to yell at the kids to quiet down, but the screaming got louder and louder until I jolted awake. I looked around at the cabin to see almost every seat filled and children running up and down the aisle, screaming. There is no better birth control than being in close quarters with obnoxious children. Luckily, our backpacks were still in the compartment above us.

We had little to no room for error at our first stop in Empoli. We had a six-minute window from the moment our train arrived until our departure to Pisa. We got off the train as quickly as the three strollers in front of us would allow, and frantically beelined to the LED monitor with departure information like we were on *The Amazing Race*.

Our next train was also packed. I guess everyone was heading to see the architectural blunder in Pisa.

When we arrived in Pisa, I thought about staying on the train. Ash woke up from yet another nap, and to add on to her anger from last night, she was hungry. This was a lethal combination for my safety. This was no time for games; I had to act fast and with the only way I knew how (and which constantly failed me): humor.

"Hey, you wanna Pisa me?" I said, throwing up my fists. She cracked a fake smile and then went back to stone face. I retreated to staring at the tracks. Ten minutes later, I tried again, "What do you call a leaning picture in the Louvre?"

It took her a few seconds of me staring at her to reply. "I really don't care, Kyle."

"Nope," I replied. "Good guess, though. You call it the Mona Pisa."

"Kyle, I am starving."

I saw the pitch and swung for the fences. "You want a piece of Pisa pizza?" I had plenty of time to think about that strikeout on my walk to McDonald's to get some fries. When I returned, it was as if a chemical reaction had taken place. Not only was she smiling and talking again, she wasn't mad at me anymore, either. It was like the fries had gotten her high off fatty acids and salt.

Our next train arrived in Genoa, and my first thought when we set foot in the station was that it looked like an outdated version of Miami.

Matteo, our next host, told us he would be waiting for us at the place, so we started the mile walk. The closer we got to our Airbnb, the cooler the city became. We became confused when Google Maps led us between two castle towers. After asking someone if this was the right place, they told us this was just the Old Town gate. I didn't even realize we had booked our Airbnb in Old Town. Hell, I didn't know anything about this Airbnb; Ash had booked it.

Matteo was a nice Italian guy in his midthirties. He acted like we were old friends when he saw us approaching the building. Sometimes this sort of thing is annoying, but he did it in an endearing way. He led us up the stairs to his top-floor apartment, taking Ash's backpack with him.

It was a studio with a great bathroom, futon, fully equipped kitchen, and an abstract porch in the shape of a triangle overlooking Genoa. As soon as we entered the quaint little studio, Matteo opened up a bottle of wine, unwrapped some fresh focaccia, and showed us maps of the city. Once we finished the bottle, he headed out with a "Ciao," and told us to e-mail him if we needed any help.

What a great first impression. We were easily won over with the bread and wine. At the end of a long day of travel, arguing, screaming kids, and silent-Ash, wine and focaccia was exactly what I needed. We made ourselves at home and got some to-go pasta and more wine from the restaurant directly below our place. We were Genoans for the next week.

8/12/15
Genoa, Italy

The futon, which took up the entire room when laid flat, was surprisingly comfortable. In the past, I would have frowned upon having to sleep on a small futon with Ash that I myself could barely fit on. However, my standards on sleeping conditions had dropped dramatically since we'd started our journey. From hot to cold bedrooms, hard beds to soft, my body was learning to treat sleep as a necessity rather than a luxury.

With our coffee jitters in full force, we rappelled down the mountain of stairs, landed safely in the streets of the Old Town, and set off in search of focaccia. Ever since that little taste we'd gotten from Matteo, we couldn't stop thinking about the herb-touched Italian bread.

Twenty yards from Matteo's place was a small focaccia shop equipped with a little woman and a large oven. We chatted with the woman, who turned out to be the owner. Her family had been making focaccia in that exact spot for 150 years.

"Well, what do you suggest we get to eat?" Ash asked sweetly. This was her *I'm trying to make friends* voice.

"Well," the woman said, elongating the *l*. "Have you ever had focaccia before?"

"Nope, and we just got to Genoa yesterday!" Ash replied, sneaking in a little white lie.

The woman went on to suggest all her favorites, and we ordered three large slices: ham and cheese, tomato and mozzarella, and her personal favorite, onion and garlic. She threw them back in the oven to warm them up and took out a huge pan of regular focaccia she had just finished baking.

Her focaccia had a texture that was a mix between pita bread and pizza dough, yet it was fluffy like a croissant but with fewer flakes and more consistency. We packed up the three breakfast treats and promised to see her tomorrow. It looked like we'd found our new local spot.

Matteo recommended we visit Boccadasse, a small neighborhood on the eastern side of Genoa. He told us we could walk the three miles if wanted, but advised taking the city bus that left from Brignole station. We were getting burned out on long walking, and the obscene amounts of bread sitting in our stomachs made this decision easy.

The Sarzano/Sant'Agostino metro was only a hundred yards away from our place. It looked like a wide phone booth that happened to have a stairwell inside. We began our descent, expecting to travel two flights at most. I felt my ears pop after the fifth flight. Why did this thing need to be in the lower mantle?

We finally came to an empty one-track station. Fifteen minutes later we were on the verge of leaving, when we felt a soft rumble beneath our feet. A gentle glow began to evolve in the tunnel, and eventually the train came rolling into the stop. I had a feeling there was only one train down here that continuously looped the eight stops.

Two stops and five short minutes later, we were at the Brignole station. We headed aboveground and approached the number 31 bus. The driver was smoking a cigarette and leaning against the side of the bus.

"Sir, how much is a bus ticket? I asked, expecting to pay a few dollars.

He checked his watch and responded, *"Un minuto,"* and then walked away to put out his cigarette. We boarded the bus—we would just cross that bridge when we needed to pay. We jumped out at the closest stop to Boccadasse on our maps and walked into the village without paying. The bridge had never presented itself.

Boccadasse was made up of brightly colored buildings that huddled around the water like cold campers around a fire. We walked through alleys and past restaurants we couldn't afford, and to the rocks jutting out over the sea, only to join some locals sunbathing and swimming.

The water was nowhere near as clear as in Croatia, but we were hot from all the walking and took turns taking dips. One of us had to watch our backpack. For some reason, as Ash backstroked in the water, a random rush of guilt/panic washed over me.

It was a Wednesday afternoon, and instead of advancing my career or doing something productive, I was watching my girlfriend frolic in the Mediterranean Sea in Italy. I could not shake this constant pull on my conscience. It was like the devil-horned Kyle on my right shoulder had shown up and said, "What are you doing here right now? It's a fucking Wednesday, dude. You might as well start applying for jobs now, because it will be *years* before you will convince someone to hire your lazy ass ever again."

Then out popped the angel Kyle on my left shoulder: "Don't listen to that asshole; why are you so worried about working? You think jobs are going anywhere? You are twenty-six, have great work experience, an education, and now a great story to tell. You are happy in this moment right now, and that is what life is all about—being happy, living in the moment, not working oneself to death. Nothing is promised in life."

You both make good points, I thought. *Thanks for the advice, guys.* Despite convincing myself in Croatia that we had made the right decision, I was still torn two and a half months into the trip. Well, there was nothing I could do about it right then; it was my turn to swim in the Mediterranean and Ash's turn to watch our backpack.

8/13/15
Genoa, Italy

The sunlight that ventured into our studio ran full speed into my vulnerable eyelids and woke me up around 8:30 a.m. I wanted to go back to sleep, but my stomach made an angry noise that sounded like "FAA-CAH-SHAAA." I rolled carefully out of our futon so as not to wake Ash, with the intention of grabbing breakfast, but without a single movement, I heard a muffled pillow voice say, "Are you going to get focaccia?" She knew me all too well. I pulled my shorts up, and they felt tighter than usual.

"Ash, did you shrink my shorts? They feel tight," I asked, sure that was the case.

"Kyle, we haven't used a dryer since Rome," she replied.

"Yeah, but we have had washers?" I replied, and received a blank stare. This was the day I learned that drying clothes was how you shrunk them.

We walked to the little woman's focaccia shop and walked in eagerly to see her moving bread in and out of the oven. When she turned to see us enter, she lit up like a lightbulb and said, "You were right! I did see you tomorrow!"

The reason we came to Genoa was not for focaccia or Boccadasse; we came here because we wanted to go to Cinque Terre. We couldn't afford to stay in the places in the five villages, but Genoa was only a short train away. We ventured down to the popular Porto Antico area to find out firsthand when we could visit the colorful villages.

When we got to the neighborhood by the port, it felt like we were in an Italian area of Berlin. The walls of every building were smothered with the graffiti of *talented* artists. We spent the first hour in Porto Antico walking around and taking pictures of our favorite graffiti. The art tour led us straight to the kiosks for whale watching. The tour guide told us to check the visitor center around the corner for ferry tickets. We found that taking a train to Cinque Terre would be far cheaper than a ferry, and we headed home.

Exhausted from the hike back to the Old Town, we grabbed a table at a restaurant near our place and exhaled deeply. This was our idea of a hard day: a long walk down to the pier to find out how to take the ferry to Cinque Terre, and a long walk back. In our defense, it was ninety-seven degrees out, and the humidity was intense. But it was still embarrassing that we were this tired. I could sense Ash was getting restless, and the fact that we couldn't go to Cinque Terre today had put her down in the dumps.

I think the real problem with Ash was we were over halfway done with our trip and stuck in Genoa for four more days. We didn't fly out of Rome until the twentieth, and could only afford a few days in Venice with the prices of their Airbnbs, so we had booked six days in Genoa to save money. This was our first big booking mistake. We both wished we were back in Siena, drinking wine in the Tuscan fields. With a lack of things to do here, our growing exhaustion from traveling, and the depressing fact that we were leaving Europe soon, Ash was not feeling good. I couldn't blame her.

8/14/15
Genoa, Italy

Matteo made us promise him that we would check out a view of Genoa from a lookout above the city. As we walked through alleys at sea level, I was trying to figure out how we were going to have a view of the city, in the city. When we were 0.3 miles away and still on flat ground, I was certain we had put the wrong place into Google Maps.

That was until we spotted the incline ahead of us zigzagging up a massive hill in the middle of the city.

By the time we climbed up and back down, Ash was not feeling good. It wasn't that she was sick; she was ashamed by our conditioning.

She turned to me, her face uneasy, and said, "Kyle, that hike this morning was a hell of a wake-up call."

"Yeah, I mean, I could have kept sleeping too. We can think about that for tomorrow," I replied, clearly misinterpreting the idiom.

"No, baby, I feel out of shape and have no energy."

This was probably the part where I was supposed to reassure her that we were not out of shape and that she looked great, but for some reason all that came out of my mouth was, "Yeah, baby, we are *definitely* out of shape."

We agreed to eat groceries tonight for the first time since Croatia. We had been so engulfed in the Italian food culture that we had been blowing up our budget and BMIs. As we walked to the market, a distant rumbling alerted us to an oncoming storm. An afternoon thunderstorm, a five-dollar bottle of Prosecco, a five-dollar bottle of Chianti, and healthy cereal sounded like our idea of the perfect evening.

We spent the rest of the day indulging in the activities that most Millennials would during a rainstorm: perusing social media, chatting with friends, and drinking cheap wine. The Prosecco wasn't bad, but the Chianti clearly showed her price. Tomorrow we were going to make Cinque Terre our bitch.

8/15/15
Genoa, Italy -> Cinque Terre, Italy

I was awakened by Ash rummaging through her toiletry bag. There was a distinct sound of makeup mirrors and lipstick cartridges colliding. Although she rarely wore makeup anymore, she kept the touch-up gear handy, just in case. I was blinking rapidly in an attempt to gain my morning vision and find my phone. My phone had become life support at this point in the trip; frankly, it was the only way of connecting to the world we once knew in America. Squinting to avoid the light of the blinding screen, I scrolled through the news of yesterday.

As I finished reading the news on my phone, I noticed Ash was putting on her thermal leggings as if we were going snowboarding back in Denver. "Why the layers?" I asked through a cracked voice, my vocal cords still getting warmed up.

"Cinque Terre only has a high of seventy degrees, with storms possible all day," she proclaimed, a bit surprised I was awake. Cinque Terre was our destination, and quite honestly, it was the place Ash had been looking forward to most on this trip. I had followed a few travel blogs since our trip had begun to find ideas for places to visit, and this string of five multicolored villages on the rugged coast of Italy was a common top destination, especially for women. I don't know if it's from a chick-flick movie or if it just rolls off the tongue well, but Cinque Terre was the Pumpkin Spice Latte of Italian destinations, and suffice to say, Ash was pumped.

We strapped on our boots, packed our rain jackets, journal, and snacks, and hit the streets of Genoa in search of one of the city's eight subway stations. We wanted to arrive by 9:00 a.m., but the Italian railway websites tended to be—how should I put this?—ambiguous. The trains very rarely arrived at the time the website proclaimed. We had no itinerary today other than to hike between the five villages, so we took the metro to the train station and asked the clerk when the next train left for Cinque Terre. "One hour," the clerk replied, handing us our tickets. We headed to platform 9 to wait.

As we sat there, I noticed menacing clouds approaching. The cumulonimbus cotton candy heading our way was worrisome. I stated to Ash, who was behind me, "Looks like a tornado is coming." I turned around to see she was busy making friends with a nice Italian woman and her five-year-old daughter, and that she had not heard me.

I am obsessed with storms and admittedly had become the "boy who cried funnel cloud" a bit too frequently. Every time I saw dark clouds, I convinced myself (and those around me) that a tornado was on the verge of dropping out of the sky.

This obsession began when I was a young boy in Michigan, a place where tornadoes are fairly common. I will never forget the eerie sound of the citywide siren that warned the residents of Ann Arbor to seek shelter or risk being taken to Oz. When the alarm sounded, my mom would rush my brother, my sister, and me to the basement, and then run upstairs and outside to see if she could see the tornado. It was rather traumatizing at the time, because as a child, you assume every tornado is going to pass right on top of your house, but as I grew up, I realized she was just as intrigued by the weather phenomenon as I was.

Our train arrived, and we took our seats on the right side of the cabin so we would have a view of the coast as we headed south. These are things we had learned to think about: there is nothing worse than missing the Italian coastal scenery because you sat on the side of the train that stares into the dirt on a hill. I sat and watched the calm water as the storm's clouds now covered the sea like a dark-blue blanket. I noticed a small spiral dipping down from the thin strip of cloud working across the water. Suddenly, there was some sort of twirling splash coming from the sea directly below the funneling cloud. I am no tornado expert (don't tell Ash), but I believe this is how a dangerous storm begins. No one else on the train seemed to notice, as everyone was entranced by the screens in front of them. I continued to watch, on the edge of my seat, until at last the moment I had been waiting for my whole life happened: the top and bottom swirls combined, and the tornado formed. I suppose it is technically a waterspout, but tomato, tornado.

I frantically awoke Ash and pointed at the beautiful funnel cloud dancing across the Mediterranean. The rest of the train's passengers must have heard my excitement when I woke her up because the cabin erupted in gasps as everyone noticed the cyclone. We watched as the waterspout matured and went through waterspout puberty, quickly picking up water and stumbling over its new feet. Soon it had become rather large, and a few passengers were growing visibly concerned. Our train passed through a tunnel, and I waited eagerly for us to emerge, my face glued to the window. I had the equivalent of a runner's high at this point.

We flew out of the tunnel, and the cute little waterspout had become a massive tornado. I didn't care if it was scientifically referred to as a waterspout; this was a full-blown tornado, and it looked ready to demolish anything in its path. It had grown four times as large, and the entire train erupted in cries of both excitement and fear at the sight of the twirling beast. With my personal storm-chasing expertise, I concluded that we had gone from an F1 to an F2 storm. I assume that scale simply means we were twice as effed as before.

A large ferry sat in the Mediterranean, directly in the path of the oncoming twister. People started murmuring in Italian, and although my Italian was a bit rusty, I thought they were saying something along the lines of: "Go faster, boat. Go faster!" I was staring at the boat, fearing for the crew's safety. Suddenly I realized I had tunnel vision. No, not on the ferry—we literally were in another tunnel, and I was staring into blackness. When we emerged, we had no view of the storm. We had turned around a peninsula and had lost sight of the boat and the tornado. We would never know what happened to that boat or that storm, but my day—hell, rather my trip—had been made.

I had forgotten the tornado was not why we'd boarded the train, and we arrived in the southernmost of the five villages, Riomaggiore. We stepped off the train, my hands still shaking with adrenaline. We, along with everyone else, were looking for some sort of direction. We knew we wanted to hike, but first we had to find the trail. I walked into the info center and asked the woman there how to hike to the next village, Manarola.

"Trail is closed," she said, a blank look on her face.

"Oh, okay, so we can't get there by foot?" I asked.

"Yes, you can," she said.

"Oh, I thought you just said it was closed?" I replied, not sure what was going on here.

"It is closed," she responded.

Okay, hmmm, let's try this again. "So the trail is closed, but we can still get there by foot?" I asked, trying to piece together all the clues.

"Yes," she responded, still staring at me blankly.

I wanted to say, *Do you care to elaborate here, or are we going to do this all damn day?*

Instead, with my last bit of patience, I asked, "Okay, so how do I get there?"

"Take the red trail; it is way steeper than the other trail. Start here," she said, pointing at the map.

I was perplexed at how long this exchange had just taken. I thanked her before walking outside to Ash.

Neither of us wanted to admit to the other that we were struggling one hundred yards into the hike. It was a blessing in disguise, and our stubbornness pushed us forward. We emerged around a corner to find a couple also moving sluggishly, and took this opportunity to pass them. I had the mind-set of a dog when it came to being the lead in the pack (and also when it came to finishing every last thing on my plate, even if it made me sick). Passing the couple made me feel better about our conditioning; at least we weren't the slowest. The trail rounded off to a plateau at last, and I slowed down when the view came into sight. I could see why this was a UNESCO World Heritage Site. We stood on the edge of the rocky cliff surrounded by vineyards and attempted to soak in the views on either side of us.

To our left was the colorful village of Riomaggiore. It was breathtaking to see the dark-blue sea colliding with the cliffs. The surprising crash sent sporadic waves of water into the air in all directions and created a white-water splash show against the side of the rocks.

To our right was the second rainbow-colored village of Cinque Terre, Manarola. The vineyard that snaked up and down the mountain was hypnotizing. The village was nestled in the valley, surrounded by the hill of a circular vineyard. We prepared for our descent into the village of Manarola to refuel the caffeine tank with espresso. Before we started down, I captured a picture of Ash gazing down on the Gatorade-colored sea and Skittles-colored village.

"Ash, check this picture out!" I said proudly.

She took the phone, but the only thing she noticed was the small area between the bottom of her sports bra and pants.

"Kyle, I hate the way I look in this picture. My back looks fat!" she said, pointing to the only possible flaw on an otherwise unbelievable picture.

Again, we had been eating nothing but carbs and gelato for weeks now, and admittedly we had both probably gained five pounds in Italy. Had she changed physically? Yes, but that was nothing in comparison to the changes she had made mentally. She was truly a happier person now that she was exploring the world and indulging in the delicacies of the local cultures. I had never seen her smile more than in the last few months, and that glow from her smile overshadowed any slight weight gain.

"What? Why are you looking at your back? Look at how awesome this picture is!" I said, laughing, trying to lighten her mood.

"It just looks so fat, Kyle. It's fine; don't worry about it," she said as she put her shirt back on to cover her exposed skin. She was also embarrassed because the two rubes we had passed earlier now walked past us on the plateau. *I know, I know, slow and steady.* But Ash still had a healthy-looking body, and although there were some soft spots, I think it was just the sports bra squeezing her skin. But whatever made her feel comfortable was fine with me, so we headed down to Manarola.

I'm not sure if it was the way she looked dejected walking down the hill, or simply the fact that I had spent enough time with her over the last two months to finally understand how her feelings worked, but it eventually hit me. This was my job. She isn't going to know how beautiful she is, inside and out, unless I explain it to her. I constantly struggle with this, and it's not that I don't think she is the prettiest girl on earth; I just assume she knows she is and I think it rather than express it to her. Normally I would let it go and move on because Ash gets over things pretty quickly if I just give her some space, but this time was different. We were on top of a mountain in Cinque Terre, Italy, overlooking the Mediterranean Sea and colorful seaside villages. If I was ever going to make her feel as beautiful as she was in my eyes, she deserved it to be right now.

"Ash, stop! Take your shirt off!" *Jesus, Kyle, this is how you convey your revelation to her? You truly are an idiot.*

"What? No, Kyle. It's okay. I just don't want to take it off. I don't want to look fat in these pictures, and I hate how my back looks," she said and continued walking.

I stopped her and grabbed her hand so she would hear what I should have told her a long time ago.

"No, it's not okay, Ash. You don't have back fat; you have a back. You don't look fat; you look happy. You are the most beautiful thing on earth when you smile. You constantly preach to me about how much self-image ruins confidence in women and plays such an acidic role in how women feel about themselves. Take your shirt off and be beautiful in your own skin."

She looked at me, confused for a few seconds, as if she were trying to figure out who I was and what Cinque Terre had done with her dork of a boyfriend. Then she smiled from ear to ear, took off her shirt again, and shoved it deep down into our backpack. It was a symbolic moment for us because putting that shirt on to cover up her back had represented all the times she'd covered up her self-consciousness rather than address it (or "undress it," in this case). I was finally able to explain to her that she didn't need to cover up anything about herself. How she carried herself and her happiness depicted how she should feel, not what she looked like to others. She proudly marched ahead, and I followed her beautiful back for the rest of the day as we traversed the coastline of Cinque Terre.

8/16/15
Genoa, Italy

As embarrassing as this is to admit, we both woke up sore today. Sure, we may have only hiked five to ten miles total yesterday, but we were far from prime hiking form. I wasn't going to tell Ash I was sore, and I was sure she wasn't going to tell me, but when I stood up from the futon, I let out a small yelp of pain.

She laughed and said, "Me too."

Thankfully, for us, it was pouring outside, to the extent that we couldn't even sit on the porch because of the squalls of sideways rain.

We were (finally) leaving Genoa tomorrow, so we spent the entire day in bed, planning our trip to Greece and watching HBO's *The Newsroom*. It was a lazy Sunday in the most honest sense, and it felt great.

8/17/15
Genoa, Italy → Venice, Italy

Our 6:30 a.m. wake-up call hurt at first, until I remembered I had a date with my German friend: Mr. FlixBus. We were having trouble finding a train from Genoa to Venice, and as a last-ditch effort, I checked the FlixBus website to see a new banner across the top, claiming they were now in Italy! How convenient. This new promotion in Italy included a direct route from Genoa to Venice for one dollar a person. We were traveling, I should note, for six hours on a luxury bus for less than it costs to pee in a public bathroom in many European cities.

I immediately fell asleep after we got comfortable in our seats on the bus. I woke up to the feeling and sound of the bus going over some bumpy road material that wasn't asphalt. I didn't even realize I had fallen asleep, but there was an ink blotch on my journal that gave away the precise moment of slumber. Ash woke up too and looked around, confused. It always takes her a few minutes to get her bearings after a six-hour nap. We had arrived in Venice and exited the bus to a hot blanket of uncomfortable moisture in the air that soaked my lower back in a matter of seconds.

Ash and I had only two days in Venice before we had to get back down to Rome to catch our flight to Greece. This meant we had to pack all our sightseeing into forty-eight hours. Eager to drop off our bags and start exploring, we raced through busy sidewalks and over the many bridges connecting the blocks of water.

Our Airbnb was located in the heart of Venice and was really more of a bed-and-breakfast. We were paying an absurd eighty-five dollars a night for this place; it was the cheapest we could find in the city.

A small woman answered the door and told us to follow her. There were other guests scattered all over the place.

There were some pros and cons to this place. Pros: the bed was large, the AC worked, and we were in the best location in Venice. The cons included a defect shower (water everywhere), very minimal natural light, a single sheet as a blanket, and the fact that the ceilings were probably five and a half feet tall. I felt like Alice in Wonderland after she drinks the damn vial.

Ash had made plans for us to meet up with her friend from high school, Annalise, and her boyfriend, Stephen. When Ash texted Annalise to meet up, they chose St. Mark's Square as a meeting point. When we got to the square, it quickly became apparent this was a poor choice for a rendezvous.

This happened to be the biggest square in Venice. Unfortunately, the thousands of people in the square weren't the bad news; the bad news was the pigeons. There was easily a thirteen-to-one ratio of pigeons to humans. The amount of pigeons was beyond sickening, and the worst part was the hundreds of people feeding the pigeons from their hands or letting them land on their limbs and heads. We made our way cautiously through the square, trying not to kick the flying rats. I went back and forth between disgusted and concerned for these people, who were letting these disease-carrying birds lounge all over them. I was busy dodging a low-flying pigeon and cursing under my breath when Ash pointed to a couple waving in the distance. She ran up to hug Annalise.

Annalise and Stephen had just finished law school at UNC and were traveling for a couple of weeks while they awaited their bar exam results. After making the initial small talk with Stephen, I discovered that he'd lived with some people from my hometown while he'd been at UNC.

Shooting the shit with Stephen was far easier than I had imagined. We instantly bonded over our strong dislike for pigeons, Duke, and the current lack of beer. There was nothing we could do about Duke right now, so we set off to handle the other two issues.

Corner stores were everywhere, so we were able to arm ourselves with tallboys. We took our beers to a pier on the Grand Canal, swapping stories from our prospective journeys. They were only here for a day before heading to Florence, so this was the only night for all of us to go out. We agreed that a ride on the gondola was the sole thing we had to do while we were here, so we found a gondolier and asked how it worked.

Well, it turned out that the gondoliers also knew it was the one thing all tourists had to do in Venice, and they charged 120 euros for a thirty-five-minute ride through the canals. Even at sixty euros a couple, this was almost as much as we were paying a night for our Airbnb. But the girls had their hearts set on a ride, and frankly, if we were in Venice, I wanted to check this off the bucket list as well. So we set off to get wine for the trip. If we were going to pay this much to ride on a boat for half an hour, we were going to be heavily inebriated while doing it.

We drank a few more beers, our wine in hand, and Stephen and I decided to break the seal, so we peed into the canal. The girls were cracking up, but it seemed pretty normal to us. Just a massive urinal everywhere you go. I imagined people did this every day. Yet another reason no one was swimming.

When we arrived back at the Grand Canal, we spotted a gondola station and walked into the small hut on the water. It was similar to catching a taxi outside of baggage claim at an airport. The manager in the hut called over one of the gondoliers from across the canal. The man arrived in a matter of seconds with a few swoops of his massive paddle. He invited us in, and we all gently stepped into the large boat and took seats on plush pillows. *They have the decor down; I'll give them that.* Stephen passed out plastic cups of the wine, and we started our tour through the streets of water.

To be honest, I was slightly disappointed. I'd expected a singing Italian man with a curled mustache wearing a striped shirt and a scarf. We ended up with a clean-shaven man who, when asked if he was going to sing, replied bluntly, "I don't sing well." He was knowledgeable, though, and pointed out Marco Polo's childhood home as he kicked off the wall to keep the boat from slamming into it. We passed under footbridges and banked sharp turns, holding on to our

Chianti for dear life as our boat fit through tight spaces. Luckily, we had the entire canal to ourselves this late at night.

With the thrill of being on a gondola with my new friends, the Chianti was quickly going down the pipe. I zoned out from the sound of the gondolier's voice as he told us about Canaletto's home, and tried to absorb what was going on. Being on a gondola in Venice with my beautiful girlfriend, who was beaming and holding my hand tightly with excitement, was something I'd never imagined would actually happen.

We neared the Grand Canal once again, and I assumed he was going to take us to the other side of the large river, but the gondolier pulled back into the dock. We looked at one another, confused. We had paid for thirty-five minutes (already a huge rip-off) and were back in nineteen minutes. The gondolier explained that with no traffic, the route goes much faster. I wanted to tell him we didn't pay for a fucking route; we paid for thirty-five minutes, and we paid a *ton of money*, but I didn't want to make a scene in front of our new friends.

But I had a feeling they were in the same boat—*ha ha*. Had we not been with them, they probably would have raised hell too, but we had just finished two bottles of wine in nineteen minutes and were having too good a time to bring any negative energy into the mix.

Would I advise you to pay 120 euros to ride a gondola when you visit Venice? No, there are much better things to do for that much money. Would I understand if you did it anyway because you were in Venice and riding gondolas is what you go there for? Yes, absolutely. Despite overpaying for an underwhelming gondola experience, our night with Annalise and Stephen was far more fun than I'd imagined. We made plans to see them when we got home, and we meant it. There aren't too many friends who you get to pee side by side with into the Grand Canal. We'd drunk far too much wine and had spent far too much money, but we didn't feel too far from home.

8/18/15

Venice, Italy -> Burano, Italy -> Venice, Italy

The semiconscious thumping in my head was replaced with the sound of pills ricocheting off plastic walls on the way to Ash's palm. Ash took some ibuprofen down the hatchet and turned to see that I was blinking awake and offered me some.

"Sure. Can I have some water?"

"No," she replied, and lay back down with a groan. She *isn't* the nurturing type.

It took us a while to get going as we both rolled around in pain from the wine and budget beatdown from last night. As we strolled along the sidewalks, the annoying tourists became unbearable. Crowds of people were either trying to look at something, find something to look at, or find their kids. I had to bulldoze through numerous groups of people who didn't respond to "Excuse me" due to the language barrier. Ash stuck closely behind me and apologized for both of us. When my temper had reached the tipping point, Ash offered an idea.

I think Ash had purposely taken us to the most congested area of Venice to get me to this point. She had her heart set on going to a place she'd found out about from travel bloggers called Burano, but it was an hour-long ferry ride away. She'd mentioned it the other day, and I'd said it would be a pain to travel all the way out there, but today I was ready to head back to Rome a day early if it meant getting away from the crowds. We bought tickets on the east side of Venice and boarded the yellow ferry to escape.

Burano is an island off the coast of Venice known for the color of its buildings. Every piece of property looked like its owner had spun a color wheel, and whatever color it had landed on, they'd painted the entire property that color. It gave the place character and uniqueness.

Neither of us wanted to leave Burano, but we were traveling to Rome early the next morning, and it was already 10:00 p.m. We both bobbed in and out of sleep on the ferry ride home.

Venice is a really cool place, but the amount of people who go there in the summer is quite overwhelming. Not to mention, Venice is a giant tease. It was scorching hot here, yet we were surrounded by water that we couldn't cool off in. That being said, I loved Burano and having to cross streets of water via bridges to get around Venice. There is something magical about Venice, and we were both glad we'd made the trip.

8/19/15
Venice, Italy → Rome, Italy

The soft sound of the rain was broken by a piercing Apple alarm. Ash and I were both so mad that our nap was over that we groaned and kicked the sheets off in a tantrum. Italy had been full of travel days, and this one in particular was going to be a pain due to our lack of sleep and the shitty weather. We reached the Santa Lucia train station on the island and bought our dollar-fifty tickets to travel inland to the Mestre station to meet our BlaBlaCar driver Karim.

Karim was a happy-go-lucky guy who was one-third Italian, one-third Moroccan, and one-third Spanish. He called himself a "Mediterranean mix." He was an Italian army ranger commander who oversaw a unit of 120 men. This surprised me because he seemed like such a gentle, goofy guy. He must have sensed my surprise, because he laughed and quickly let us know that he was more of the brains of the operations than a fighter.

Karim drove BlaBlaCar when he traveled to and from Rome and Venice for the sole purpose of having company on the trip. We started heading out when he told us he had to pick up two more people, a small Italian guy named Matteo and a small Chinese girl named Anna. With our melting pot of passengers safely on board, we set off for Rome once again.

With Karim and Matteo chatting in Italian in the front seat, and Anna and Ash swapping traveling stories, I tried to get some writing done. It didn't go very well because I couldn't help but tune into the conversation in English. Anna was on a two-week holiday from her job in China and was traveling alone. She had couch-surfed from Sweden to London and now was doing the same through Italy.

Eventually, when Ash started telling our story, I dozed off against the window.

Karim stopped to get gas soon after I awoke. This also happened to be Matteo's stop. We said good-bye to the little Italian fella, and I jumped in to sit shotgun, excited to stretch my legs.

"Off to my hometown, Perugia, for lunch—is that okay?" exclaimed Karim. None of us knew where or what Perugia was, but we were all hungry and still had three hours to go before Rome, so we all cheered "Yes!" and set off. Karim took us to a restaurant that he claimed had the "best food in Italy."

Karim went up to the counter to order for us because he said it would be much easier. He returned to our table with three beers and a bottle of red wine (Anna wasn't drinking). We drank the small beers as an appetizer and chatted about his girlfriend issues. Ash was especially interested in this topic, and Karim was more than happy to seek advice.

"She just wants to get married right away," he explained, clearly distraught.

"Well, why don't you marry her?" Ash responded, looking at me while she said it.

"See, man, girls are all the same. It doesn't matter the nationality," I said playfully.

Karim and Anna laughed, and Anna clasped her hands together, leaning in and looking back and forth between Ash, Karim, and me, smiling like she was watching a hilarious sitcom. I could tell she was really getting quite the international experience here: sassy Southern girl, animated Italian guy, and cocky Sasquatch.

Karim opened the bottle of wine to let it breathe and then said, "Well, a wedding will cost me thirty thousand euros. Plus, I want children first, but she wants a wedding before children! I bought a Doberman puppy named Javelin, and her coworkers just say, 'He is only buying you a puppy to avoid getting married!'"

The way that he mimicked his girlfriend's coworkers almost made me spit out my beer, I was laughing so hard. He'd sounded *exactly* like a nagging Italian woman.

After letting the wine breathe, Karim poured each of us a glass and gave Anna one more look and motioned to fill hers.

She said, "Okay, okay, I will have one!"

We all cheered and raised our glasses to Anna just as our food arrived.

The food did not disappoint. The double-crust pizza was home-made by the owner's grandmother. Karim told us that the kid always said his grandma's secret recipe was so good that he could sell it and make a fortune, and here he was with a packed restaurant.

As we headed out the door, I handed Karim twenty euros at the same time Anna gave him ten euros. But he refused our money and said, "You guys are my guests, and this is how we do it in Italy!"

I could not believe how generous this man was. Not only was he BlaBlaCar driving simply to have company, he took that company to a secret gem of a restaurant *and* paid for the meal. Karim was not just driving us across Italy; he was forming friendships along the way.

The remainder of the wine-fueled drive was much more fun than the first leg. I introduced Karim to my DJ friend Nevy's "Sun 'n' Shades" mixtape, and all four of us danced the entire ride to Rome. Karim was screaming over the loud music, "This is the best DJ I've ever heard!"

When we reached Rome, we were all sad to say good-bye to one another. We were such an unlikely foursome, but we promised to stay in touch via Facebook.

Then Anna blurted out sadly, "I can't find you on Facebook. We aren't allowed to use it in China."

So Ash wrote down our e-mails and phone numbers in the book she had just finished and gave it to Anna. Anna held the book in her hands and tears filled her eyes. She bear-hugged Ash so hard, it made Ash squeak like an inflatable toy being deflated. Karim looked at me, confused, and then bear-hugged me so hard, I made the same noise.

We were leaving Italy tomorrow, which meant this was the last BlaBlaCar trip of our journey. After all the BlaBlaCar disasters, we couldn't have ended on a higher note.

8/20/15
Rome, Italy → Rhodes, Greece

We woke up in Italy for the very last time. The boot of Europe had kicked our asses from a budget standpoint, but we'd enjoyed great food, amazing scenery, and new friendships. But it was time to escape the land of pizza and pasta and enter a world where salad was in the name of the country's staple item.

We had to be out of the Airbnb by 11:00 a.m., but our flight wasn't until 6:30 p.m. We decided that, rather than walk around Rome, sweating for four hours with our backpacks, we would just head to the airport. We were also in a bit of a flight predicament. We'd bought our flights to Rhodes for seventy-five dollars from an airline called Blu-express, and we'd paid for them via PayPal.

We arrived at the station and immediately got to the bottom of this Blu-express mystery so that we could buy other tickets if we had to. I walked up to the first airline kiosk we came to and asked, "Where can I find the Blu-express kiosk?"

The woman in the kiosk responded bluntly, "I have never heard of a Blu-express."

Yeah, neither have we. Ash and I looked at each other, afraid of the worst.

We asked a man at the next desk just to be sure, and the man laughed and replied, "Ah yes, Blu-express, over there," and pointed at a six-foot desk in between a vending machine and another airline whose name was in a language I didn't recognize.

I approached the woman behind the small counter and explained our situation with the PayPal receipt as if it were an uncommon scenario, and begged her to let us on the plane. She looked at me oddly and searched the names on her computer that looked like it belonged in 1997. She found our names and acted like the PayPal receipt was normal.

We got in line, and the other 150 passengers rushed to line up behind us. I wasn't sure why; we still had two hours before departure. But once we reached the ticket counter, it all made sense. The Blu-express woman handed me my boarding pass and said, "Here is your boarding pass. There are no assigned seats. Sit wherever you'd like."

Oh shit. At least Southwest had some sort of order; this was a good ol'-fashioned free-for-all. I didn't want to resort to the old me, but who are we kidding? I was born to compete.

As we eagerly rode the transfer bus, I spotted our plane. There was good news and bad news. The bad news: the plane looked like it was most likely going to crash into the Mediterranean. The good news: we would have plenty of space to sprawl out and scream when we went down. The plane was on my side of the bus. We slowly screeched to a stop. Game time.

I flew out of the gate, practically prying the sliding doors open. The plane had two sets of stairs, one in the front and one in the back. The back was the obvious choice, so I could avoid small talk with the airline attendants. I was surprised at my lack of competition, and easily reached the stairs first. I took the steps two at a time and sprinted down the aisle to the exit row, where I plopped down and put my bag on Ash's seat. I let out a deep exhale. Mission accomplished.

I wasn't proud of being this competitive, but when my mom repeatedly kicked my ass at Monopoly when I was six years old, I learned to hate losing. I sat proudly in my chair and spread my legs out. The plane started to fill up, with no one taking the other ten exit row seats yet. I looked around, confused. A flight attendant walked up the aisle, checking the luggage bins, and I asked her if these seats were reserved.

"Nope, sit anywhere you would like," she said.

By the grace of God, our rinky-dink plane survived takeoff and we were on the way to the Greek isles. The three-hour flight was glorious with the extra legroom. Eventually I heard the *ding* announcing our descent into Rhodes. When the plane touched down, the weirdest thing I've ever experienced on an aircraft took place. *At least* 95 percent of the people on the plane erupted into full-blown applause. I mean, a few people even broke the no-seat-belt-loosening rule and stood up to give the pilot a standing ovation. I thought someone had proposed in the front.

I came up with two theories: one, this just happened to be an entire plane full of unimaginably nice people who wanted to make the pilot feel truly special; or two, this was a group of very inexperienced travelers who thought they had about a fifty-fifty chance of not landing safely. I am going with the latter.

Immediately after stepping off the small plane, I could smell and taste the sea. It had only been a couple of weeks since we were in Croatia, but the salt in the air felt great on my sun-beaten skin. It also felt great to sit down on the bus to the terminal; I couldn't care less when we got to baggage claim.

Once we had secured our backpacks, we took a public bus to the Old Town of Rhodes. We were exhausted at this point, but the excitement of being in Greece gave us that jittery, intoxicated feeling. The Greek isles sounded like something that existed in a world that I would never go to, like Hogwarts or Harvard.

On the way to Old Town, our bus pulled through the New Town, which looked like a mix between a small American beach town and downtown Florence, Italy. We weren't staying in the New Town, though; we'd booked our Airbnb inside the castle walls of the Old Town.

We had to get ice cream to get Wi-Fi. We had to, okay? Once we'd secured our destination, we started the mile walk along the water and entered the large stone castle walls of ancient Rhodes. The streets were as lively at midnight as most cities are at 8:00 p.m. It seemed like every restaurant and shop was open and filled with consumers.

Our Airbnb host, Stefano, had his property manager meet us on a moped, and he let us into our building, which was four hundred years old. The place had obviously been renovated on the inside— except for the bathroom. The toilet was in the shower. It was sort of a one-space-fits-all.

8/21/15
Rhodes, Greece

I got out of bed and stepped into the all-in-one shower to bathe, brush my teeth, and pee. Ash was running around the room, radiating excitement as she lathered on sunscreen. Neither of us had seen the Old Town or the water in the daytime, so this was essentially our first time seeing Greece.

The first thing we had to do was indulge in the local cuisine. After thorough research (you only get one first meal in Greece in your life), we found that a gyro place called Pita Fan had the best prices and reviews. Venturing down the cobblestone road among the sand-beaten buildings toward the Old Town festivities made us feel like we were venturing back in time. The Old Town strip was full of people, many of whom were trying to corral the masses into their restaurants. It seemed like every ten steps someone was trying to persuade us with a four-second pitch in their best English, "Food, drinks here!" or "Maybe snack?"

We reached Pita Fan and ordered their traditional gyro. The cook grabbed a warm pita from the grill, shaved off some lamb and chicken from the meat rotating around the burner, and topped it with fresh tomatoes, onions, and tzatziki sauce. The portions were much bigger than we'd expected, and it was ready in twenty seconds.

With our stomachs sufficiently filled, we were eager to show off our new baby bumps at the beach. We followed the main path out of the Old Town to the large castle gates and stared across the blue sea to Turkey. Turkey was only thirty miles away, and if you looked at Rhodes on a map, it would make much more sense if this were a Turkish island instead of a Greek one.

We crossed the road to our destination for the day and most likely week from the looks of it: Elli Beach. *The hype of Greek beaches is real,* I thought. We both reached the perfect vantage point of the beach and stopped in our tracks. It would have been completely silent, but Ash blurted out, "Shut the fuck up." *Never fails.*

The beach was covered in small, soft pebbles that massaged our feet as we walked toward the water and a café right on the beach. We sat down and ordered two large Alfas, a Greek beer brewed in Athens. It wasn't great beer, but it was cold. As I sipped my drink and listened to the sound of seabirds singing, I spotted something that made the child in me do backflips. A few hundred yards out in the middle of the light-blue water was a massive three-level diving platform. It was pretty far from shore and would definitely be a ten-minute swim, but there was no way we weren't going to be jumping from it in the near future. After we finished our beers, I paid Thanassius, the owner, and tipped him very well, as I imagined we would find ourselves here often this week.

Ash and I found what looked like a safe place for our backpack and raced like eight-year-olds, diving into the cool water. I could feel my body breathe a sigh of relief as my tight, sun-beaten skin instantly began healing in the salty medicine. After floating and laughing for a few minutes, we swam out to the platform. Normally, I wouldn't swim into deep water, but that was because of the fear of the unknown. There was no *unknown* in Greece. The water was transparent, and even while disrupting the surface with my arms as I swam, I could see the fifteen feet down to the bottom and pick out individual shells. When we reached the platform, we watched people jumping.

The first level of the platform was about three feet above water to the right. Then a second level to the left was ten feet up. The highest level was a long platform twenty feet above the sea. We obviously climbed to the top first and crept to the edge. We were expert jumpers at this point, and before long we jumped as hard as we could and soared through the air before crashing into the water. We enjoyed the clear blue sea for hours before deciding to head back to check on our backpack.

The swim back felt much longer than the swim out to the platform. To our slight surprise, our backpack was still there, and we sat on the beach in relief. It wasn't until dark that we started back toward our castle for the evening. My neck and back were sore from jumping all day, but I couldn't wait to wake up tomorrow and jump again. *What a great feeling,* I thought.

8/22/15
Rhodes, Greece

I woke up and felt like I had spent the night in a washing machine. What an awful feeling. Apparently, fifty jumps into the Aegean Sea from twenty feet in the air had taken a toll on my body. The muscles in my neck were strained, and the area between my elbows and armpits was bruised from flailing my arms when hitting the water. We decided we would do what any sane people would do—grab two gyros from Pita Fan, walk back to Elli Beach, and swim to the platform and jump off it.

I was always taught not to swim on a full stomach, so I washed down my gyro with a beer at Thanassius's place. Ash wasn't in the mood for a noon beer after three gyros in two days, so she set off to find sea glass. It was a quiet Monday morning in Rhodes, and I was the only person in the restaurant, so Thanassius came over to chat.

Thanassius was the owner, bartender, and main waiter at the Meltemi Café, and he spoke English, Italian, French, German, and Greek. I was in awe at this achievement, and he explained, smiling, that once you learn two, the rest came easy. (*Damn*, I am still struggling to learn one.)

I told him about our journey and asked him what we should do while we were in Greece. He recommended we go to the other major city on the island of Rhodes—Lindos—and a few other restaurants. I loved that Thanassius was not a salesman or chasing ulterior motives. This was refreshing in a place where people constantly tried to corral you into their restaurants. He also offered to hold our backpack behind the counter while we jumped off the platform. *My man.*

In just two days we had a local friend, a favorite gyro place, and a home in the heart of the Old Town. Most people would venture out to explore a difference beach today, but Ash and I loved being part of a community. We preferred to get to know a few people and make lasting relationships than get to know a ton of people as acquaintances.

I was working on relaxing on this trip, something I constantly struggle with. It's not that I don't have the time; I just don't have the patience. Technology and social media have created a world that we feel so connected to that both have become an addiction. It is hard to go off the grid, and I don't mean for a lifetime—I mean for a few hours.

I floated in the shallow water, picking up handfuls of pebbles and looking for sea glass. I tried to let the sea floor massage my feet as I used my legs as anchors in the small waves.

We had been reading about the rafts of migrants washing up on Kos, the large island directly north of us. I scanned the horizon in front of us, expecting to see people coming to shore to escape the atrocities of their country. This meditation worked for half an hour, but the need for excitement overpowered my foot massage and I started for the platform. Relaxing was a work in progress.

I dove off the five-foot platform a few times to get my diving confidence back up before reaching the ten-foot platform. I peered over the edge and laughed out loud at the thought of diving off this platform. There was no way I could dive headfirst from this high up.

The rest of the day was a repeat of the morning. We cycled between drinking, swimming, sea-glass searching, and more drinking.

8/23/15
Rhodes, Greece

We didn't reach Thanassius's place until around noon after sleeping in. He noticed us arrive and brought us beers immediately. Not sure if I felt embarrassed or flattered.

Ash decided to lie out on the beach for a while. This sounded far from appealing to me, so I swam up to the platform. I had only been there for a minute when a little chubby Greek kid walked up to me and said, "Will you face-to-face with me?"

Face-to-face with you? I thought. *I just met you.*

So I asked the obvious question to an inquiry such as this and he replied, "We jump at same time and face each other in the air."

Well, this seemed weird, but there were five to ten young kids out here jumping, and no one was playing with this little guy. "I don't see why not," I said, smiling.

"So, yes?" he asked, confused.

I forgot I was talking to a little Greek kid. "Yes, come on," I said, leading the way.

We counted down from three and jumped. I watched his face inflate like a blowfish as he held his nose with his fingers. It was actually much scarier than I thought it was going to be because I couldn't see when I would land. I came up to the surface, laughing, as did he.

"Again?" he asked, concerned that this was a one-time thing.

"Yeah, let's go!" I said. His face lit up, and the other kids noticed that we were having much more fun than they were now. *You guys should have played with him when you had the chance,* I thought.

Chris was from Rhodes. If I had to guess, I would say he was probably about eight years old. I asked him if he knew any of the other kids and he replied, "Yes, but they don't play with me."

I felt bad, but I knew if I played with him, it would be more fun anyway. I was great at playing like an eight-year-old.

After too many face-to-face jumps to count, Chris saw his mom waving from shore and said, "My mom is calling me for dinner. I have to go. Thanks for being my friend," and took off swimming.

"Thanks for being my friend, too!" I yelled back. Chris had brightened up my day, and to see the looks of the cool kids' faces when Chris was playing with the older guy and having more fun than them was priceless.

8/24/15
Rhodes, Greece

We made sure to be up bright and early to have a full day of exploration up to Lindos. There were far fewer people out here at 7:30 a.m., and the Old Town was actually visible. I felt like I was seeing the cool shops and white buildings for the first time.

We reached the moped rental shop, and I asked to rent a 250cc moped. "Sure, I will just need your license," the owner replied. I handed him my license and started looking at the massive scooters to pick out the color we wanted. "I will actually need your moped license," he said.

What the hell is a moped license? "Uhh, they don't have those in the US. This license covers everything," I said, confused.

"Sorry, man; in Greece, a moped license is required, but you can rent a car if you want."

Are you shitting me? I thought. We thanked him and tried a few more places, but they were all the same—each one required a moped license.

As we headed to the beach, dejected, we passed a kiosk for the Blue Star Ferry. Ash wanted to go get tickets to Santorini, and I tried to convince her we could just get them online later, but she was relentless. The ferry to Santorini only ran on Mondays and Wednesdays, so she wanted to get it out of the way.

"Two tickets to Santorini please," I said to the woman at the only desk. She replied with the five worst words since the curator said, "*David*? In a different museum."

"The tickets are sold out."

"Excuse me?" I politely asked, hoping she had said, "The tickets are so cool."

"Yes, sold out, unfortunately," she said, looking at me blankly.

"They are already sold out for Wednesday?" I asked, just to confirm.

"Oh no, just sold out for today," she said. "You are in luck: there are only five tickets left for the Wednesday ferry. Had you waited any longer, you would have had to wait until next Monday."

I tried not to look at Ash, but I could feel her eyes branding *I told you so* into my skin.

With it apparent that we weren't going to be visiting Lindos today, we started the walk to home base. No, not our Airbnb. Ellie Beach. We took naps on the beach.

I woke up at ten thirty and immediately swam out to the platform to jump my brains out. As I approached the platform, I saw

Chris pacing on the lowest level, smiling at me and waving. When I got closer, he jumped and nearly landed on me.

We played some jumping games, and, as Chris and I ran up the steps to the top to jump again, I noticed a Greek man in his forties literally trembling on the middle platform.

"Sir, are you okay?" I asked him.

"Oh yeah," he said, half smiling. "I want to jump, but I am very nervous."

"Oh, okay! Well, good luck, man!" I said encouragingly. "It's not scary at all."

Eventually he jumped off the middle platform a couple of times, and I congratulated him between each one with a fist-pump, to which he smiled back and gave me the thumbs-up. He tried to make his way up to the top platform, but halfway up he would start trembling again like he was having a seizure, and then return to the middle platform. This man had an actual fear of heights. I had never seen anything like it. Chris and I passed him on the way back up to the top, and I assured him of two things: one, it really wasn't that bad; and two, he definitely didn't have to jump. I was trying to make him feel better with either decision he chose to make.

This was when Spidos, the trembling man, told me the story of him jumping off this very platform as a ten-year-old kid and hitting his arms so hard, they bruised. I nodded and casually put my black-and-blue arms behind my back. He told me this had haunted him, and he *had* to jump to get over this fear. I told him if he just pinned his arms by his sides and jumped like a pencil, he would carve right through the water and feel nothing but euphoria. I may not utilize this method, but I was sure it worked.

Poor Chris had no interest in this man's trials and tribulations and was tugging on my arm to come jump face-to-face. I told Spidos I would be right back, and jumped with Chris, laughing the whole way to the sea. When we climbed back up to the top, Spidos pulled me aside and said, with the most serious face a human could put on: "Hey, Kyle, will you face-to-face with me?"

It took all my power not to burst out laughing. Not at Spidos, of course; I was more than happy to help him overcome his fear. I was trying not to laugh at the fact that in a matter of twenty-four hours, both an eight-year-old and a forty-year-old had sincerely asked me to "face-to-face" with them.

"Of course, Spidos, follow me." We positioned ourselves on the edge and made sure our feet were in the prime position to jump. He was sweating profusely, and his face was white. "You ready?" I asked, smiling and trying to reassure him.

"Yes, I am ready," he said, and exhaled loudly.

"Okay, on the count of three, we jump. One . . . two . . . three!"

For the rest of my life I will remember the next five seconds. Spidos and I left the platform, and his face flashed a fear I have never seen in a human before—not like being frightened by a spider, but true fear. I just wanted it to be over, for his sake. We hit the water, and I think I may have audibly said, "Thank God," underwater as if it would have been my fault if we'd somehow defied gravity and didn't make it.

I hurried to the surface. Spidos emerged from the water, flailing with laughter and tears of joy. Not the kind of joy when you hit one hundred Instagram likes, but true elation that only comes with changing your own life. He half hugged me, half high-fived me in the water, and I couldn't stop laughing.

"I did it!" he screamed.

"You did it, and it wasn't that bad, was it?"

"Yes," he screamed. "Yes, it was—it was awful!"

As the sun set, we all decided to swim back and go our separate ways.

"Hey, Kyle!" Spidos screamed from across the bay.

"Yeah?" I yelled back, treading water.

"Thank you so much. I will never forget what you did for me!"

Before I could respond, he began swimming away again.

8/25/15
Rhodes, Greece

I ventured into the bathroom, half-asleep, and looked in the mirror to see red staring back at me. I rubbed my eyes, shook my head, and refocused. My haphazard sunscreen application yesterday had not kept my skin safe from the blazing star in the sky. "Ashhhh . . ." I whined. When I walked out of the shower, I found her staring in the mirror at herself. She looked like a beet wearing a blond wig. We both lathered up for half an hour before leaving the room. Sunburn sucked, but sunburned sunburn was sleep suicide.

Ash and I played some cards at Thanassius's, and the game got a bit heated. I was crushing her. We decided to give each other a little space, so I left for the platform, and she stayed to read at the café.

To both my disappointment and delight, Chris was not there. I loved the little kid, but he was exhausting. I walked to the top of the platform, and for some reason I just didn't feel like jumping. I let my legs dangle and meditated. As I was deep in thought, the warm air and soft music of swimmers put me in a trance. My mind wandered from fantasy football, to my family, to what we would do when we got home. I lay down on the platform and fell asleep. I woke up to the sound of nothing but water hitting the platform. I looked around and realized it was dark out and everyone had left. I had a moment of panic.

It wasn't going to get any lighter (unless I spent the night), so I got a running start and tried to cover half the swim with my jump. I landed in the sea, and the fear of sharks filled my thoughts to the point that I swam back like my life depended on it, which it very well could have. Who was the last person to leave the platform? I knew they'd seen me sleeping. *Dick move, last person. Dick move.*

8/26/15
Rhodes, Greece → Santorini, Greece

My day started with a migraine. With twelve-plus hours of travel ahead of us, my head had picked a poor day to act up. To make matters worse, we had to be out of our place by 11:00 a.m., but we couldn't board the ferry until 2:00 p.m. These purgatory travel periods were the absolute worst, because we had to haul our backpacks with us wherever we went.

After forcing myself to eat a Greek salad, pop ibuprofen like Skittles, consume two cups of coffee, and drink water like I was being paid to, the headache subsided. We reached the port and had nothing but time to kill, so we joined the other early birds and sat in a shaded area against a fence. I watched as cars and trucks drove onto the ferry cargo area. This ferry was massive. It looked like a cruise ship that had eaten another cruise ship.

We were the first passengers to board the ferry, and we rushed up the flight of stairs to the seating area. We weren't sure how hard it would be to find outlets near seats, so we wanted to get a head start in the scavenger hunt. When traveling, outlets were as important as food.

We found a plush love seat and rotating chair with a round table in the middle and set up camp. Ash sprawled across the love seat and set a new trip record as she took an hour-and-a-half nap and woke up before we had left the port.

Our ship sailed north for an hour or so before we slowed down and pulled into port. Someone speaking Greek came over the intercom. I waited patiently for the English version: "We have arrived in Kos."

I hadn't realized our ferry was stopping at the island of Greece where most of the immigrants were fleeing to from their war-torn countries.

I zoomed out of the map that had our current location pinned, and it really hit me how close we were to Libya and Syria. According to Google Maps, we were only 350 miles from Libya and 430 miles from Syria. To put that into perspective, it is 800 miles from San Francisco to Seattle.

When we were safely anchored in the port, a good chunk of people exited the boat and a much larger chunk boarded. Obviously no one had on shirts that read I AM A FLEEING IMMIGRANT, but it was safe to say that the majority of these passengers fit the category. I couldn't have been happier to see them board.

Every person on this boat who was running from something horrible was a success story in my eyes. Can you imagine what the conditions must be like for people to gladly risk their lives and their children's lives to board a raft and cross the Mediterranean, where the odds of surviving were probably not great? I can't either, but I know it was something worse than a bad economy or poor living conditions. These people were escaping rape, murder, or a combination of the two. These people were living in hell, and the fact that they had made it this far in their escape made me proud to share this boat with them.

I stood up to go to the bathroom and realized the boat was rocking furiously. I opened one of the cabin doors to the balcony outside and saw waves that were *much* larger than I was comfortable with. Kids who looked to be immigrants were crying as their mothers consoled them by rocking them back and forth. All I could think of was how absolutely petrifying it must have been for the people on rafts. The waves were easily rolling fifteen feet over the surface of the already rough water.

We reached Santorini several hours later, and stepped off the ferry into chilly, howling winds. It was midnight, and the port was located at the bottom of a large cliff. There was one road that switchbacked all the way to the top of the island. We scanned the small crowd for our Airbnb host, Petros, who had offered to pick us up for twenty dollars. We spotted a shorter Greek man with a great beard holding a sign with Ashley's name on it. He greeted us with big hugs and two-cheek kisses.

We drove to Kamari, where Petros's hotel on the hill was. He brought us into the lobby excitedly, being sure to open the door for Ash. Because it was midnight, he didn't have to be awake, but he poured us each a glass of OJ and outlined the map of Santorini. I was having trouble listening to his advice because of his thick Greek accent and because I was so stunned at how kind he was being. I tuned back in when he said the words *complimentary breakfast*. "Come here from 8:30 to 10:30 a.m. for unlimited breakfast. We can talk about renting mopeds in the morning. Now follow me!"

We reached our room, and it had all the essentials: big bed, Wi-Fi, AC, bathroom, and a porch with a view of the Mediterranean below. Santorini was a place Ash had been looking forward to her entire life, and I was starting to see why. After twenty-five years of dreaming and a ten-hour boat ride, she had finally made it.

8/27/15
Santorini, Greece

Something in my mind was telling me to wake up. I couldn't figure out why, but I was actively trying to break through the chains of unconsciousness. When I finally stirred awake, my eyes naturally followed the only provider of light and stared out the window in a trance at the sunrise. The oranges and reds were more vibrant and passionate than I had ever experienced. The sun was not yet over the curtain of the sea, so the plants outside our windows served as silhouettes against the fiery sky. I took it in for a few seconds and then woke up Ash to share the experience. She grumpily stirred, groaning, and then followed my finger to the sky outside and whispered, "Shut . . . the . . . fuck . . . up . . ." in a soft, sleepy voice. I went back to sleep. My work here was done.

I awoke again to the sound of our 8:30 a.m. alarm. I was not in the mood to be awake, but we (literally) couldn't afford to miss a free breakfast.

I threw on my UNC jersey and gym shorts and sleepwalked into the lobby. We took seats, and a beautiful woman immediately came over, smiled, and dropped off a carafe of OJ and a plate with little biscuit crackers and Nutella. She also brought a basket of bread and asked if we wanted coffee or tea. "Coffee would be great. Thank you so much!" Ash and I said in unison. The woman seemed taken aback by our response and beamed at us once again.

When we had sufficiently filled our tanks, we set off down the steep road to Kamari. *Road* is a bit of an overstatement; it was more of a group of rocks that had been pounded flat after thousands of years of being traveled on.

Kamari was Ash's dream world. A nicely paved street lined with boutiques, affordable jewelry shops with items from the local volcanoes, and other stores full of clothes and trinkets. Where there weren't boutiques there were cafés and bars that all led to the sea. There was a very specific demographic walking around. The people in Santorini were all on vacation and all had money to spend. (Well, everyone except us.) We watched from our café porch as people jumped from the cliff ledge and disappeared into the blue sea. It was time for us to make a name for ourselves.

We reached the platform where people were leaping off. Someone jumped near us, and it was much longer than I would have liked before I heard the body hit the water. I looked down. Big mistake. The scary part wasn't the ten more feet of height than the platform in Rhodes; the scary part was that we were on a cliff on a mountainside, and the waves were crashing against the cliff.

Oh well, no time to think, I ironically thought, and jumped as far as I could out to sea. For some reason, it was not scary at all. I was so used to jumping off things at this point that it just felt natural. I swam in the rough water and back up to the ledge.

After three or four jumps at this height, I was ready to take it a step further. I wanted a little adrenaline, and this jump was just giving me a long swim back to shore. I watched a local guy scale the mountainside and climb up a few easy rocks that gave him another fifteen feet of air time.

"Kyle . . ." Ash warned when she noticed me studying the Greek acrobat's steps.

"Baby, it doesn't look that hard," I replied.

He leaped to the cheers of the crowd, and to be honest, I wanted the limelight. I climbed up to his exact spot and peered over the edge. Okay, well, shit. This was why he got paid the big bucks. This was probably forty-five to fifty feet above some pretty rough water. I took a deep breath, gained my composure, secured my footing, and propelled myself out as far as my body would allow.

I had forgotten the feeling of true free-falling until then. Even with the last jump, which was only fifteen feet or so shorter, I felt like there was an end in sight as soon as I left. From this point on the mountain, I was flying. I could hear the faint sound of cheers and clapping right before I hit the water. I wish I could have paused before the surface and basked in the applause. People only like you while you are flying; no one cares when you go under. Ash and I spent the entire afternoon jumping until it became time to go to Thira for the sunset.

I thought Kamari was a nice village, but Thira was a step beyond Kamari on the bougie spectrum. We walked until we found a restaurant that had a view of the sea, and took seats. Our table sat on a balcony seven hundred feet above the water. We could see the Nea Kameni volcano a short distance away. We drank two glasses of red wine each and watched the sun take her sweet time setting on the Greek isles.

8/28/15
Santorini, Greece

Immediately after waking up, I knew I was sick. My nose was sprinting, my head was pounding, and the amount of pressure in my sinuses made my hearing distorted. I could tell it wasn't allergies. There was one jump yesterday when I'd closed my eyes and hit the water later than I had anticipated. Water shot up my nose and came out my mouth. The salt had burned my nasal passage and throat for ten minutes. I think this was the recipe for a sinus infection.

We took our same seats in the lobby and discovered the breakfast was identical to yesterday's. This was great news. We could use a little stability in our lives. Petros walked over to our table and let us know that the moped rental guy would be here in half an hour to take us to the rental shop.

A twenty-year-old kid entered the building and waved at us to follow him. He didn't speak very good English, and the extent of our conversation was "Moped?" "Yes." "Good." He dropped us off at the rental spot down the hill and immediately left to get other tourists.

I was worried they were going to ask me for a moped license, but it was still worth a try. There were plenty of parts of this island we wanted to explore. The owner did not seem to give a single shit. "Which one do you want?" he asked, barely looking up from his computer.

Ash sat on the back of the red bike and gave me directions as I tried to avoid large rocks. We were not in Mljet anymore. These roads were exponentially more dangerous than the nicely paved roads in Croatia. The asphalt had been taking a beating for a long time now. The worst part was our helmets—they were like horseback-riding helmets, and mine that slid up my head with the oncoming wind.

We decided to drive around Santorini and explore aimlessly. We climbed to a steep part of the island, where we came to an overlook and pulled over. We walked to the cliffside and gazed out over the water far below. I strolled to the edge to pee while Ash took pictures behind me. All of a sudden, a massive gust of wind hit me as I turned to ask Ash a question. The pee suddenly took off toward her. She screamed, "Kyle, you're peeing on me!"

I tried to straighten the stream out, but then it hit me: *You can't just pee on yourself; that's ridiculous.*

"Run, Ash!" I yelled as if I had no control over the stream. When I'd finished, I walked up the hill to find a very unhappy Ash.

When we got home, the woman who'd served us breakfast was in the lobby/living room area. We sat down on the couches and must have exhaled loudly from our day because she walked over, smiled, and asked if I wanted some coffee. It was like she could read my mind. She brewed three cups and sat down to chat.

Tina was a Nigerian woman who now lived in Athens in the winter and worked here seven days a week in the summer. She was divorced but had a thirty-two-year-old daughter who was still living in Nigeria. I could feel how kind of a soul she was just by talking to her. She was one of those universal mothers.

After spending the evening with Tina, we were dying to eat some seafood. Petros had recommended a great, affordable place on Kamari Beach. We each ordered an entire sea bream and ate the fish from head to tail, leaving only a cartoon fish skeleton. We were walking home after a great meal, looking at the sunset, when Ash tripped over her Zara maxi dress for the thirty-sixth time since she'd bought it. It took all my power not to say, "I told you so." I still failed. I knew that full-length dress was going to be trouble.

8/29/15
Santorini, Greece

Being sick at night blows. Being sick at night in a foreign bed in a foreign land really blows. Being sick at night in a foreign bed in a foreign land with no medicine really, really blows. The worst part about being this sick on the road is that rest is a necessary component to getting healthy. The opportunity cost of lying in bed all day to rest was far too high. I would be sacrificing spending time on the beach in the Greek isles.

It was apparent after my first few bites of breakfast that I needed to be in bed and that I needed medication. I was burning up, and my head and body ached. Tina came by with OJ and the first course of bread and asked if we wanted coffee or tea. She knew the answer; she was just going through protocol. When I responded, "No, thank you. I am going to try to go back to sleep," she became concerned. Ash reassured her that I just had a cold; it was no big deal. Tina walked away slowly, as if she were thinking deeply, and then came back with green tea and lemon. She stood by me to make sure I drank it.

We finished eating and returned to our room so that I could try to rest until noon. I got back in my pajamas and was about to crash when there was a knock at the door. I opened it to find Tina holding another cup of tea. *Universal mother.*

Yesterday when we were talking to Tina, we found out that she was a very religious woman. She said she woke up every morning at sunrise to sit outside and pray. When she handed me the tea, she said, "You will be okay," and recited a small prayer under her breath and crossed her chest. Then she looked up and smiled like she had just received good news and said again cheerfully, "You will be okay!"

The combination of the warm food, green tea, and Tina's prayer sent me on a one-way flight back to REM sleep. Two hours later, we were getting ready to leave the hotel and head to Oia, the most famous town on the island of Santorini. I heard a knock at our door. Ash and I looked at each other and smiled, and when we opened the door, there was Tina with a bowl of noodles.

"For your sickness," she said, holding out the bowl and smiling. She had clearly been worried about me, and I didn't know how to thank her for being so kind. We kept trying to pay her for the food, but she would not allow it. The noodles were cooked with some sort of spice that truly opened up my nasal passages. I was leaking from the nose for a few minutes, but at least I could blow my nose.

Oia is the village you see on Google if you type in "Santorini" and search images. The massive cliffside village was covered with houses that looked like marshmallows with dark-blue tops. The drive to Oia was forty-five minutes of dodging bumps, buses, and busy drivers.

When we arrived, I felt like I was driving right into a Pinterest page. This was Cinque Terre 2.0 as far as girly bucket list places go. We parked the moped along the main strip and started walking up the single road that zigzagged through town. The buildings looked like white Play-Doh, and about halfway down the cliff they stopped as the earth became too steep to build on.

We agreed that if we were going to spend the money to eat on this cliffside balcony, we were really going to fucking do it. We ordered wine with appetizer dips and pita bread. The dips were exquisite, made with local olives and hummus. Ash ordered risotto and I had a chicken fillet. My dish was good, but Ashley's was on another level. She had two large shrimp swimming in the sea of risotto and a single clamshell coming vertically out of the rice. It looked like it belonged on a magazine cover. The dessert menu had cigars on it, and it took every last ounce of my better thinking to not get one. My throat was still throbbing from my nasal faucet dripping all day.

It was a long and stressful ride, but we arrived home safe and sound. When we walked inside the hotel around 10:00 p.m., Tina was watching TV in the lobby and we sat down to watch with her. Before I could even think about it, she asked if I wanted more tea. I didn't like her getting up to get me anything, but she refused to hear me out. My Santorini mom.

Tina called back into the lobby from the kitchen, "Princess, do you want some too?" I had thought I'd heard her call Ash *Princess* earlier in the day but wasn't sure. Ash looked like her heart had just melted and she was trying to grasp it.

"No, thank you!" she said in her sweet voice.

While Tina boiled water, I thought about how great our Greek experience had been so far. Everyone we had met both here and in Rhodes had been kind and sincere. I was so glad we'd decided to make the trip despite the economical dilemma of "Grexit." Greece had a surplus of good people, and just because the economy was in the shitter, didn't mean we shouldn't experience what this culture had to offer.

We hung out with Tina all night, and eventually Petros joined us. We watched some spin-off of *The Hunger Games* similar to *Scary Movie*, and it was surprisingly funny. At one point we were all gut-laughing, and I looked around to see my girlfriend, a short Greek man, and a tall Nigerian woman laughing at 1:00 a.m. at a spin-off in Santorini. These were the moments we were traveling for.

8/30/15
Santorini, Greece

It was another long night of snoring, sneezing, and coughing. I lied and told Tina I was feeling much better at breakfast so she didn't feel like she had to take care of me. Petros recommended we visit a beach on the other side of the island called Perissa.

While we lay on cabanas for the price of two beers, we decided that we were going to watch the sunset at the Santos Wines Winery tonight. Petros made it clear this was the best sunset spot in Santorini.

It was our last night, so this was our last sunset. Hopefully we had saved the best for last.

We hopped back on the moped, this time wearing our "nice outfits." The drive to the winery was more sketch than the drive to Oia, but in a different way. The road that ascended to the plateau looked like a letter *S* that never ended. On one of the turns, the side of our moped actually touched the ground. It was a close call, but my superb driving skills prevailed and we made it to the Santos Wines Winery.

It is going to be hard for me to describe the beauty of the backdrop to the winery. We were clearly late to the party, and searched the balcony seating up and down for a place to sit. I was hardly looking for seats as I couldn't stop gazing up at the golden coast of the cliff, spotting both Oia's and Thira's white-capped villages miles away.

We sat down at a table on the cliffside and remained transfixed on the sun calling it a night. We hadn't planned on ordering anything other than a glass of wine, but when we glanced at the menu, there was a twelve-wine sampler for twenty-two euros—cheaper than two glasses of wine in most places. We ordered the sampler and waited for it to arrive.

When the waiter returned, he had twelve large cups of various wines. I became extremely jealous that Ash wouldn't have to drive us home on the moped. She started rubbing her hands together like someone getting ready to take on a mega-burrito for a T-shirt. She read each wine description out loud, and we sipped them, trying to pinpoint the acidity, aroma, and dryness levels in the tastes. After we got through sipping the twelve wines, I resorted to eating all the olives and cheeses while Ash went back to finish the remaining wine.

I can say with complete sincerity that this experience in Santorini, Greece, was the best twenty-five dollars I had ever spent. The view alone was worth every dime. The olive and cheese tray alone was worth every dime. The wine alone was worth four times every dime.

When it was time to leave, we got on the moped and I put Ash's arms around my chest as a seat belt. I was pretty certain she fell asleep on my back within minutes. I noticed that the headlights on our moped shone the brightest when I accelerated, clearly a malfunction of the bike. They barely lit up when I wasn't accelerating. It was like the gas powered my vision.

This wasn't overly difficult to work with until we got to the final descent. I jokingly said to Ash through the wind, "Please put your tray tables and seats in the upright position as we begin our descent into Kamari." I turned back to see if she was laughing, but my suspicions had been confirmed: she was fast asleep.

The turns were actually much harder to manage than I'd thought they would be, and I had to accelerate for a quick second to get the lights on and then slam the brakes and use my feet to walk us around the corner slowly. There were no streetlights, and if I didn't do this, I couldn't see. The moon was hiding behind clouds and provided very little help. Soon we were finally home free and had made it to the bottom. *I thought.*

I accelerated in the direction of our home, but all of a sudden the road disappeared in front of me. The road banked 180 degrees to the right, and it was too late to stop. I tried to slam the brakes and put my food down to try and catch the road. The turn was full of gravel, and I am still unsure what exactly happened next, but I think I was running at some point. The moped slid out from under us on the gravel-covered turn, and the next thing I knew, I was on lying on the asphalt in the middle of the road.

I blacked out, and the only thought that fought its way through the adrenaline to my brain was: *find Ashley.* I scrambled to my feet and screamed, "Ashley! Are you okay?" At the precise moment I yelled this, I heard a cry come from across the road.

"Kyle! Are you okay?"

She told me she was fine and wasn't hurt so I came back to life and started assessing our situation. We had to get off the road immediately. I grabbed the still-running moped and dragged it over to the side. The turn was so steep, I could barely get the moped off the road without picking up speed. On the side of the road, I did a quick check for injuries on both of us, and aside from a scratched knee each, we were fine. This was semi-remarkable to me. Nothing left to do but jump back on the horse.

I was shaking as we drove along the beach to the villas. I could feel my forearm and leg burn a little, and expected to find a bit of a road rash. Upon arrival to the hotel, we checked the moped for any damage and found nothing but a little scratch that might have even been there before we got it. I was just happy to be alive.

8/31/15
Santorini, Greece → Athens, Greece

I woke up at 4:00 a.m. to prep for my 5:00 a.m. fantasy football draft. I was in the war room (patio porch) ready to draft. The twelve cups of wine had gotten to Ash, and I picked my head up to hear her running to the bathroom.

We had to be out of our room by 1:00 p.m. today. I blew my nose, and a rust-colored amoeba-looking glob found its way into the tissues. It was time I took the moped down to the pharmacy. We were heading to Athens for two nights and then to Thailand. I had to go into Asia with a clean bill of health if I wanted a chance at not dying.

When I reached the pharmacy, I walked in and told the pharmacist I was pretty certain I had a sinus infection, and he threw me an antibiotic off the shelf and asked for six dollars. I have done this a few times now since we got to Europe, and it blows my mind every time. I grabbed a Sprite for Ash's stomach, and jetted up the hill in good spirits. An antibiotic to a sick traveler is like a new video game to a teenager.

We were deciding between going down to the beach one more time or spending time with Tina and Petros. It was an easy decision. We watched a National Geographic show on snakes, and at one point Tina fell out of her chair when the snake attacked the camera. We all laughed until our sides hurt. My side already hurt from the crash, but I laughed through the pain.

Eventually Petros checked his clock and said we should get on the road. We both hugged Tina and exchanged e-mails. Tina had given us something we had not had in a long time: she had given us the love and care of a mother.

This place may have beaten us up a little bit, but it was a give-and-take world. It gave us cliffs to jump and pee off of, sunsets indescribable by the written word, and people who became like family. We were going to miss Santorini; the Acropole Sunrise Hotel had truly felt like home. We double-cheek kissed Petros and his beard and set off to Athens for our last stop in Europe.

I was into my third Lord's Prayer during takeoff when my head felt like it had exploded. I grabbed my ears to make sure they were still attached. I had completely forgotten I had enough pressure in my head to make Michael Jordan miss a game-winner. I tried popping my ears, but it was no use; the pain was unbearable. I survived the flight, but we had twelve hours of flying coming up, and I was deeply concerned.

It was 2:00 a.m. when we landed in Athens due to a delay. We felt awful for our Airbnb host for keeping him up this late. We asked him if he could just leave the key somewhere, but he told us Athens was too dangerous for that. *Well, that's comforting.*

Our sixth-floor Airbnb studio was spacious and, most important, cold. It was ninety-five degrees in Athens, even at nighttime. After showing us all the amenities of the place, our host opened up a bottle of liquor from the freezer, poured three double shots the size of Jell-O containers, and said a Greek toast. Ash and I looked at each other, shocked. It was 2:30 a.m. and neither of us was in the physical condition for shots, but we couldn't say no. The man had just recited an epic Greek toast, picked us up from the airport, and kindly showed us around in the middle of the night. Cheers to our last European city—*gulp, gulp, gulp.*

9/1/15
Athens, Greece

I awoke at noon expecting to feel much better, but I was still in bad shape. It was as if the flight had stirred up and intensified all my symptoms. My ears were clogged with pressure, and my head was burning up. I really wanted to go out and see the Acropolis, but my health was my first priority at this point.

We left the studio only to get food and orange juice, and the heat outside was unlike any I had ever experienced: take the humidity of a Deep South summer day and combine it with the heat of an Arizona desert and you might find what we were experiencing in Athens. In the daytime, this place looked much more run-down and beat-up than it had last night. Most of the buildings were vacant and covered in graffiti, and there was trash everywhere. I am sure there are nicer parts of Athens; we just couldn't afford to stay there. We grabbed a few groceries to get us through the next twenty-four hours, and headed home so I could take the second installment of my Z-Pak.

Ash was as bored as a kid at a Homeowners Association meeting. She decided to go to Zara. I didn't like the idea of her going alone to a store half a mile away, but I had little energy to argue with her. She is an expert arguer, like me, but being at half health, I was no match. I soon fell asleep and tried to let my antibodies go to war.

I awoke to Ash wiping drool off my face. She had the look of a dog that had just shit all over your Persian rug. *Oh no.* "How much did you spend?"

"I made you some pasta!" she said, skipping into the kitchen. I knew I was in trouble when she was in a nurturing mood. Eventually she admitted she'd spent 150 dollars on clothes from that Spanish asshole Zara. Midway through her extensive explanation on why she needed all these rompers and already ripped overalls, I told her I just didn't have the energy to care.

I couldn't believe I had spent the only day we were in Athens in bed, but I didn't have much of a choice. We did have a nice view of the Parthenon from our window. I just hoped this rest and relaxation was going to pay off in Thailand.

We watched the finale of *Game of Thrones* and called it a night in preparation for Bangkok.

9/2/15
Athens, Greece → Cairo, Egyp

When we awoke, and the reality that we would be flying from Europe to Africa to Asia today set in, we packed extra carefully. Our backpacks would be traveling through three continents, and I didn't anticipate anyone giving a shit about them along the way. Once we had everything securely fastened, we set off into the streets of Athens and headed to the metro that would take us to the airport.

The airport was way east of the city, and as we traveled beyond the outskirts of Athens, I thought about the fact that we were leaving Europe today after three months. We might have only been here for ninety days, but we had adapted to many of the European ways of life. It was hard to believe it was over, and even harder to believe we'd made it. It seemed like just yesterday we had conquered our first metro and made it to Bastille in Paris. I can still feel the gratification and sense of accomplishment we'd felt after completing our first travel day. At the time, we didn't know this was going to be one of the easiest ones of our trip. All we had to do was get from the airport to our Airbnb. There was no BlaBlaCar driver to rendezvous with in the middle of nowhere, no eight-hour bus ride full of bad smells (and little English), and certainly no ferries without air conditioning in the heat of Croatia.

We had visited world wonders like the Eiffel Tower and the Colosseum, immersed ourselves in historical triumphs and tragedies at the Berlin Wall and Auschwitz. We had indulged in hearty beer in Belgium and Tuscan wine in Italy; we'd fallen in love again in Prague and fought on kayaks in Croatia. We felt the lows of sickness in Athens and experienced the many highs of Amsterdam. Europe had been both a great challenge and even better victory for us as it changed our views on life and happiness. We'd done it; we had made it to Athens by September 2. So long, Europe; you've been fantastic.

9/3/15
Cairo, Egypt → Bangkok, Thailand

We landed, and a woman announced, "Welcome to Africa." That was a first for me. We went through a variety of customs, and at almost every checkpoint, we had to pull out our passports and tickets. This was easily the most heightened security we had experienced yet. Even the waiting room for our flight had a security checkpoint. We entered the room and sat along the wall with the other three hundred passengers heading to Bangkok.

We were two out of four white folks on this plane. I'd never felt nervous or scared by this fact, but I could definitely feel many eyes on us, as if we were the minorities here—we were. Cairo is 90 percent Muslim, and I was sure most of the people in that room were Muslim as well. A sudden wave of embarrassment washed over me.

In our current political and global state, many Americans hate all Muslims for the violent acts of a small percentage. I couldn't imagine how scary it must be to live in a place where you were blamed for the acts of others. I was so grateful these people weren't treating us with animosity simply because we were Americans. Sadly, I couldn't say they would receive the same respect if they were in the United States.

As soon as we took seats on the massive 777, an airline attendant handed us a bag containing eye masks, earphones, and tube socks. Who would wear all these things? The woman came back shortly after and asked if we wanted chicken or beef for dinner. We went with the chicken and steamed veggies, and it was actually really good. "This food isn't bad, is it?" I asked Ash as I devoured the veggies. She didn't answer, and when I looked up, I saw her bobbing her head to Taylor Swift in her earphones, eye mask on, her feet covered in the gratis socks. I guess I answered my own question.

I took a nap on Wednesday and woke up on Thursday.

"Finally," Ash said, popping some EgyptAir snacks into her mouth.

I was just happy my ears weren't clogged and I could sleep. I felt like I was finally coming out of the sickness that had been bringing me down for a week now. We were only two hours from Bangkok, so I must have been asleep for six hours.

Two hours later we landed in Bangkok. As soon as we stepped off the plane, the humid jungle air filled my lungs. I could *taste* that we weren't in Europe anymore.

I was still trying to wake up from my sleep, and rubbed my eyes at the bright lights of the terminal. As soon as my vision reappeared, I saw that inside the door there were five Thai women screaming at us. "Transfers here!" screamed one while another stepped up to out-shout her. "Immigration, this way!" she yelled, using her hands like the orange neon bars that led planes into the terminal. *Why don't you guys just use signs like the rest of the world?* This was a bit ambitious for 6:00 a.m.

Our taxi sped out of the airport, passing Buddhist temples and a Bangkok Bank billboard the size of a football field. We got an Airbnb two miles from the airport because we were leaving to fly to Chiang Mai in the morning and didn't want to go all the way to the city for only twelve hours. Our Airbnb was located in a pretty run-down area, but we were exhausted and decided to wait to experience Bangkok when we came back at the end of the month.

The ride cost us only three dollars, and being a taxi, this was probably a rip-off. Three-dollar rip-offs were the best kind. An eighteen-year-old kid in front of the Airbnb greeted us with a *wai* (when someone puts their hands together like they are praying and bows) and said, *"Sawadee kap."* We had read about this greeting but completely froze when the time came to say it back. The kid took our bags and led us up to our room. On the way out, he once again gave us a wai. This time we both gave a wai.

We had finally made it. We were showered and lying in our king-sized bed, ready to eat and then go to bed for the night. Part of me never really imagined us making it to Thailand. It was so far down the list of places we had to book accommodations for that it was such an afterthought. We both took naps until 7:00 p.m. and woke up only to order food. The jet lag was real. When we looked at the room service menu and saw that every bowl of food was a dollar fifty, we ordered five plates. We tried a little bit of everything, from pad Thai to spicy shrimp, and set the plates outside our room to call it a night.

9/4/15
Bangkok, Thailand -> Chiang Mai, Thailand

I woke up in the middle of the night and had to sprint to the bathroom with only seconds before a massive blowout. Apparently, my stomach was having trouble acclimating to the Thai food. Let's be honest: we all knew this was coming. I just didn't think it would be so soon after our first meal.

By the time Ash woke up for good, my condition had worsened. Ash yelled into the bathroom, "Kyle, don't use the water to brush your teeth! You could get sick. Turn the faucet off."

I yelled back to her, "I am not brushing my teeth, and the faucet is not on!" (Not my proudest moment, but it gives you perspective on what real diarrhea sounds like.) I had to mentally prepare myself for another travel day, but this time with bubble guts.

The security line at the airport was short. I tried to refrain from being a wide-eyed, bearded American covered in sweat, but there wasn't much I could do. I almost had to leave my belongings behind as they came out at a snail's speed. I threw my shoes on untied and ran off, my belt in hand. (I didn't need a belt where I was going.)

I spent the entire hour-long trip with my head in my hands. When we landed, we rushed off the plane to get to our next checkpoint. The Chiang Mai terminal reminded me of Santorini in its size and casualness. It also looked like a high school cafeteria. We had been corresponding with our Airbnb host, Richard, who was waiting for us outside of the room with the single baggage claim belt. He held up a sign that read KYLE JAMES.

Richard was cooler than the other side of the pillow. He was a savvy man in his sixties who was originally from Boston, but he'd left the US to work in the French film industry when he was twenty-one. He'd moved to Chiang Mai ten years ago to acquire and rent out real estate.

He gave the taxi driver directions to his house and sped off in front of us on his motorcycle. Our taxi drove us the four miles through the lush jungle setting of Chiang Mai, the second biggest city in Thailand after Bangkok. The city center is a perfect one-by-one-mile square of roads. There is a moat around the square, and bridges connected the outskirts of Chiang Mai.

We walked cautiously through the gate, unsure what to expect. We followed Richard inside. We both dropped our bags and jaws at the same time. We had walked into a crazy, modern, funky house that looked like a rich person on LSD had furnished it. There were huge angel statues with various scarves draped on them and six-foot film production lights in corners.

We chatted with Richard about life for a while before he left. Once we were settled and unpacked, we did what everyone should do immediately when they get to Thailand: we headed to a massage parlor.

As we walked to one of the main strips, we passed schools with children playing outside. There seemed to be a large Buddhist temple every few blocks. We peered into one of the temples from the road and saw people kneeling and praying.

Even from afar I could tell that these people took their religion very seriously. Many people in the US go to church simply for the community and social aspect, myself included. It was more of a routine than a true burning passion and desire. From the looks of these people praying, I couldn't imagine that was the case in Thailand.

On the walk to the massage parlor, Ash was so excited about getting pampered, she decided we needed to get pedicures before anyone massaged our feet, which we'd beaten up for the last three months. I had never had a massage or a pedicure, so I didn't care what the order of operations was. We picked a place that looked nice, and the women gave us a wai and led us to big comfy chairs. Ash ordered some special procedure for us, and they really brought out the power tools for this one.

Ash had a petite woman who couldn't have been more than five feet tall. My woman came out and was a much bigger lady, a huge grin on her face. They had to find someone strong for these feet. She cracked her knuckles, assessed my feet, and prepared to go to work.

She soaked my feet in warm water and rubbed off all the dirt. I felt bad for this poor woman. These feet had seen more mileage than most twenty-six-year-olds', and they'd never received any treatment other than soap in a shower. She continued to survey them. When we stood up and walked to the register to pay an hour later, the woman told us it was four hundred baht total (ten dollars). It took all my power not to blurt out, "Shut the fuck up."

We walked home on our new feet to get ready for our trip to the famous Chiang Mai night bazaar. Richard had told us it was the Chiang Mai version of Times Square. We hailed a red pickup truck and bartered with the man on price. Richard also told us that the drivers would spot tourists and try to charge forty or sixty baht per person, knowing that tourists wouldn't be aware of the local prices. He said the locals only pay twenty baht, and that if you proposed that price first, the driver would usually agree. If not, simply wait for the next one.

The first truck agreed to twenty baht each, and drove through the square of the city, crossing the bridge to the outskirts, where the Chiang Mai night bazaar lived. It was a half-mile stretch of street markets and hustling vendors. There were trinkets, bootleg watches and purses, and clothes and accessories. There were indeed large billboards lit up with ads for McDonald's and other large American chains. It had the rush and energy of Times Square but lacked the money and Starbucks.

We walked down the strip as night fell, but the temperature did not. We were dripping sweat, but it didn't matter; walking through an Asian street market like this was exactly what we had envisioned. Ash and I bartered with almost every vendor just to see what we could get. We would haggle back and forth between a dollar and fifty cents, and no matter where we landed, it was absurdly cheap. By the time we had finished walking up and down each side of the street, we had probably spent ten to fifteen dollars and accumulated pillow covers, hanging ornaments, fake Ray-Bans, bracelets, and a purse.

It was now 11:30 p.m., and between my sickness episode this morning and traveling, we were pretty exhausted. As we walked home, bats flew all around our heads and roaches covered the roads. It looked like the asphalt was moving. We ducked and jumped to avoid the respective pests all the way home. We had only been here for one day, but I could tell it was going to be quite different from our time in Europe. I was ready for the change of scenery.

9/5/15
Chiang Mai, Thailand

There is always that one sleep that completely kills a sickness. I had both the few remaining symptoms from my sinus infection and the twenty-four hours of explosive diarrhea kicked out of my system in the same night. I was feeling better, finally.

After a little research, we decided on getting breakfast at Simple Thai Cafe—the name left nothing to wonder. The café was built with bamboo and had a hipster/Seattle vibe inside. We ordered two iced lattes to combat the humidity, an appetizer, and two cashew nut chicken dishes. Our meal came out to be ten dollars.

We spent the rest of the afternoon roaming the streets in the bottom-right quadrant of the city, popping in and out of stores. We had to be home around 5:00 p.m., as some of Ash's friends from college who were teaching English in Chiang Mai were coming over to go out to dinner with us. After all, it was Saturday night.

We made it home and cleaned up the house for our guests. *We haven't done this in a while,* I thought. Aarin, Becky, and Chelsea arrived on their mopeds at 6:30 p.m. They were all teachers at a primary school around the corner from us. Aarin and Becky had gone to App State with us, and Chelsea was a friend of theirs from the school who was also from the US. We drank tallboy Chang beers, the local Thai beer, and caught up on each other's lives.

We ate dinner at a place they had nicknamed the Treehouse. The best part about Thailand so far wasn't the cheap massages; it was the fact that you could buy handles of whiskey at a restaurant and order the mixers separately.

After dinner, we jumped on the backs of the girls' mopeds and ventured to the northeast corner of the city and to the North Gate Jazz Co-Op. I didn't really know what to expect from a jazz club in Chiang Mai. The venue looked like a living room, with couches and tables facing a stage area in the corner. There was a one-person bar where everyone seemed to be buying soft drinks and handles of SamgSom whiskey to mix at their tables.

During a break in the open mic sets, I went to the bathroom, and similar to most American dive bars, there was writing all over the stalls. However, unlike in American dive bars, all the writing and quotes were encouraging. There was not a *single* negative thing written on the stall walls. It was refreshing to see such positivity.

We finished up our last drinks. The bar closed at midnight, earlier than we would have thought. Someone had been shot in Chiang Mai last month, so the government was cracking down on bars' hours. We took our fresh bottle of whiskey and headed to the girls' favorite late-night food spot, Tacos Bell. No, there is no typo there.

Tacos Bell was a food stand on wheels that a man had been operating for years. There were three options: taco, burrito, or quesadilla. We each grabbed two items and chatted with some other drunken people who had walked over from the jazz club. We took our food to go and headed back to our house.

I had a moment when I woke up from how much I had had to drink, and realized I was sitting on the back of a moped, flying through Thailand with a fifth of liquor in one hand and a bag of tacos in the other. The vibe might have been different in Asia, but in the nighttime hours, all nightlife seemed similar.

We had a good ol'-fashioned after party at our house with only five people. We blasted music and played college-style drinking games, getting far drunker than we had anticipated, and laughing until we were crying. It was an incredible night, and Chiang Mai had already blown away our expectations. Although it was the farthest away we had traveled yet, Chiang Mai felt like home.

9/6/15
Chiang Mai, Thailand

Ash went to the Sunday market with the girls while I wrote in Simple Thai Cafe. It felt good for me to be working on this project. There were times when I still felt guilty for not working and advancing my career somehow, but it had made me start thinking about what my career really was. Since I left college, I've trained athletes in sports performance, planned corporate meetings all over the country, and fundraised for a nonprofit. I don't have a career; I have experiences. I don't think traveling the world and writing a book about this travel was necessarily a bad next step in life. This book was giving me a different kind of experience; it was giving me a sense of purpose.

Apparently, shopping was giving my girlfriend purpose. I returned to find Ash with a bed full of clothes, umbrellas, and blankets. "Ashhhhh . . ."

"Kyle, I don't know what happened. One minute I was just perusing the vendors, and the next thing I know, I had bags full of stuff." So what do you do when your girlfriend goes somewhere so cool that she blacks out and buys tons of things? You go check it out for yourself.

This Sunday market made the night bazaar look like a yard sale. It was only four blocks from our place, and hosted a long stretch of vendors selling their crafts. It was like Etsy had come to life. Unfortunately, we continued buying things because the value-to-price ratio was just too good. We bought gifts for people, a wedding present for my sister, and a few things for ourselves. The reality set in when we got home that we were leaving this house tomorrow morning at 7:00 a.m. and all the stuff we had just purchased had to come with us. What the hell were we thinking?

Ash told me to get out of the way and just let her go to work because I "packed like an asshole." Fair enough—I'll accept the insult for the lack of work I had to do. I hit the steam room, and when I returned, she had packed every single item into our two bags. *Wow, I really do pack like an asshole,* I thought.

We tried to get some sleep, but the excitement level of what we were doing tomorrow was far too high. Tomorrow we were going to spend the night at the Elephant Nature Park (ENP), deep in the jungles of Thailand. This was unequivocally the aspect of the trip I was most excited for.

9/7/15
Chiang Mai, Thailand → Elephant Nature Park, Thailand

We did a final sweep of Richard's house before heading out to find a taxi. The city was certainly different during the week. The road was packed with people rushing to work or getting their children to school. We hailed a red truck taxi and climbed in the back with a Buddhist monk. He smiled at us. Riding in rush-hour traffic with a Buddhist monk—just another day in Thailand.

The truck dropped us off at the office of ENP, where we walked in to join other people heading into the jungle and boarded a van. It was early in the morning, so there was very little small talk, and everyone fell asleep as we drove an hour and a half north toward Myanmar. The busy roads and buildings were quickly replaced by jungles and small villages.

This was the part of Thailand I wanted to experience: Chiang Mai and Bangkok were cool cities, but there was nothing like this in the US. As the road became bumpier and the jungle became denser, elephants began to appear. Seeing the massive animals walking around freely in the jungle was surreal. Our driver explained that there was a string of elephant parks out here; some were kind to the animals, but most were not.

We arrived at the park and followed the guide to a wooden platform that stood ten feet in the air and was the home base of the camp. We took seats at a picnic table underneath. Our driver/counselor gave us an overview of the home base. Along the main hallway there was water, a coffee shop, a gift shop, and bathrooms. There was also a small canteen where beer, drinks, and snacks were available. This place was basically a grown-up elephant summer camp. I couldn't be happier.

The driver told us we would begin the "experience" soon, and he set off to handle some loose ends. As we chatted with some German people from our van, a big beautiful elephant searching for food walked right up to the railing ten feet away from us. This was why the platform was elevated: to feed the elephants from above. Our guide came back with a bucket of watermelon. He showed us how to gently place the pieces where the lady elephant could grab them out of our hands.

I noticed a man below the platform rubbing the elephant's side casually as the elephant chewed on some grass. He was neither worried nor excited to be around an animal of this size and beauty. Our guide explained that he was the elephant's mahout.

A mahout was the person who stayed with the elephants almost twenty-four hours a day. The only breaks being six hours while they slept. Each of the thirty-one elephants had the same mahout from the time they got to ENP until one or the other passed away. They were life partners.

I immediately wanted to be a mahout, and my mind raced on how I could make this a possibility. I lacked about 90 percent of the qualifications; being a male was my only promising quality.

It was our turn to feed the elephants, and we walked cautiously up to the area of the platform where they were waiting. As soon as I reached into the bucket, the elephant knew what was coming next and reached her trunk right up to me, sniffed out the melon, and grabbed it by pinning it between her thumb-like nub and the rest of her trunk. Once she had a firm grip, she pulled it to her mouth with a brisk swoop. We fed her ten watermelons and didn't skip a beat.

Next up on our itinerary was to explore the area where the elephants could roam freely. I glanced around and could see herds of elephants all over the park. We started our elephant-networking event with the two oldest gals. The two females were eighty and seventy-seven years old. It looked like most mahouts were very cautious when people were around their elephants, but these two just sat together under a tree, chatting. These old women were of no worry to anyone. Elephants acted very similar to humans with respect to age, and these grandmothers were too old to be up to no good.

We approached them and felt their soft, thick leathery skin, which was covered in little hard bristles every few inches. When we left the two grandmas, our guide let us know those two were the only exception to the ENP golden rule that this was their world and we were just living in it. If an elephant approached us, we could let them check us out and then touch them gently. We were not to approach them. The babies were also tricky because they got spooked quickly. We were not to interact with the babies because, while they might have seemed like they were having fun, one yelp and the herd would come running. It wouldn't matter who or what was in their way.

The next group we met on our tour was three large elephants that had bonded over common injuries. One had stepped on a land mine in Myanmar and had a mangled leg, another had a broken leg from a trap, and the third had a broken back from people riding her. I loved that they could sense another elephant in pain and bond over their commonalities. These animals were emotionally superior beings.

After a large buffet-style lunch, we walked out to the river that formed an outer barrier to the park. As we walked and talked, a few elephants passed us on either side. It wasn't every day you were part of an elephant herd walking to the river.

We walked up to an elephant in the water and were instructed to bathe her. I had no problems being on the ground with the large animals, but it was bit unnerving to be waist deep next to one. But it was far too epic to pass up, so I led the way in and earned the trust of the elephant by walking to where she could see me. I rubbed her face and trunk.

I scooped up a bucket full of the brown water and launched it onto her dirt-covered back. She did a little shimmy—similar to anyone who'd had water thrown on him or her. They reminded me more and more of humans every minute.

Our guide pointed to a scene up the river that was out of National Geographic. Three elephants rolled around and dunked one another like summer friends at a public pool. When they were ready for their next meal, the three elephants charged right out of the water, and we all made a path for them to stroll up to the fields between us.

We wrapped up the afternoon by hanging out in a group as one of the elephant herds meandered around us before heading home to the platform to call it a day. This is when we met Apple, our overnight guide/tour guide for tomorrow. She was a local Thai girl who'd grown up with elephants for as long as she could remember. She really wanted to be a mahout, but girls were not allowed to be mahouts in the Thai culture. This was the closest she could get, and she was fine with that. Apple walked us down the path from the platform and showed us to our huts for the night.

Our hut was perched off the ground like a beach house and had a bathroom that was essentially an outdoor shower with a toilet attached. The beds were thankfully covered with mosquito nets. The one-room bungalow had a great porch overlooking the compound where the elephants slept at night so wild animals couldn't bother them. There were still wild tigers that roamed Thailand. Although scarce, they were out there.

Then we discovered we had a serious problem. We could not find our passports. Apple asked us to get them out, as they had to document everyone who spent the night here, and we assumed they were in our bags, but when we got to the hut, they were nowhere to be found. This was pretty much the worst-case traveler scenario, aside from, you know, dying. We didn't have time to handle it now; we had to be at the welcoming ceremony.

There was a top floor above the base of the platform where the ceremony took place. We sat on pillows in the front row, listening intently as the director of the camp explained the Thai ritual that a local Buddhist shaman would perform on us tonight. He would round up all the bad luck and energy in us and put it in a box to send down the river. He explained that we would then be sprayed with holy water and given a white cloth bracelet for good luck. He said that the actual ritual would only be performed on four people because of time, but the rest would participate and be given bracelets. He pointed to two girls in the front row and then looked around and called up Ash and me. We were shocked. There were probably one hundred people here. We sat crisscross applesauce on pillows, and the shaman entered the room and began the ceremony.

The old man recited Buddhist chants and prayers in Thai as we sat with our eyes closed. His voice was powerful beyond measure. I felt like I could understand the language. Not the words, obviously, but the feeling. I became lost in his words, and my mind cleared. He grabbed my hand first and rubbed off all the bad luck. This was going to take him a while. Then he proceeded to sprinkle holy water from a golden cup. The experience lasted half an hour, and when he was finished, he tied a white string bracelet on my right wrist and smiled at me. The girls received them on their left wrists. *This culture is very gender conscious,* I thought.

Ash and I agreed that after sixteen years each in churches, this was *easily* the most powerful religious feeling we had every felt. The shaman's assistants were all little old women in their seventies and eighties and nicer than anyone should be at that age. We thanked them over and over. The shaman didn't speak any English, but continued to wai and smile, our hands in his. We walked downstairs eventually, still in awe, and I have to admit: I could feel all my bad luck floating down the river to be eaten by fish. Ash checked her phone at the platform, and Richard had e-mailed us: *I found your passports! They were in the driveway; they must have fallen out of your bags.*

I am not going to say this had anything to do with the ritual we just went through, but I am also not going to say it didn't. We capped off the night by drinking beers with our new German friends, who were brothers, chatting about the differences between growing up in Germany and growing up in the US. Turns out we have more similarities than we'd imagined. Today was one of the best days of our entire trip—and our lives, for that matter. Elephant trunks and Buddhist shamans had truly moved us.

9/8/15
Elephant Nature Park, Thailand -> Chiang Mai, Thailand

We were packing our gear at 6:30 a.m. when we heard the elephants being extremely vocal with their mahouts. They were clearly ready to get moving on their eighteen hours of eating. We sat on our back porch and soaked in the sound of roaring elephants. I had a hunch we weren't going to wake up to this sound again for a very long time.

The German brothers were already at the breakfast table when we arrived. We grabbed plates of stir-fried rice with eggs, toast, and fruit. When we wrapped up breakfast, Apple came by to take us on our private walk with the elephants. The weeklong volunteers were all doing the chores for the park, and the daily visitors wouldn't arrive until around 11:00 a.m. We had the park to ourselves.

We started down to the river and began looping the park and stopping where herds were hanging out. Apple told us the stories of the first three elephants we passed, and unfortunately, none of them were good. The first female broke her back from being used as a riding elephant. I felt awful because, although I had never ridden an elephant, I'd always wanted to. I had no idea it was just a tourist trap and hurt them.

The second elephant had a digestion problem. She could not keep weight on because food went right through her. The third elephant in this group had both of her back legs broken. They were bow shaped, and she walked with a serious limp. She'd had a case of forced breeding, and her weak body could not handle the weight of the large male that had mounted her. I felt bad for these poor girls, but at the same time, they were the lucky ones. This was happening all over Southeast Asia, and most elephants remained in these awful conditions until they were either sold or they died.

Our group moved on to the next herd along the river that was rolling deep. There were five big girls and a baby. The baby was up to no good, running around and driving everyone crazy. His mahout was steering him in the right direction with the help of his mother when all of a sudden we heard a crack of a whip and then a blood-curdling elephant roar. It made the hair on my body stand up.

The baby started crying immediately, and all the elephants looked across the river and started roaring back.

"What was that?" we asked Apple.

She explained to us that there were riding camps on the other side of the river, and there the elephants were beaten if they didn't obey. "It breaks my heart," she said, "but there is nothing we can do. They own the elephants and can do what they want."

I really wish they would stampede those sick sons of bitches. How on earth could you whip any animal, let alone an animal as peaceful and majestic as these creatures?

We got back to the platform for lunch just as a batch of daily visitors and overnight guests were arriving. They were getting their orientation on the platform, and I spotted our guide from yesterday prepping the buckets of watermelon with his new group. They were all wide-eyed and giddy with excitement. We shook hands, and he asked if I would show his group how to feed the eighty-year-old gal. *Step aside, rookies,* I thought as I walked up, rubbed the elephant's forehead, and gave her watermelon. Ash looked at me and rolled her eyes, and then we hit a noodle station for lunch.

I built a mountain of food I knew I couldn't finish, but it was hard to be around other mammals that ate their body weight in food every day and not do the same. After lunch, Apple thanked us for coming to her home at the ENP and hugged all of us before we departed.

Spending two days at the Elephant Nature Park was an eye-opening and rich experience I would recommend to anyone who visits this part of the world. We didn't just learn about elephants here; we learned about the Thai culture, Buddhism, and how humans can still make a difference. These elephants came from carnivals, abusive owners, riding camps, and other places where they were left to die. Here they roamed freely and got eighteen hours of meals a day in peace—a vast improvement. Tonight we would be going to sleep better humans than we had been before we got here.

When we returned to Chiang Mai, we went back to the jazz bar. Our day had started with the trumpeting of elephants and ended with a saxophone solo.

9/9/15
Chiang Mai, Thailand

It was another early morning for me, as I had to meet Richard at the ol' mansion to get our passports. He would only be in town at 8:00 a.m., so I didn't have much negotiation power. I just wished I hadn't drunk six Changs last night.

On my walk home, it began pouring and didn't let up for hours. This was the best case for working on my book. I wouldn't feel guilty about not sightseeing. I wrote and sipped cool drinks for hours as Ash got a massage and shopped. We called it an early night to get good sleep before our 6:00 a.m. flight tomorrow morning.

It was hard to believe we were leaving. When we'd returned from the ENP yesterday, it felt like we were coming home from summer camp. This was our first true love in Thailand, and when people ask what was our favorite place, this hipster mecca filled with kind people and jazz stars may come spilling out of my mouth before I have a chance to think about it. Your gut is usually right anyway, isn't it? We used the rest of the day's budget to get one more massage and then headed home for good. We hopscotched roaches and did the limbo under bars of bats. It wasn't out of fear; it was just the Chiang Mai Shuffle.

9/10/15
Chiang Mai, Thailand → Railay Beach, Thailand

We quietly snuck out of the Airbnb in search of a taxi in the deserted streets. There wasn't a single vehicle in the road. It was 4:30 a.m. on a Thursday. We had not thought this part through. We were screwed. I mean, even the roaches and bats were sleeping at this point.

We decided that our only option was to start walking in the direction of the busiest street, which was obviously one of the four roads that made up the square. We reached the east border and saw a single light speeding down the other side of the road across the median. I told Ash I was going after it, then ran with my backpack across the road, flagging the car down just in case it was a taxi. It was, and the driver saw me and stopped in the middle of the road. We didn't see another car of any type the entire way to the airport. You would have thought we had good luck or something.

I have never been through a quicker airline process. We went from the taxi to our airline gate in three minutes. There was only one 6:00 a.m. flight leaving Chiang Mai.

We boarded the AirAsia aircraft and took our seats in the suspect plane. This flight was fifty dollars for a reason. I was prepared for this plane to go down. After listening to the safety instructions, I determined that the oxygen masks weren't going to help us when we hit the earth at three hundred miles per hour. Time to catch up on some sleep.

When the plane landed and we stepped off the stairs and onto the runway, I couldn't believe how chilly it was. The sky was gray and filled with rain, and it was only sixty-eight degrees outside. We stepped inside the terminal to wait on our trusty bags.

REI needs no endorsement from some amateur traveler, but if there was one thing we had that had saved us on this trip, it was our backpacks. My blue Crestrail 70 pack was part of me at this point. REI is the king of backpacks, and mine was worth its cost five times over.

This is where the trip to Railay Beach got tricky. Railay Beach was unreachable by road, so we had to find a bus that would take us to the port where the boats waited. We had found taxi and transfer services online for twenty dollars total, and knew this was a tourist trap. Sure enough, there was a bus outside for three dollars.

When we arrived at the beach, the man at the dock told us, "Sixty baht each. Run down and catch boat seven." We paid him the equivalent of about four dollars and hurried down to the flawless blue water. Sure enough, there was a long boat with 7 on it like a NASCAR car. These were the prototypical Thai boats you see on Google Images. I will never forget the look on Ash's face when the longboat taxi driver waved us over as he stood out in the waist-deep water.

Do not expect these boats to come pick you up on a dock. Two thoughts went through my head as we prepared to enter the warm waters of the Indian Ocean. One, I wish I hadn't worn my hiking boots that were laced up like boxing gloves; and two, I wish we hadn't bought all that shit in Chiang Mai. I held both of our fifty-pound backpacks over my head to keep our electronics dry as we waded out to our taxi.

The ride to our beach was rough, but I didn't care about the bouncing. I didn't get seasick, and I was far too preoccupied with staring at the coastline. There were massive rocks covered in trees and moss sitting in the neon-blue water. Greece and Croatia had clear blue water, but Thailand's water had a teal-green tint to it. When it hit the lush green islands, it looked like two vibrant paints colliding on an artist's easel.

We pulled up to our beach and slowly got to where the boat was in three feet of water. I felt like we had just washed ashore from being lost at sea for months. I looked like Tom Hanks in *Castaway*, and we walked barefoot on the long white sandy beach until we reached the Railay Beach Resort. Ash spotted it and said, "Here we are!"

As Ash checked in, I looked around. There was a half-mile-long beach that had *maybe* six people on it. We were surrounded by an amphitheater of cliffs, including the famous rocky cliff jutting out from the beach that looked like a mix between Pride Rock from *The Lion King* and a tower made of grass. It paid to be here in the low season.

I showered off the travel day and walked into our massive suite to find Ash sitting on one of the two queen beds, watching TV and wearing her complimentary robe and slippers. I was surprised. Not that she had the robe and slippers on, but that she didn't have the EgyptAir socks on as well.

I had to take a siesta. Getting only two hours of sleep had left me exhausted. Ash told me to come find her later and left for the pool.

I awoke an hour later and had absolutely no idea where I was. I had probably slept in more places over the last four months than the last four years combined. I walked to the beach and saw Ash sitting on the sand. There were zero other people around. This was one of the nicest beaches in Thailand and probably the world, and we had it all to ourselves.

We ate dinner along the water at the resort restaurant. It was pricey, but we didn't have many options. After dinner, Ash went to shower and I sat along the pool, writing. The sunset was beyond stunning over the water and cliffs. I hoped Ash wouldn't make it back in time to see this because I knew I would get summoned for pictures.

But she arrived back and saw it from miles away. I quickly tried to snap her out of the hypnosis. "What time is our bus tomorrow morning?"

"Yeah, sure," she replied, gazing longingly at the sky.

Shit . . . I've lost her. The glowing sun receded into the horizon and painted the sea a mixture of orange, red, and yellow. I watched as girls with cameras flocked to the beach, dragging their Instagram husbands/boyfriends behind them.

"Hey, we should go take pictures!" she said enthusiastically, and left the pool to dry off.

Damn you, Sun. Why can't you ever just pull an Irish good-bye and disappear without showboating? I sighed heavily, pounded my beer, grabbed the Canon, and followed Ash to the beach, where other fellas were snapping shots of their girls pretending to be walking casually out toward the sea.

We had left the northern jungle of Chiang Mai and the busy life-style with it. We had another ten-hour travel day that had consisted of walking, riding in the bed of a truck, flying, busing, wading, and boating. As exhausting as these days could be, we were always rewarded in the end. I was starting to realize how much we were going to miss this. It was happening too fast.

I watched Ash skip out to sea with joy I had never seen before. It was almost as if this was where she belonged. "Slow down, Ash!" I yelled as she set off to the beach. "Let's take it all in before it disappears."

She ran toward the sunset and said, "It's going to be over soon, Kyle. Come on!"

I know it is, baby, I know it is.

9/11/15
Railay Beach, Thailand

I glanced at my phone during breakfast, and the date was the first thing I noticed. The phrase synonymous with 9/11 is "Never Forget," but how could anyone? I still remember exactly where I was on that awful day in 2001, and I am positive you do too. Despite the terror, fear, and uncertainty our entire country experienced on that fall day in September, it was beyond inspiring to see our country come together afterward. Unfortunately, I feel like our country is split now more than ever.

Ash and I told our 9/11 stories to each other, as we did every year, and left to swim in the Indian Ocean for the first time. This left only the Southern and Arctic Oceans for me to swim in. I didn't anticipate either of those happening, and when the hell did they come up with the Southern Ocean? I definitely missed that geography memo.

Ash had read somewhere that Railay Beach was famous for its rock climbing, and she signed us up for it through the hotel. We were instructed to meet at the front desk at noon, where our guide would pick us up. At twelve on the dot, a small man with dreads down to his butt arrived. He greeted us both, and we followed him to the other side of the Railay Beach peninsula.

"Have you guys ever rock climbed before?" he asked.

We replied simultaneously yes/no, and looked at each other, confused at the other's response.

He smiled back at us and told us it was no problem; there were routes for everyone. We passed through a small village with a few shops and restaurants that sat in the middle of the peninsula between the two beaches. Ash began to get nervous as we got closer. She is always so good at things, especially athletic things, but she gets so embarrassed to do things in front of people.

We emerged from the jungle to another beach that was much less glamorous than the one on our side. He led us to a small hut and gave us our belts, shoes, and chalk. He then introduced us to our guide for the day, Paul. We also had one other solo climber coming with us today. He walked up to us and introduced himself.

Danny was an experienced climber who did this often as a hobby. He had done a good bit of outdoor climbing in Arizona, where he'd grown up. He was in medical school at Ohio State.

"There she is!" Paul then exclaimed, pointing to a rock face in front of us.

What, that cliff going straight into the sky? No way in hell we were climbing that shit, right? Danny belayed for Paul as he climbed up to get the hooks for the carabineers ready. Paul looked like an actual monkey climbing a tree, utilizing his freakishly long arms to swing from rock to rock. He brought his legs up simultaneously in one fluid motion and reached the top of the wall we were climbing in a matter of minutes. I was cursing myself under my breath for the three months of beer, gelato, and food that were about to weigh me down. I was here with my girlfriend, an expert local climber, and Danny the muscular climbing med student. *Fuck.*

Paul came down and switched sides with Danny, who climbed the wall at almost the same speed as Paul. Dammit, Danny. I was hoping you were bullshitting and were actually going to suck. It was my turn. Ash looked at me with encouragement. I couldn't let her down now. So I acted like I knew what I was doing and took the approach I took in all things in life: I faked it until I made it. I started up the wall, and after only a few minutes had made it to the top easily.

When Ash was prepping for her turn, she became nervous and I assured her she would be great. Sure enough, she was a natural and glided up the wall with ease. She made it back down, and we all high-fived at our first wall victory.

Paul undid the harness, and we all walked to the next wall. It took him a while to climb the next rock. When he got down, he was sweating profusely and out of breath. He fought words through his frequent exhales and said to us, "This one is just for Danny; it is very advanced."

Come again, Paul? I thought: *I was not about to get bitched in front of my girlfriend.*

"I want to try it," I told Paul confidently, and put my knot on first before he could say no.

"Are you sure?" he asked. "This is the most difficult climb of the day."

"Yeah, I'm positive. I will go first."

From the first hold, I knew I had outkicked my coverage here. The grips were small, and many were only wide enough for a few fingers. I knew Ash was down there watching me with hope, and Danny and Paul with doubt. I had reached a point where the only grip was going to be a jump. I prepped my legs for action and did a few practice squats before lunging up. I managed to get three fingers in the slight indentation, but I was slipping fast; I put all my weight into those three fingers and lifted a leg quickly, just as my hand slipped away. I lunged again and found a secure grip at the last millisecond. It was a bit of a combo move, and when I made the jump, I heard the three of them cheering and clapping below. I made it to the top minutes later, and when I came down, it was both a great and embarrassing feeling to hear the surprise in their voices as they congratulated me.

Ash started climbing the next wall as it began to rain. She still killed it. It was inspiring to see her use her arms and legs to propel herself up. When she came back down, she warned me that this wall was more difficult to climb than it looked. I should have listened. I got cocky and injured my forearm falling four feet down the cliff. Idiot.

Railay Beach is on the bucket list of the most serious climbers around the world, and we knew we were lucky to have experienced it. We went to bed that night and realized we had not yet booked a place to stay in Ko Samui the next night. Most people might panic, but we were too busy basking in our climbing victories. What was the worst that could happen? We'd sleep on the beach in the Gulf of Thailand? Everything would work itself out. The panic and planning could wait for another day.

9/12/15
Railay Beach, Thailand → Ko Samui, Thailand

When our alarm went off at nine, we remembered the crucial fact that we had nowhere to stay tonight. We quickly did some research and booked a resort in Ko Samui before taking one of the boats to the mainland.

Our boat pulled into the same port we had arrived in, and we walked up to a bus station full of travelers. When it came time for our trip, we entered the bus, and I was pleasantly surprised by how nice it was. I mean, it was no FlixBus, but it did have reclining seats and AC. We had a six-hour ride from one coast of Thailand to the other.

I took a nap and awoke a few hours later to the sound of raindrops pelting the bus. I looked out the window and saw nothing but palm trees and deep brush. We were far in the jungle at this point, and every break in the trees showed people walking in fields and riding motorbikes through paths. It dawned on me as I gazed out at the lush green colors how many different landscapes I had observed from bus windows.

Soon the rainy lullaby and dark sky put me right back to sleep in my reclined chair. I didn't wake again until we'd arrived in Ko Samui.

When we arrived at the station, we waited in the shade for our ferry. We'd chosen to explore the three islands in the Gulf of Thailand rather than stay on the Indian Ocean. Ko Samui was the first and biggest of the islands in the gulf. It was the second biggest island in Thailand after Phuket.

We were surprised at how busy the streets of Ko Samui were. I guess I'd imagined something similar to Railay Beach. This was a busy island, and there was plenty of opportunities for business with all the tourists. Our taxi driver must have had all the resorts memorized because he sped off at our first two syllables.

"Fair House Resort," the driver said when we reached our destination. We tipped him and walked up to one of those typical hotel check-in roundabouts. The resort was rated four stars on TripAdvisor, but you could tell it had been five stars in the nineties and they just hadn't upgraded anything.

We checked in, and the woman at the front desk drove us on a golf cart to our fifty-eight-dollar-a-night suite. Admittedly, our room was in an odd area of the resort, and Ash gave me a nervous glance. "Well, it does have character," I told her. We were beginning to second-guess our stay on the island.

To get some fresh air and escape our outdated room, we hailed a red taxi from the main road and headed to Chaweng Beach.

The man dropped us off in a very vibrant scene full of shopping, nightlife, and massages: three of Ash's favorite things. We ordered mai tais from a liquor cart on the side of the road and strolled the promenade. Shopping always lifted Ash's mood.

At the end of the market was a makeshift food court. We walked along the path and perused the menus. All the owners were standing in front of their shops, yelling their specials at us. We smiled and continued walking until we came to a guy the size of a sumo wrestler. He was standing with a five-foot-tall guy who could have fit in my backpack. It was the oddest duo I had seen in a while. They both smiled sincerely and bowed their heads as a greeting, not saying a word. Finally, people who let their food speak for itself. We sat down in their restaurant, and they both looked at each other like they had just won the lottery. All the other owners threw their hands up in disbelief.

We both ordered our favorite dish, cashew chicken stir-fry, and two large beers. Before the sumo wrestler left our table, he said, "I will make sure our mom makes it especially good for you two." This was when I knew we'd made the right choice; not only were we supporting a mother and her sons, they were honored to have our business.

It had been quite a day, and I could tell we were both getting tired. Not just from today but from the last three months. Sleeping in different beds every few nights and spending long hours crunched on buses, planes, boats, and cars was finally catching up to us. Not to mention being sick numerous times. These last few weeks on the islands in the gulf were going to be a great way to reset before we returned to the US.

9/13/15
Ko Samui, Thailand

We had truly only experienced one day at the beach so far in Thailand, and even that had been cut short by rock climbing. We were eager to find the beach and spend the day doing nothing. I didn't know what to expect as we walked down the pathways of the nineties resort. There were pools everywhere, but there was no one in them. This place really shut down during the rainy season.

As soon as we emerged from the resort grounds, we were immediately ashamed of ourselves for being unhappy last night. The beach looked like a postcard. The white sand was untouched, and the water was just calm enough to be gentle yet had enough waves to avoid looking like a lake. There were even beach chairs and umbrellas set up for the guests. We were the only guests, so we picked the chairs in the very front. That way, even if anyone came later, we would still be staring at the sea.

We spread out towels on the chairs and got situated. Once we were comfortable, I turned to Ash and said, "Now what?" But she had rolled over to take a nap.

I decided to get in the water and dove into the warm sea. It felt amazing, and I can honestly say the water was warmer than shower water. I think it just felt that way because the clouds had covered the sky, and there was a light drizzle every ten minutes or so.

Eventually I retreated to the chairs to lie out. I was only doing this so I didn't have to write. It is amazing what humans will find joy in doing while procrastinating.

The struggle I was having with writing this book was timing. When I had time to write, I wasn't in the mood. I was usually drinking at a bar with Ash when the creative juices started flowing. This was why I'd decided to write this book in handwritten journals. I brought my journal with me everywhere, and found myself writing at bars and restaurants, and in massage chairs. I have a newfound respect for people who write for a living. Deadlines don't give a shit what mood you're in.

With not much motivation to write, we headed back to the Chaweng Beach downtown area. Our first stop was, of course, our local food shack. When the two guys standing at the front saw us, they immediately gave a wai and shook our hands with both hands. The looks on their faces when they realized they had loyal customers who were coming on back-to-back nights were priceless.

After our second night in Ko Samui, our outlook on the island had completely changed. It just goes to show how much your view on something can change when you get to know it. We had arrived in the darkness last night and had chosen to let our moods be ruined by our first impression. The light of the morning had brought us a bright new view on Ko Samui.

9/14/15
Ko Samui, Thailand

We awoke and immediately headed to the beach for breakfast. As we lay on our chairs, I started thinking about our return home. We would be ending this journey in two weeks, and I couldn't tell if it felt like we had been gone for years or days. The one thing I was sure of was how proud I was of us. Not only had we decided not to be okay with our average lives, we'd acted on it. Ash was a teacher and I worked for a nonprofit; it wasn't like we were bankers who'd left to live this lavish traveling life. We'd saved every dime we'd made for months. I was proud of us for surviving this trip as a couple and for surviving this trip in general. I was proud of us for learning and trying new things and for learning from each other and those around us.

It turns out that the whole rainy season thing carried weight. It started pouring on us again around four, so we decided to leave the beach and get ready for our routine night in Chaweng Beach. Without mopeds, it was hard to be motivated to pay for taxis to any of the surrounding villages.

Our taxi dropped us off in Chaweng Beach, and we strolled down the streets. We had cashew chicken to eat, locals to please, and massages to get. The food was as good as expected, and the sumo wrestler and small guy were as nice as always. The massage was a bit more painful than expected. We got the traditional Thai massage, and it felt like a UFC fight with our hands tied behind our back. It would be leg massages only from here on out.

9/15/15
Ko Samui, Thailand

Our morning was spent on the beach, floating in the shallows of the gulf. We talked about our plans for the rest of the trip and our plans for the rest of life. We reminisced on our days in Denver and in Eastern Europe. We promised ourselves things we would do when we got home and things we wouldn't. The warm waters of the Gulf of Thailand were a great place to make plans.

After showering off sweat, salt, and sand, we decided to do something different tonight. There was a famous Buddha statue on the island of Ko Samui, and after our powerful experience in Chiang Mai, we were interested in seeing it. It took some negotiating, but we found a taxi that would take us there for six dollars. We were about halfway there and, like clockwork, the rain showed up. The truck was covered with a makeshift tarp, but it didn't even come close to keeping us dry.

The driver must have put two and two together and asked us if we needed a ride back. We said yes, and he agreed to wait for us.

The temple area was set up like a courtyard, with meditation altars and small temples on both sides. In front of us was a golden staircase that led up to a forty-foot gold Buddha statue sitting cross-legged. The cold rain poured down on us, but we were mesmerized by the beauty of this forty-three-year-old relic. It was almost eerie in the darkness, but we felt safe with the large Buddha looking down on us. I heard a noise and turned to see an old monk sweeping one of the altars. He looked over at us and we locked eyes. He gave me a smile that could only be described as pure peacefulness. The aura of positive energy he put off warmed me in the cold rain, and I smiled back. He continued to sweep, and I could tell he was happier sweeping rain off these temple steps than many people were ever. I bottled up as much energy as I could, and we raced back to the taxi, avoiding as many puddles as possible.

The taxi driver waved when he saw us and started the truck once again.

"I am glad you got to see the Buddha. Would you like to see another great temple?"

Normally, I would think he was just trying to extend our fare, but for some reason, I trusted this guy, and the people of this country in general. "Sure, that sounds awesome," we said in unison—for once.

He drove us across the island to a temple next to a Buddha. Both were on a platform out over the water and had a long walkway leading up to them. We walked in the pouring rain out to the large majestic Buddha, where we heard a sound coming from the temple. I looked across the water and saw dozens of monks singing in prayer inside. Standing in the cold rain, the dark, stormy sky sitting closely above, and listening to monks recite a prayer was beyond powerful and very spiritual.

This was a moment I would never forget. The combination of the monks' prayers and the rain bouncing off the water produced a natural music that put me into a deep trance. I let the music take me away and stared at the massive Buddha in front of me. I felt wholesome, I felt positive, and I felt cleansed. It was as if my life were starting from this point forward, and everything that had happened up until now was simply to get me to this moment. The small things disappeared, and the clouded space in my mind clogged with meaningless media and social norms was pushed away by this feeling of pureness. I was refreshed and energized. Then the monks stopped praying. The rain stopped moments later.

I opened my eyes. Ash was staring at me, intrigued by my absence and asking if I was okay.

"I've never been better," I told her.

9/16/15
Ko Samui, Thailand → Ko Pha Ngan, Thailand

Packing had become an excruciating assignment this late in the trip. Ash was our project manager, and she assigned me the task of staying out of her way. Once we had every inch of our backpacks loaded, we went to check out. We noticed that the rain was not only coming down in waves, but it was whipping the trees back and forth. Not ideal for travel by boat.

Our travel day started with a taxi that inevitably got us wetter than we wanted. When we reached the port, we got our tickets and squeezed under the small awning to try to stay dry. Our ferry arrived; it looked a little out of its league in the rough waters. I asked the lady at the desk if the boat was still going to make the trip in this storm and she said, "Oh yes, it will be fine."

When it was time to board, we were ushered to the front of the boat where we walked downstairs and sat in seats under the cabin. When it was time to set sail, I felt the boat jerk as the anchor was lifted, and we started backing up slowly in the choppy, angry sea. We had windows on either side of us that showed water splashing up to meet them. This ferry wasn't going to make its way to Ko Pha Ngan, though; we had to turn around.

As the boat rotated slowly, we found ourselves in the exact spot we didn't want to be. All of a sudden, people around us began to scream; the ship had reached that purgatory zone directly between the waves. They slammed the boat, and one side of the ship raised high in the air as the other sank to the sea. My stomach lurched, and I grabbed on to Ash. We looked out the windows. To the left I saw nothing but water, and to the right I saw nothing but sky. We were about to flip and everyone on the boat knew it. Then the boat came rocking back to the other side, and everyone held on to something to avoid falling. This was a helpless feeling. I couldn't move because we were swinging down to our apparent demise and gravity was pinning me down. Even if I could have moved, what could I do?

Just as fast, the boat straightened out. It was back to the choppy bumps coming head on and water splashing the windows. Everyone on the boat who was previously crying or screaming was silent and looking around at one another with horrified faces that could only ask, *Do you think it's over?*

A few people laughed nervously. I wiped my forehead, which was absolutely coated with sweat. The thing that scared me the most was everyone else's panic. When you are on an airplane and there is extreme turbulence, there are always people who are afraid; however, there are also many more calm passengers who ride the bumps and never even look up from their Kindles.

The ferry began heading north, and before we could all catch our breaths from the teetering terror episode, we started bouncing. Our choppy ride became bumpy, and the boat settled into a uniform terror. Every three seconds it felt like we were being propelled off a wave and sent airborne. After only a few minutes of the gut-wrenching bouncing, complete chaos ensued.

We had reached deep water, and our vessel rose up the large swells with enough speed that the front of our boat, and our current seating location, took off like we'd hit a ramp. Then we would free-fall for three seconds to the sounds of shrieking passengers until we smashed into the concrete-like water. My concern turned to terror, and I stood up to try to help. I didn't know why I'd stood up; there was nothing I could do from the bottom of this boat. I just felt like I was sitting and waiting to die down there.

Standing up was the wrong decision, as the next free fall threw me onto the floor. I got up quickly as the adrenaline took over, and crawled back into my seat as we were tossed again. The trend continued over and over. Rise, rise, rise, screams, and then a three-second free fall as everyone tried to hold on, then *crash*.

I had read numerous reports of ferries capsizing in Southeast Asia, but I'd never understood how that had happened. They had not run into anything—how did they capsize? It all made sense now; they ventured out into a storm with waves they were not equipped to take on. Our ferry had absolutely no business being in these waters. It had been storming all week, and today was the worst yet. I was furious at myself for allowing us to be in this position. As I looked around the boat, I felt like time had stopped. I watched as women cried and held their children close to them, I watched as people were now throwing up onto the ground that was now quickly taking on water, and I watched as crewmembers screamed orders in Thai at one another. I decided if this ship was going to capsize, we weren't going to be sitting down here waiting for it.

I told Ash to stay put and hold on while I tried to survey the situation to see if there was a better place for us to sit. The last place I wanted to be when we blew open the boat was in the holding cell at the bottom of it. I had to time my dismount with the pending slam of the boat. We rose up into the sky, and I braced for impact as we flew down and crashed into the sea. As soon as I had held on long enough not to fly into the seat behind me, I burst up the hole like Barry Sanders, and ran to the back of the seating area, grabbing the handrail just as we lifted off again.

I put a death grip on the stair railing and was able to see the entire front of the boat from this perspective, similar to looking up the aisle on a plane. The nose of our ferry rose up with nothing but a view of the dark sky and then fell in violent fashion, assaulting the sea with a brutal slam. *This* was when I truly understood the magnitude of how dire our predicament was.

The waves outside were colossal, and the sight of the rolling white caps thrashing about filled my mouth with vomit. *I guess I do get seasick.* These waves were not only *much* larger than our boat, but moving in all different directions. It was two in the afternoon, and it looked like it was midnight outside. We looked like a rubber toy boat in a bathtub that a two-year-old was thrashing in. I had a sense of blackness with no noise. My panic had blacked me out, but when it switched to survival mode, I came to.

Focus, Kyle. First, I had to get Ash out of the lower cabin. If we didn't capsize by tipping over, we would surely sink with the amount of water we were taking on. That lower cabin was going to fill up first. I got back to the stairwell after carefully timing the crashing of our boat on the waves and motioned for her to come up here immediately. I wanted us to be right next to the door so that we could get out if we had to.

"Kyle, what are we going to do?" Ash asked in a surprisingly calm tone as she reached me. When Ash gets really freaked out, she shuts down. I kind of like that about her. I prefer it to a frantically screaming person.

"Ash, I am about"—holding railing for impact—"sixty-five percent sure we are going to capsize. In the event that this happens we are going to"—holding railing for impact—"have to swim."

"Swim? Okay, swim where?" Her calmness was borderline concerning.

We both turned as a girl threw up in her lap right next us. The entire boat was in distress because we were enduring the stomach-dropping feeling every five seconds.

The waves were growing larger as we got to the deeper water, which meant the gut-wrenching stomach feeling was getting worse. Our stomachs lifted as a wall of water showered the boat. The crew was rushing around the cabin with anything they could find to try to get water off the boat. The crewmember next to us on the stairs was using a dustpan.

I pointed out the only island in sight to Ash and told her that was where we were going to swim if this thing went down. We had no life jackets, but it couldn't have been more than a few miles if I could see it through the rain. As I was pointing out the island, I saw her approaching: the queen of the sea—the rogue wave. She was slowly rolling toward us and growing every one hundred feet. I blacked out with fear and felt a shot of adrenaline unlike any other. This was what it must have felt like when you knew you were about to die but there was nothing that could save you.

I grabbed Ashley's hand and wrapped it between the railing and mine. I wanted to have her hand in mine in case the boat went underwater or we flipped upside down. The boat began to rise, and it seemed like everyone had figured out at the same moment that we had risen much higher in the air than on any previous wave. Normally we would be starting our descent, but we continued to rise for two more seconds. We reached the top, and there was a euphoric moment where nothing mattered. We were airborne and free, and I had never in my life been more afraid of the fall.

I heard a blood-curdling scream from below as we fell headfirst into the outstretched arms of the angry sea. I held on to the rail and Ashley with all my power as we free-fell for what felt like ten seconds. The *bang* that ensued had to have been the bow of the ship being obliterated by the water. Water poured down the stairwell as we bounced off the surface and then stabilized beneath the behemoth wave. The next few seconds were like the climax in a horror movie. I heard multiple people throwing up. At this point, I was becoming more nauseous from the sound and smell of vomit than from the waves. The crew rushed down into the cabin to try to get their buckets full of water. Meanwhile, my 65 percent capsize rate had risen to 90 percent, and I told Ash to be ready to swim and to stay with me no matter what. At this point, we had no phones, no wallets, and no backpacks. I wasn't sure if the boat had broken in half or if we were taking on water from below as well as from above.

We went over the game plan one last time in between swells: get away from the boat as fast as possible. This thing would be a death trap once it stopped floating, eager to take us down with it. The open water was rough, but we could swim in the water— we couldn't escape a sinking boat. As we prepared for the worst, I felt the engine slow down. *This must be it.* I looked out the other window and saw heaven on earth. I saw our island. Well, I'll be damned. . . . We'd made it.

We rocked back and forth into the bay at a level that before today would have concerned me, but we were no longer getting air time. I was ecstatic. Ash and I hugged each other and laughed at the fact that we had survived. I would have kissed the dock when we stepped foot off the boat, but someone had just thrown up on it.

When we arrived at our next resort, I was reminded that we'd booked a deluxe suite. This essentially means we paid an extra eighteen dollars a night for a "dirty bed." I wish it'd meant what you are thinking, but I meant it in the literal sense. I am a neat freak when it comes to our bed. I hate when there is any sand, dirt, or crumbs in it. Our room had a queen bed for us to sleep in and a dirty bed for Ash to keep her clothes on and for us to nap in after the beach. We both took a dirty nap in the dirty bed and slept the stress of our trip away before heading to the beach village for dinner.

At dinner we met an Israeli couple who I could tell we would like. Sivan told us how her husband, Yoav, had stayed up until 3:00 a.m. nightly on this trip to watch his fantasy soccer team. *My fucking man.* Yoav and Sivan were easy to talk to, and we had great conversations about Israel and the United States. They knew a lot more about the US than we did about Israel, but that is usually how it goes. If the countries of the world were TV shows, the US would be *Keeping Up with the Kardashians.* Nobody likes their antics, but everyone knows about them.

We taxied home with a sweet Thai woman whose shop sign read GROCERIES, GAS, CLOTHES, AND TAXI. She was an all-purpose lady. Her taxi was simply her personal pickup truck, but we didn't mind whose car it was. We trusted these people with our lives (which almost came back to bite us in the ass today). When we got home, she didn't have any change for our large bills, so she smiled and told us to just pay her tomorrow.

Today was probably the most polar day of our trip. We had the absolute lowest of the lows on that ferry, but then we made great friends, experienced kindness and trust in its purest form, and had a resort suite with a dirty bed to come home to. This was what traveling was about: no day was ever the same, and our comfort zone was constantly being blown up. We appreciated life more than usual tonight. We showered and crawled into the clean bed for a good night's rest.

9/17/15
Ko Pha Ngan, Thailand

I woke up to what I thought was an alarm but was in fact a steady rain hitting our window. Our suite was up on stilts in the jungle with a large porch overlooking the lush island. I never wanted to leave this moment in our comfortable bed in the jungle, receiving a concert from the clouds above.

The jungle rain was a drug for me. It helped me think, it soothed my mind and soul, and it seemed to lower my stress levels. I know some people say that constant rain depresses them, but it has the opposite effect on me. The rain heals me and provides steady background noise for me to calm my thoughts. Ash and I took this opportunity to plan our last week, as there was nowhere else we could go but this breakfast hut on the beach.

Ko Tao would be our last island, and it was supposed to be the best one. The smallest of the three and the farthest from shore, it was truly a slice of earth in the middle of nowhere. We decided to spoil ourselves and book a really nice place for our final destination. The idea of this being the end depressed Ash immensely. She started to break down a little at the thought of only booking one last Airbnb, so we decided to get off the resort and venture into town.

Our trek required going up a very steep hill in the beginning and then down a steep hill right into town. We could have taxied here, but it was two hundred baht; we preferred to just get two big Changs at the 7-Eleven halfway there for one hundred baht and get some exercise.

It didn't take long for us to discover that these were some of the strong Changs, and we would be drunker sooner than we wanted to be. You see, Chang Beer, like many other things in Thailand, is unregulated. This means that despite the twenty-one-ounce bottle saying it is only 5 percent alcohol, many can be even twice that amount. With beers in hand, we looked for places to eat. We read restaurant signs until we saw the word *hacienda* in big letters. My god. Mexican food.

More than burgers, BBQ, steaks, or Bojangles', we missed Mexican food. I was salivating like a hungry dog as I looked over the menu of quesadillas, nachos, tacos, and burritos. The lone white guy sitting at the bar on his MacBook came over to take our order. He then walked back into the kitchen, relayed the message to a woman, and went back to work on his laptop. I assumed he was the owner.

It wasn't the best Mexican food we'd ever had, but it still hit the spot and gave us the fix we needed. After dinner, Ash decided to get a pedicure, and I left to get a massage at a different establishment.

We split off across the street from each other and pampered ourselves. I say *pampered* because it had been at least three days since our last massage. This was a long stretch for us. Not compared to the twenty-six-year stretch I'd had before that.

9/18/15
Ko Pha Ngan, Thailand

In my dream I was searching a large store for the bathroom because my stomach hurt. I continued to search in a panic, and after being unsuccessful to the point where I was going to have a major accident, I stirred awake in a bed full of hot sweats. I came to my senses to find a gut-wrenching gut wrenching. I scooted to the bathroom like a scared dog and made it just in time as my bowel faucet turned on.

I had to cut my losses while I was still somewhat ahead, and pounded one of our two large water bottles. This routine happened every thirty minutes until the morning, three hours later. Well, except for the water-pounding part. I ran out of water shortly.

Ash woke up around 8:00 a.m. as I was in the bathroom and came in to apologize for sleeping in. She always seemed to feel bad if I was up first.

"It's okay, baby. Don't worry about that," I said with my last bit of energy. "I need water," I added, desperately dehydrated.

"My god, you look awful," she said as she saw my white face dripping with sweat.

I was trying to figure out how I'd gotten sick and she hadn't. This wasn't just my body reacting weirdly to the food. This was a parasite, a disease, a virus, *something serious*. Then it all came back to me. *You idiot.* After my massage, the masseuse had handed me a cup of tea and watermelon as I put my shoes and socks back on. They had either washed the watermelon with water or had used unfiltered water for the tea.

Ash returned with bottles of water. I drank as much as I could and tried to get some rest. I had been awake since 3:00 a.m. and was exhausted by the fluid loss. Once she knew I was comfortable in the clean bed, she headed down to the beach.

Ash was so much better about doing things on her own since we'd left Denver. In the beginning of the trip and even when we were back at home, she probably would have just stayed with me, but she had been meditating a lot lately. I think she had truly found confidence in her self-image and worth since she had been around so many kind people who weren't competitive or lost in a world of supermodels and shows that portray women as objects. I was just happy to be able to experience her transformation firsthand.

I rushed to the bathroom, deep in thought and shallow in hydration.

After a few hours of napping, I mustered up the strength to venture to the beach. As I walked slowly down the path, I truly realized how weak I had become in the last twelve hours. Diarrhea is a deadly force. It literally drains you of water, energy, and butt softness. This was when I truly appreciated the wiping hose of Thailand.

In the States I would have wiped my butt raw at this point, but here, with a plumbing system not built for toilet paper, people had to throw their toilet paper away in a trash can. There was a hose to spray before wiping so you avoided the smell of shit in your trash. I had grown to love these hoses. I laughed at the thought of being in Europe and not wanting to use a bidet, but here I was in a mosquito-infested outhouse in the jungle in the pouring rain, spraying my butt with a water gun.

I returned to Ash and took shelter under a cabana. It truly had been raining all types of rain since we'd arrived. "Ash, let's go in the water!" I suggested.

We rushed out into the warm sea together and took seats in the water, crisscross applesauce. The white sand underneath was soft, the warm water was soaking my chilled body, and the rain massaged my head and shoulders. We both sat in silence as the rain pounded the water around us. I stared at the surface of the waves and let my mind escape. Instead of focusing on anything, I watched the silhouette of the rain hitting the water. My mind watched the drops rise rather than fall, similar to when tires look like they are rotating in reverse at high speeds. It now looked like thousands of drops were slowly rising out of the water. This self-created hallucination mixed with the humming sounds of the earth's shower gave me a natural high that no drug could replicate. The rain let up after fifteen minutes, and I snapped out of the lucid trip.

"Wow," Ash said softly.

"Yeah, that was intense," I replied.

"Do you want to look for seashells for Madi?" she asked.

"Of course," I said. "Just as long as there's a bathroom in sight."

Ash's niece, Madi, was basically like her little sister. Ash's parents had been helping raise Madi since she was a young girl. I could tell this was who Ash missed the most. We walked along the beach, collecting seashells for the rest of the afternoon.

9/19/15
Ko Pha Ngan, Thailand

Another sleepless night. I didn't mind not being able to eat, but not being able to sleep was going to be the death of me. My stomach would wake me up semi-hourly to dispel all the water I'd just drunk. I drank as many liters of water as I could throughout the night and never peed once. These sleepless nights were catching up to me, but my priority remained hydration.

I woke up and was happy to discover that the three-day rainstorm had *finally* passed. (No, not the diarrhea; that was alive and well.) It was sunny outside. I found a note on the dirty bed from Ash saying she was at the beach.

I had been in the shower for so long that my water had gone cold. I heard a knock on the door; I forgot I had the only key. I knew I was going to get the floor wet, but Ash was rather impatient when she was outside in mosquito country. I tiptoed over and opened the door. Hmm, Ash looked a lot like two housekeeping ladies. *Oh shit!* I slammed the door and apologized through it as I stood there naked and cringing. They were probably scarred for life.

When Ash got home a few minutes later, I told her what had happened.

Her response: "Those poor women."

We ate takeout for dinner in the dirty bed and watched the only channel in English on TV. Which also happened to be the best channel on TV—Nat Geo, baby. This was our idea of a great night. We cuddled in bed, our bellies full of pasta, and watched epic wild animal battles. My stomach had kept us from doing too much the last few days, but it felt like a blessing in disguise. Sometimes we took quantity over quality and tried to do so much that we failed to see the beauty in what was right in front of us. We had a lot to process in the coming weeks, and it wasn't going to be easy without rest.

9/20/15
Ko Pha Ngan, Thailand

Let's just say the gun hose next to the toilet was out of ammo. I didn't know how much longer this could go on before I couldn't keep up with the hydration. I had promised Ash we would rent a moped tomorrow to find the waterfalls. I still had a bit of moped post-traumatic stress disorder from our crash in Greece, and a bit of pre-traumatic stress disorder from my pending diarrhea. This accumulated to one hell of a stress disorder. We really didn't have much of a choice, though; the taxis were four hundred baht to the other villages, and a moped for the entire day was only 250.

The guy at the front desk ordered us a moped, and two Thai girls showed up minutes later, each on a moped. They dropped one off with us, and both drove off on the other. Before we set off, Ash asked where our helmets were. I assumed they were under the seat like with most mopeds, but they had not given us any. Luckily, our resort had extras. (If I died on a moped without a helmet on, my mom would kill me.) We sped up the hill, chasing waterfalls against TLC's advice.

It was really tough for me to get used to driving on the left side of the road. I would have it down for a mile or two, but then, when I pulled out of a turn, I would naturally merge into the right lane.

It also was tough for me to get used to driving as chaotically as the Thai drivers. We reached a two-lane roundabout, and I didn't even attempt to figure it out. I just beelined diagonally to the road we wanted, as did a Thai truck next to me. I think I was learning.

We spotted what looked like the area where we were supposed to pull over, and I slowed down onto the rock-covered parking lot. There were no signs around, but we saw a truck full of guys pulling out of the parking lot. I pointed to the trailhead across the street and tried to ask with my facial expressions if that was the waterfall. Every single guy on the truck pointed and nodded. The truck pulled away, and they all smiled sincerely and waved good-bye.

The trail was an easy one, and we came to the first small series of falls within a few hundred feet. I was treading carefully to keep an eye out for poisonous snakes, scorpions, and centipedes. I was sick enough with this norovirus (what I deducted after researching this morning); I couldn't afford to add poison to the mix.

As I took pictures of Ash on the waterfall (Instagram gold), I noticed that I was getting red and overheated for some reason and found that my bootleg sunscreen from 7-Eleven was simply clogging my pores. Instead of allowing my sweat to cool me down, the sunscreen was trapping it and overheating me.

This was the luxury of being on an island: you could drive in any direction and eventually reach water. Soaking in the sea turned out to be a futile attempt at cooling off. The water on this beach felt like it had been sitting in a teakettle on the stove. We did succeed in washing off the white paste that was sold to us as sunscreen. Then we dried off and sat at a beach restaurant to try to cool down and let our sweat go to work for us.

Ash ordered a sandwich, and I set off to the bathroom behind the café. It was a cinder-block room that looked like a torture chamber. It had no mosquitos, though, which meant it was perfect in my book. My standards on bathrooms had dropped so sharply that as long as the bathrooms didn't have mosquitos, they could be much worse.

We finished our food and got back on the moped to get some wind in our faces. We passed lines of coconut groves and elephant camps, where the elephants were either doing work or being ridden around on by tourists. This broke my heart as I thought back to the stories we'd heard at ENP. I wanted to throw a coconut at the riders and knock them off the poor animals.

The island was absolutely gorgeous. We cruised through small villages, waving and smiling at as many people as we could. We were trying to feed back into the positive energy grid that we had been using for weeks now.

It was our last night in Ko Pha Ngan and our best day yet. This island was improving our spirits immensely. I'd spent much of our time in Ko Pha Ngan deep in thought, and that was exactly what I'd needed out of Thailand. We were going to be leaving this magical place soon, and I wanted to be able to capture and bottle up the kind nature and energy of the souls who inhabited it.

We lay in the dirty bed before showering, discussing our time here and how it had been another great piece of our puzzle. As we chatted, Ash leaned in and pulled something out of my beard. That something was a large beetle. I had no idea it was in there, as I hadn't felt a thing. Well, there went my shot at romance tonight. Ash was dry heaving in the bathroom. I really wish our helmets had had visors.

9/21/15
Ko Pha Ngan, Thailand → Ko Tao, Thailand

This was it. The night where my immune system held a press conference with the rest of my body to let it know we had defeated the norovirus. I awoke and glanced at my clock to see what time it was and figured it would be around 8:00 a.m. When I saw 11:15 staring back at me, I knew we had to move quickly. Our boat to Ko Tao was at 12:45 p.m. We threw everything haphazardly into our bags and started running to the village.

As we hurried to the pier (in the bed of a laundromat owner's truck who agreed to take us for ten dollars), I was having vivid, lucid flashbacks of water rushing into our boat as we thrashed about in the sea. I couldn't believe we were going to venture back into this water.

But we didn't have much of a choice; we couldn't stay out in the middle of the gulf forever.

The clear skies and calm water gave us ideal cruising conditions. Other than an occasional bump, it was literally smooth sailing. This was good for my mental state. I couldn't afford to lose that; my physical state had already deteriorated.

The sea looked like a scatterplot with no correlation as multicolored boats hunted fish in all directions. We waved to captains on boats that looked like Forrest Gump's boat, *Jenny*. (I don't know if you've noticed, but that is my third reference to *Forrest Gump*. Somehow our trip reminded me a lot of that movie, and I couldn't begin to tell you how, but I felt good about it.)

I felt the boat drop gear and slow down as we cruised toward Mae Haad Pier. I glanced over the edge of the railing and saw the clearest water yet; it looked like our boat was gliding on air. I could make out every single fish, rock, and piece of coral. This place felt unreal. I was glad that bartender in Antwerp had told us to come here. It looked like we had saved the best for last in Ko Tao (Turtle Island). Just how we'd planned it.

Our hosts, Alan and Heidi, were a British couple who had lived in Ko Tao for ten years. They seemed to be in their midforties or fifties, and were a rare combination of quirky, sweet, and smart. Alan used to be a financial advisor, and Heidi had been in customer service. They greeted us with the two-cheek kiss. *This greeting seems like a distant memory.*

We followed behind them to their small pickup truck, and Alan asked, "Do you want to ride the boring way or the dangerous way?"

That was like asking a person with an excruciating hangover if they wanted one ibuprofen or three.

We climbed onto the back of the pickup truck that had a handlebar above the cab. Ash and I stood on the bed and held on to the bar as Alan backed out of the pier parking lot. We laughed with excitement as we rode the truck like a roller coaster through the coconut groves. The tall palm trees grew to be forty to fifty feet tall here. Many still had a full chamber of coconuts. If we took one of those to the head. we'd be scre—

Thwap.

"I'm hit, Ash! I'm hit!" I screamed.

"You idiot, that was just a branch. Keep your head down when we pass the trees!" Ash responded while laughing with joy from the thrill of the ride.

In my defense, it had felt like a coconut. I kept my head on a swivel from that point forward.

We turned onto a dirt road that must have been the driveway to our place, the Star Villa. It was basically a mountain, and it took more power than I cared to use to keep my bag and myself from flying off the truck. I felt like I was doing a pull-up hold at the top of the bar as we climbed. We reached a point where I could feel Alan holding down the gas, and we barely made it over a lip before flattening out and stopping abruptly.

Once we got out of the truck, Alan led the way up steep steps and told us to have a seat on the rocking chairs at the top on the porch. I slid off my backpack and felt a surge of relief. Our view was unreal. We were on top of a mountain, looking down over the coconut grove and all the way out to sea.

Alan did a rundown of the swanky villa, from electronics to AC, to food and drinks. There were surround-sound speakers and a DVR system. We'd been lucky if we had a TV with English channels up to this point.

Even better than the place itself was the phone they provided. They gave us an old-school "burner" phone and told us that all the taxis and good restaurants were contacts in there. They also told us to call them twice a day to get a ride down to the village. *Thank God,* I thought. We were trying to figure out how we were going to get to and from this place.

We thanked them for the hospitality and took time to unwind. After four months of traveling, Ko Tao was our last real stop. Just writing those words made me sick to my stomach. Almost everything in Thailand made me sick to my stomach, but this was a different kind of nausea.

9/22/15
Ko Tao, Thailand

This morning we walked to the porch and looked at the view, then drank coffee and ate toasties (ham-and-cheese paninis made famous by 7-Eleven) and omelets that Alan had made for us.

After breakfast and enough coffee to get us moving, we packed our day backpack with towels, sunscreen, the GoPro, and snorkels that Alan and Heidi were letting us borrow. Alan drove us down the steep hill as we held on for dear life in the back and watched for coconuts and trees. He dropped us off at the moped rental place. After mapping out what we wanted to do this week, we found that renting a moped for three days would be cheaper than taking taxis.

Our first beach was called Aow Leuk Bay. Alan and Heidi said it was their absolute favorite and that they had spotted many sea turtles and stingrays there. Before we left, he warned me that it was a very tricky drive on a moped but it was doable. That was concerning, but we had already crashed once and lived.

Driving in Thailand is essentially just a series of near misses. There were few rules here. I hadn't seen a police officer since we'd arrived, and people had very little concern for mopeds. Cars and SUV taxis blew past me, giving us a foot of space. It was honestly terrifying, having Ash on the back. I wouldn't mind if it were just my life at stake. After a stressful fifteen minutes, we reached the turnoff for Aow Leuk Bay.

Now let me set the scene when we reached the beach. We had been to the gorgeous beaches of Greece, the rocky coast of Croatia, and three other beaches in Thailand. After a short discussion, we decided that Aow Leuk Bay in Ko Tao, with its white sand, took the cake.

We walked onto a magazine cover, plopped our stuff down in the sand, and waded into the water to snorkel. I put my mask on and went underwater to make sure it worked. When I dropped below the surface, I found myself staring into the eyes of at least forty fish.

The bay was overpopulated with fish. I didn't even know where to look. The farther out into the bay we got, the more coral and sea life there were, with at least two dozen different types of fish in sight at all times.

There were plenty of your usual clear and white fish with black stripes, but we were gravitating toward the school of neon fish. It felt like we were those people you always wanted to be as a kid: the ones in the large tanks at the aquarium. Every time one of us spotted a large fish, we pointed and made awkward drowning noises to each other.

After casually floating through the hallways of the coral reef for an hour, we hit the snorkeling jackpot. The prize was hundreds of foot-long multicolored fish that were swarming a piece of coral like a group of four-year-olds attacking a recently exploded piñata. We took turns diving toward them to pose for GoPro pictures for the obvious reason that if we didn't document it, it didn't happen. After half an hour we took a break. We had been treading water for an hour now, and were losing steam.

When we reached the beach, we frantically recapped what just happened as if the other wasn't there. Ash went down for an afternoon nap. I headed back out to the shallows to float and do my daily meditation. The only difference was, this time I did it underwater. I breathed through the snorkel and let my mind swim instead of my body.

When the sun was beginning to set, we headed home. I was not looking forward to this drive, as I was exhausted from swimming all day. It was much harder on the way home because I had to maneuver through valleys and rocks and use the acceleration to get us up the hill. If I got going too fast, we were chalked, but if I took my hand off the accelerator, we went backward. We had a few close calls where I had to put my feet down and propel us to keep us from tipping, but we made it to the concrete. All that was left was a very steep hill leading to the main road. I started revving the engine and gave it all I had when suddenly the worst-case scenario played out right in front of us.

A large truck taking up the entire lane came careening over the road, and while we could have slid past it on the side, it would have been tight. The shock of the truck made me take my hand off the accelerator, and before I could start again, we began rolling backward. I tried to hit both the brake and the accelerator, but it was too late. I could not catch the ground with my foot because we were moving too fast. The front tire turned a bit and the moped tumbled right into the bushes. We went flying over the side and launched into the brush.

It was a casual fall and neither of us was hurt, but I was embarrassed as I tried to get the moped out of the bushes. I had gotten frantic and was slipping and stumbling when Ash stood up and said, "Baby, it's okay. Just relax!" She was more mad than rattled. I finally got the moped up and she kept saying, "Why didn't you just keep going?" I tried to explain that the truck had spooked me, and once I took my hand off the accelerator, we'd started going backward on the hill. But she didn't understand, because she hadn't driven one of these with someone on the back. They are heavy.

I was in no mood to be lectured. I was furious with myself, and there was no way I was simply going to apologize—that would be too mature. I yelled back at her to just let me drive; I was far too rattled to have a backseat driver at this point and had to focus on oncoming trucks and driving on the other side of the road. I spent the remainder of the ride home in utter fear of crashing once again, and when we got to the bottom of our driveway, I pulled over. There was no way I was driving up that treacherous gravel hill.

We began the walk in silence, and I watched above, hoping a coconut would fall toward Ash's head. Obviously I didn't want it to hit her; I just wanted to have an opportunity to catch it before it did and save her life so she would know I still loved her and wanted to protect her. I wanted to apologize for crashing our moped by saving her life.

By the time we reached our villa, we were both extremely out of breath and aching from the steep incline. Neither of us spoke due to the constant inhaling and exhaling and the situation we'd just escaped. That was two strikes on the moped in two different countries, and it had me shook. We had escaped serious injury twice, but how many times were we going to get lucky?

We ate delivery pizza, watched *Boardwalk Empire*, and recapped the crash into the woods now that we were in a better mood.

"What are the chances we'd fall twice on this trip?" I asked.

"Well, honestly, pretty damn high," Ash responded.

9/23/15
Ko Tao, Thailand

Rarely does one know the extent of one's injuries from a vehicle crash until the morning after. I walked into the bathroom gingerly and evaluated all the areas screaming at me.

We ordered a taxi to Tanote Bay from our burner phone to check out the snorkeling. Tanote Bay did not have nearly the sand or the water that Aow Leuk Bay had, but the snorkeling was unrivaled. We only had to swim twenty-five yards into the bay and the seafloor went from casual sand to Little Mermaid real quick.

I was so busy looking down that I almost swam directly into a barracuda that was taking in the sun on the surface. I backed away slowly and made the X sign with my two index fingers to Ash and pointed to the silver fish with the razor teeth.

We continued our tour, circling the large boulder in the middle of the bay. On the surface it was a large rock with people bathing and a rope ladder to get to the top and jump. But underwater it was a metropolis of fish, coral, sea slugs, crabs, and jellyfish.

It took us much longer to get back to shore, as the barracuda was lingering in the route we wanted to take. The swim back around the boulder exhausted us, and we hit the sand and crashed onto our towels like we had been lost at sea for days. As I lay there throwing little pebbles up and trying to land them on my stomach, I realized my stress levels were nonexistent. I was almost stressed that I had nothing to stress about.

We arrived home and sat on the porch. Soon we heard Alan and Heidi going through the orientation with another couple who must have just arrived. They came out to the shared porch afterward, and we chatted with them. They seemed like fun people, and we each cracked a beer to ring in the evening and their first night in Ko Tao.

Ned and Heather were from England and currently on a two-week holiday. They had been together for a couple of years now, but they'd still never lived in the same city. I couldn't believe they had endured a long-distance relationship until I watched them interact. They were clearly deeply in love, and distance didn't seem to affect that. One Chang quickly became two, and when Alan came up to take us to dinner, he asked if we were ready for our Chang-over.

We headed home after dinner and planted ourselves on the rocking chairs for a nightcap with our new friends. They were bright people, and it was awesome to engage in conversations comparing and contrasting the education systems in England and the US. Ash, being a teacher, was leading the discussion, and I sat back and listened as she described the inner-city school systems she had worked for. Her public speaking and debating confidence had skyrocketed since we'd left Denver. Everything about her seemed to be changing in the best way possible.

Ash and I went to bed and both excitedly agreed that Ned and Heather were the perfect people to share this villa with. The best part about them was that they loved to laugh. Being around humans whose goal in the conversation was to laugh as much as possible was infectious. It was certainly a great recipe for the last stop of our trip.

9/24/15
Ko Tao, Thailand

The sky had completely cleared for the first time since we had been in Ko Tao, and with the haze gone, we could see the mainland across the sea. We ate our breakfast of two toasties, a view unlike any other in front of us, and struggled to leave the porch. Our natural tendency as humans is to seek more, but I couldn't imagine finding something better than this. When the sun rose higher, my theory was debunked by water. We needed to cool off, so we chose to go to Sairee Beach, the biggest beach on the island.

To both avoid the moped and to try to get some much needed exercise, we decided to walk to the beach. It was only about a mile away, but going down the hill was knee-buckling. I kept an eye on the bomb-releasing palm trees above to avoid being one of the 150 people who supposedly die from falling coconuts a year.

We rushed to the north side of the beach across the main road and got in the water ASAP to cool off. This once again was not possible, as the water was hotter than the air. I had daily meditation to do and floated in the shallows as the sound of distant boats and near waves served as my backdrop noise until evening reached the island.

Tonight we were getting food with Heather and Ned. We met them on the porch and drank a pre-dinner beer while they told us about their diving excursion. Ko Tao was famous for diving, and the diver-coveted whale shark was prevalent out here.

Pong, our taxi driver, drove us down to Sairee Beach and dropped us off in a crowded area. We strolled aimlessly, looking for a place to eat and turning down taxis and massage owners every five feet. I respected the hustle and didn't get annoyed by this anymore. They were just trying to make a living and weren't pestering anyone. I simply said, "No, thank you, *kaap*," and kept walking. They always smiled and let us go without further pestering. *Except* the suit guys. *Do not*—and I repeated *do not*—engage in a conversation with the tailors. Those dudes are ruthless and won't let you leave without a damn fight or a suit.

We found a restaurant that served a little bit of everything, and ordered an assortment of food between the four of us. Ash got spaghetti, Ned ordered pizza, Heather ate a traditional Thai dish (smart woman), and I got ballsy and ordered the combo of ribs and chicken. I was in a good mood, drinking with new friends.

When we reached the villa, we all played pool in the game room below our apartments and drank Chang-overs while listening to Stevie Wonder's *Greatest Hits*. We had turned our relaxing island getaway into another beach week with friends, and we were okay with that. We had planned on resting up until we went home, but we could rest all year. Spending this time partying with Ned and Heather felt priceless.

9/25/15
Ko Tao, Thailand

So, in hindsight, the combo platter of ribs and chicken might have been a bit too ballsy. I suppose you live and you . . . Well, this is the third or fourth time I have gotten sick over consuming something stupid, so I suppose I'll just focus on the living part. I spent the entire night violently throwing up. Just another night in Thailand. Every time I went to sleep, there was about a fifty-fifty chance I would wake up and have to empty my stomach.

Our breakfast on the porch was a somber one as we said good-bye to Ned and Heather. We had loved having them as neighbors and friends, and this place wasn't going to feel the same without them. Ash and Heather had a particularly strong connection, and I feel like Heather was Ash's spirit animal and vice versa. To put some context to this, Heather was a sweet Southern woman who just happened to have a thick British accent. Ned and I bonded over our business minds and political interests. We were sure to be in touch as soon as we got back to the States.

As we sat and tried to determine what to do today, we settled on Aow Leuk again. It was going to be hard to beat, and with only two days left, we wanted to spend them somewhere we *knew* was amazing. We hit up our taxi brother Pong and rode over to Aow Leuk. He told us he would be back at five when the beach closed and to just pay him for both rides then.

We threw on our gear and floated into the land of scales. For some reason, Ash and I were not on the same page, and we kept bumping into each other as we treaded water. The last thing you wanted to do when looking at huge fish and fearing sharks was bump into someone unexpectedly. We both became irritated quickly, and Ash finally headed in after cursing me out in bubbles.

We had been struggling a lot lately as we prepared to go home. I think we were both just so scared to take on life after this journey that we were taking it out on each other. I had not planned to even make it this far. Not that I thought I was going to die; I just didn't have time to think this far ahead with so much planning to do for cities only days away. Like I said, when we'd discovered that our final Airbnb was booked and our planning was over, it had Ash pretty rattled. She always coped with leaving a city by looking forward to the next one. It was easy to leave Berlin when Prague was next. Saying good-bye to Croatia was hard, but we had Italy and Greece right around the corner. Now we had come to the realization that we weren't just leaving Thailand—we were leaving our journey.

Around 5:00 p.m. it looked like it was going to start to rain, and Pong was waiting patiently for us outside the beach. He beat the rain on the way home and stopped so we could grab pizza.

When we got home, I took a shower. And it was when I was in the shower that I noticed the apartment felt hot.

"Hey, Ash, what is the temp set to?" I yelled through the water, quickly spitting it out so I didn't get sick again.

She responded with the five worst words since the woman at the ferry kiosk in Croatia said, "The tickets are sold out."

"Our air conditioning is broken."

We called Alan and Heidi, and they told us they would have a guy come first thing in the morning. Back to the days of fans and open windows with screens. We didn't have AC in Denver, either, but it wasn't ninety-five degrees and humid in Denver. Tonight we would be sleeping like the locals.

9/26/15
Ko Tao, Thailand

Believe it or not, last night with no AC was our best sleep in Thailand. The mixture of the open windows, semi-cool jungle breeze, and humming fan made for great background sounds. Maybe this whole closed-window, AC thing was overrated after all? We took our time getting up, and prepared ourselves for our final destination of the week, the porch. It was our last day in paradise, and we didn't want to let it go by fast.

We read the news over coffee and gobbled up our toasties and omelets. This morning routine was great for us because we got to wake up slowly. We didn't have to scarf down food and coffee while rushing to get ready for a day we didn't want to live. Despite being in different cities, countries, and cultures for the last four months, we'd had the same routine every morning.

Our bodies ached from repeated sunburns, bugbites, and moped crashes. Our clothes smelled moldy, and our hair and my beard were a step past unkempt. We were just tired, and decided today we would enjoy the view. The breeze was the tipping point; a cold gust collided with our leathery, sun-beaten skin every few seconds and cooled us.

We left the comfort of our porch only to get one last massage in town. When we finished, Alan came down to pick us up. We held on to the back of the handlebar and casually ducked all the trees and branches and watched for coconuts on the way up, only holding on with one hand. In one week, we'd become expert truck-standing riders.

As we headed up through the coconut grove for the last time, I turned to see Ash crying. It broke my heart. I felt the same way, but this was her journey. This was her trip. My journey and dream were to write this book and document this experience; hers was to grow from it in a way I didn't need to. I put my arm around her and held on to the rail on the other side and she fell into my weight. This was our last trip up the hill to our villa.

We watched the sunset over the gulf, hoping it would slow down and just stay put for once. I broke the silence between us as we looked out over the sea: "Hey, we still have a night in Bangkok." But we both knew this was it. This was the last water we would see after spending months at sea. We had soaked up enough salt and sun this summer for a lifetime, but we still didn't want to say good-bye. I fell asleep to the sound of Ash whimpering in my arms next to me. The AC was fixed, but we left it off.

9/27/15
Ko Tao, Thailand -> Bangkok, Thailand

This morning was hard on both of us. It was a depressing day, and knowing we had to leave Turtle Island, not even our toasties tasted good. Ash finished packing while I filled out the paperwork for our final bill with Alan. Shortly after, Alan and Heidi took us down the hill. Ash softly teared up once again. I decided to take matters into my own hands and take the humor approach. I looked Ash in the face and made eye contact with her puppy eyes seconds before I took a branch to the face. It worked temporarily. She laughed for a few seconds, and my face hurt much longer than anticipated.

Our truck reached the pier, and we bid farewell to Alan and Heidi. We let them know that this place had been like a home away from home for us. We double-cheek kissed and then Ash gave a wai out of instinct. Then we all laughed and gave wais to one another.

Today was our final travel day, and it certainly epitomized the phrase *going out with a bang*. We would be traveling for ten hours up the entire coast of Thailand by catamaran, bus, and taxi. As our large boat backed out of the port, we waved to the people of Turtle Island like we were leaving for America on the *Titanic*. This was a much nicer ferry than the previous ones, and we took seats in the air-conditioned main cabin.

As long as the weather stayed nice, I was happy. We had endured some tough traveling days. From the Murder Mobile in Poland to the Light Show Escapade in Florence, and who could forget the multiple moped debacles and nightmares on the water? A clear, uneventful ride to the mainland was fine with me.

Before long we had reached the Chumphon pier and finished leg one of our journey. Unfortunately, leg one did not carry significant weight on the total trip time. It was only two of the ten hours of travel. This next leg was going to be a pain in the traveling ass. We had not been on a single vehicle for more than eight hours the entire trip. Even the long flights had been between six and eight. We had saved the longest for last.

The pier had a bus station with a market attached, and we both ordered stir-fry. Ash sat on the picnic table, her hand on her face, and moved the rice and veggies around with a sole chopstick, only putting it down to wipe the beads of sweat from her brow and forehead.

Our bus arrived, and Ash turned to me and asked, "What if we just don't get on?" *I love this girl.*

This bus was far from as nice as the first one and wasn't clean. We sat in old seats on the bottom deck of the double-decker and settled in. A trail of ants was walking along the walls in front of me. I fell asleep within the first half an hour and didn't wake up for four hours. I dreamed of elephants and kayaks.

When I awoke, I turned to see Ash wide awake, staring out the window. I wondered what she was thinking about, but I didn't want to ask. She needed this time to process this just as I had in the sea. Our future was nothing but uncertainty, and it was scary. It was also scary to go back to being around and relying on other people. All Ash and I had had was each other for the last four months. Through the good and bad, we'd shared every moment of the most exciting time of our lives and couldn't have survived without each other. We had become partners and teammates. We had become family.

We both fell back asleep on each other's heads until we arrived in Bangkok. I had been dozing in and out of sleep as the sun went down and darkness captured the bus. The bright lights of the city woke me up. I could not believe how big the city was. It reminded me of New York.

When we stepped outside, I immediately smelled the stench of the city. It was both disgusting *and* inviting. We bartered with a taxi driver and got a ride in a tuk-tuk and sputtered off into the traffic. Our Airbnb was basically in a mall, located downtown in an apartment complex. We found the code from our messages and walked into the high-rise apartment. It was on the forty-second floor, and we had a view of the entire city.

We both dropped our packs and checked our texts. Ash had a message from her friend Becca from college who was also in Bangkok. Ash knew her and her boyfriend, Ajay, were here, but she wasn't sure if we would be up for going out with them after traveling all day. We stood in our Airbnb room, looked out at the towers and lights, and decided that if we were going to be traveling for one last night, we might as well go out and spend time with friends. This would ease our pain a bit, and every night we'd spent with other people on this trip thus far had been great.

We didn't even bother unpacking. We only got out the clothes we would wear tonight and for our travel day home tomorrow. Once we were all set to leave, we started the half-mile walk to the skyscraper with a bar on top, where we were meeting Ajay and Becca. When we arrived, we got into an elevator that took what felt like five minutes to get to the sixtieth floor. My ears were doing backflips every few seconds.

As soon as we saw Becca and Ajay, I realized I recognized them both. App State was a school of around sixteen thousand students, but it felt small, and if you were out and about often, you felt like you knew everyone. I had played basketball with Ajay plenty of times.

They had a seat along the balcony that made my stomach quiver instantly. I suppose they called it a sky bar because we were literally in the sky.

I was glad we'd decided to come and hang out with Becca and Ajay. They had been teaching in Thailand but were heading home to start their postgraduate degrees. What a great experience for them to graduate from school, teach abroad in a place where you acquire a new perspective and appreciation for life, and then take those rich experiences and use them as ammo in your next phase. I was proud to have met up with these two.

After we left the bar, Becca and Ajay took us to their favorite outdoor market for dinner, and we sat and ate bowls of food on the steps of a large building. As we filled our faces with noodles, I looked around and noticed how hot, loud, and humid Bangkok was. It reminded me of being back in one of the big cities at the beginning of our trip.

Many of Becca and Ajay's stories were very similar to ours. We talked about making toasties, one of the main food groups in the pyramid, and the craziness of the drivers and lawless roads. We laughed at the fact we'd sweat from the moment we got here until now, and I pulled my shirt out and let it snap back in a wet smack on my chest. We all sighed deeply at the thought of paying anything more than three dollars for a massage and no longer getting taxis for pocket change. It was a sad day for all of us, but we also had the pride and sense of accomplishment of surviving it all. We said our good-byes and knew we would see them soon in North Carolina.

A deep feeling of sadness passed over me as we walked back to our Airbnb, sweaty hand in sweaty hand. This was actually it: this was the last night of the journey that had changed our lives forever. Nothing would ever be the same after this for either of us. That was a bittersweet pill to swallow. On one hand, we didn't want to leave. We didn't want to go back to a world of deadlines; we didn't want to go back to where we weren't side by side, tackling travel days and hangovers and botched logistics. On the other hand, life would never be the same for us because we had stretched our comfort zones so far, we could never wear the life pants we'd once fit into.

When we got home, we packed all our belongings into our luggage. This arsenal had grown into two backpacks, a suitcase we'd bought on the side of the road for five dollars, and two smaller backpacks that we strapped to our chests. We hadn't unpacked much when we got here, so it wasn't hard, but we had to be at the airport semi-early tomorrow and didn't want to have to do it in the morning.

We got in bed and left the blinds open so we could utilize the night-light of the Bangkok skyline. The bed was extremely uncomfortable, the AC was subpar, my beard/hair was taking up half my pillow in a giant ball of fur, and I had not stopped sweating even after the cold shower. *We slept great.*

9/28/15
Bangkok, Thailand →

Our alarm went off, and the beeping felt more like a siren alerting us that life was on its way and to take cover. There wasn't much talking between us this morning because it was too hard. Talking about going home and this journey becoming a memory hurt too much. Neither of us had the words to comfort the other.

We used the last two large water bottles we had to brush our teeth and hydrate before our twenty-four hours of flying. You could never, it seems, *overhydrate* in Thailand. We did what we always did when we left Airbnbs and checked to make sure we had our phones, wallets, and chargers. Lastly we used the Wi-Fi to make sure there were no specific checkout instructions.

The only thing we had to do was drop the key off at the front desk at the bottom of the building. When I handed the Thai woman our key, she grabbed it and gave a wai to me. I felt like I was dropping off the key to happiness as our four months of travel had ended. Ash was at the corner, checking for transportation to the airport, and when I returned, she reported back to me that Bangkok had Uber and it would be a cheap ride to the airport. As she was about to press the button to request the Uber, I noticed a single tear fall from her big beautiful eyes. I stopped her hand and asked, "Do they have a metro?"

I noticed a slight smile form in the corner of her mouth, and she quickly googled the Bangkok public transit routes.

"The closest station that goes to the airport is only a mile and a half away," she said, looking at me with a glimpse of hope in her eyes at the prospect of one last travel day.

Our bodies were exhausted and depleted from four months of rigorous travel. I had lost twenty pounds since arriving in Thailand due to sickness. Not to mention we now had sixty pounds of luggage on our backs, on our chests, and dragging behind us. Neither of us had eaten a thing this morning, and there was an alert on my weather app warning us about the heat and air-quality index. The streets were flooded with crowded markets and hectic traffic. This was still no match for us; we were backpackers, after all.

"Let's do it," I said, smiling at her. She became as excited as that first morning in Clemence's Airbnb in Paris. Then she took my hand in hers and led me back onto the streets of Bangkok for one last adventure.

ACKNOWLEDGMENTS

To Ash: We did it. Thanks for being there every step of the way, from Denver to Bangkok. Reading these journal entries every night to you was the best part of making this book.

To the friends, family, and strangers who helped me crowd-fund this book: This could not have happened without your support. *Not Afraid of the Fall* began as a dream of mine, and I am forever indebted to those who helped push this book to become a reality.

To Mom, Dad, Sara, and Carter: Thank you for putting up with me as I fought with these words night after night for the last two years. I will never forget the sacrifices you four made to give me the time to adequately work on this.

To Emily and JJ: thanks for passing along the travel bug and sharing your family with us.

Angie and Jeff: your love and support was instrumental in helping me publish this book.

To Avalon, Angela, Adam, Thad, and the rest of the team at Inkshares: You guys are unbelievable. The time you put into *Not Afraid of the Fall*, even on nights and weekends, truly showed that you care about these books as much as the authors. This is a family, and the sky is the limit for Inkshares. I am glad to be part of something this special.

To my editor, J.C.: Those countless hours we spent on the phone envisioning the final product of this book helped me beyond measure. I can't thank you enough for being the first person to fully read this book and for rolling up your sleeves to make it what it is today. You are amazing, my man.

To my copy editor, Kaitlin: I apologize for the puzzle of grammar you had to decode to find *Not Afraid of the Fall*. Simply put, this book wouldn't be here without your help. Thank you so much, Kaitlin.

To Tay and Paul: The original cover and promotional video are the reason anyone originally gave this book a second glance, and I owe my thanks to you two. You guys helped me create those pieces without a second of hesitation.

Tyler, Dave, and Pat: You three helped me edit long before there was an opportunity for editors. Each of you saw my vision for this book and helped me chisel away the pieces to get it there. Thank you for believing in me and this story.

LIST OF PATRONS

Alex Mette
Amber Wilson
Angela Melamud
Annalise Farris and
Stephen Perry
Ashley Grigsby
Avalon Radys
Beau Long
Ben Roush
Brendan and Laura Kerr
Bruce and Susan Riebe
Carter James
Cole H Page
Dennis R Greene
Emily James
Gordon Gibbs
Grama James
Heather and Ned
Jackie Bridges
Jeff and Angela Grigsby
Jessica Glasser
Jon and Molly James
Jordan Smith
Josh Canon
Joyce Mason
Kaitlin M Grigsby
Karen D. Williams

Keith Shockley and
Breanna Brown
Ken and Marla Bridges
Kenneth Jjombwe
Kerry King
Kobla Hargett
Luke and Jess Blitchington
Marius Feldmeier
Matt Kaye
Mike du Toit
Neil Peters and Bryony Stewart
Patrick and Jordie Kerwin
Patrick Garvey and
Ritchlyn Mohammed
Phil and Cathy James
Rachel Blackwelder
Richard King
Rock and Jeannine Bridges
Roger E. Nahum
Tarron and Kathryn Robinson
The Doherty Family
Todd, Kathy, Sara and
Shayna Webber
Tom Withers Green &
Laura Capel
Walker Wells
Wanda and Robert Crocker,
Acorn Hill

INKSHARES

INKSHARES is a reader-driven publisher and producer based in Oakland, California. Our books are selected not by a group of editors, but by readers worldwide.

While we've published books by established writers like *Big Fish* author Daniel Wallace and *Star Wars: Rogue One* scribe Gary Whitta, our aim remains surfacing and developing the new author voices of tomorrow.

Previously unknown Inkshares authors have received starred reviews and been featured in *The New York Times*. Their books are on the front tables of Barnes & Noble and hundreds of independents nationwide, and many have been licensed by publishers in other major markets. They are also being adapted by Oscar-winning screenwriters at the biggest studios and networks.

Interested in making your own story a reality? Visit Inkshares. com to start your own project or find other great books.

CPSIA information can be obtained
at www.ICGtesting.com
Printed in the USA
BVOW03s0240300617
488187BV00002B/2/P